HOW TO WRITE FICTION (AND THINK /

Related titles from Palgrave Macmillan

Amanda Boulter, *Writing Fiction: Creative & Critical Approaches*
Julia Casterton, *Creative Writing: A Practical Guide*, 3rd edition
Robert Graham *et al.*, *The Road to Somewhere: A Creative Writing Companion*
Celia Hunt and Fiona Sampson, *Writing: Self and Reflexivity*
John Singleton and Mary Luckhurst (eds), *The Creative Writing Handbook*, 2nd edition
John Singleton, *The Creative Writing Workbook*
Jayne Steel (ed.), *Wordsmithery: The Writer's Craft and Practice*

How To Write Fiction (And Think About It)

ROBERT GRAHAM

Guest Contributors
Gareth Creer
James Friel
Ursula Hurley
Heather Leach
Helen Newall
Jenny Newman

First published 2007 by
PALGRAVE MACMILLAN
Houndmills, Basingstoke, Hampshire RG21 6XS and
175 Fifth Avenue, New York, N.Y. 10010
Companies and representatives throughout the world

PALGRAVE MACMILLAN is the global academic imprint of the Palgrave Macmillan division of St. Martin's Press, LLC and of Palgrave Macmillan Ltd. Macmillan® is a registered trademark in the United States, United Kingdom and other countries. Palgrave is a registered trademark in the European Union and other countries.

ISBN-13: 978–1–4039–9314–4 hardback
ISBN-10: 1–4039–9314–9 hardback
ISBN-13: 978–1–4039–9315–1 paperback
ISBN-10: 1–4039–9315–7 paperback

This book is printed on paper suitable for recycling and made from fully managed and sustained forest sources.

A catalogue record for this book is available from the British Library.

A catalog record for this book is available from the Library of Congress.

10   9   8   7   6   5   4   3   2   1
16   15   14   13   12   11   10   09   08   07

Printed and bound in China

Contents

Acknowledgements

I want to thank the Learning & Teaching Committee at MMU Cheshire and MMU's English Research Institute and the Department of Contemporary Arts for funding, which released me from some teaching to work on this book.

Robert Graham

Notes on Contributors

Robert Graham is Programme Leader for Creative Writing at Manchester Metropolitan University, Cheshire. His short stories have appeared in a variety of magazines and anthologies and have been broadcast on Radio 4. He is the co-author, with Keith Baty, of *Elvis – The Novel*. Over a dozen of Robert's plays for youth theatres have been staged, including *If You Have Five Seconds to Spare*, which Contact Theatre, Manchester, produced. He is co-author and co-editor of *The Road to Somewhere*: *A Creative Writing Companion* (Palgrave, 2005) and of *An A–Z of Creative Writing*. His first novel, *Holy Joe*, was published in February, 2006.

Gareth Creer runs Free To Write, a project which works with inmates and ex-offenders. He lectures in Imaginative Writing at Liverpool John Moores University and his novels, *Skin and Bone*, *Cradle To Grave*, and *Big Sky* are published by Transworld and in translation. He has also written for the *New Statesman*, *Sunday Times* and *Daily Telegraph*. His short fiction has been published by *Penguin*, *City Life*, *Headland*, and *Waterside*.

James Friel leads the MA in Writing at Liverpool John Moores University. His novels include *Left of North*, and *Careless Talk*. His work has appeared in *Blithe House Quarterly*, *The Writers' Workbook*, *Time Out*, *Harpers & Queen*, *Fable*, *The Universe*, *Cercles*, *Pretext*, *Pool*, *Boomerang*, *Harrington's* and BBC Radio 3 and 4.

Ursula Hurley teaches Creative Writing at the University of Salford. She has published poetry, articles and short stories widely and is currently working on a novel as part of her PhD thesis.

Heather Leach teaches Creative Writing at Manchester Metropolitan University. Her short fiction and non-fiction work has appeared in a variety of media including The Big Issue and BBC Radio and she won the Times Higher Education Essay Competition in 2004. She is co-editor of *The Road to Somewhere: A Creative Writing Companion* (Palgrave, 2005), and of *An A to Z of Creative Writing* (forthcoming 2007).

Helen Newall is the Programme Leader for the Drama, Physical Theatre and Dance degree at Edge Hill University. She's written plays for The Nuffield Theatre, Southampton. She was writer in Residence at The Chester Gateway Theatre. Her short fiction has appeared in *Myslexia*, *Pool* and *Pretext*. She is co-editor of *The Road to Somewhere: A Creative Writing Companion*.

Jenny Newman is a Reader in Creative Writing at Liverpool John Moores University. She has published two novels, *Going In* (1994) and *Life Class* (2000). She is a contributing co-editor of *The Writer's Workbook* (2004) and of *British and Irish Novelists: An Introduction Through Interviews* (2004). Her short fiction has appeared in *The London Magazine* and BBC Radio 4.

Introduction

How To Write Fiction (And Think About It) is for people like you, people who want to learn how to write fiction. In the early stages, the book introduces some primary writer's disciplines: reading as a writer, writing practice and using a writer's journal, for example. Following on from that, you will develop your fiction writing by examining some thoughts on the craft of fiction, through studying examples of good practice and practising the craft of fiction yourself. For instance, when we come to look at dialogue, you will be offered suggestions about what makes for good dialogue. You will have the chance to analyse the use of dialogue in Sarah Water's novel, *Affinity*. Finally, you will be given a writing exercise in which you may practise writing dialogue yourself, to emulate, perhaps, what you have learnt from looking at the suggested theory and the good practice. In this way, over time, my hope is that this book will help you acquire a portfolio of skills and techniques – a writer's toolbox, if you like.

I have studied a few aspects of fiction writing to help me improve my writing and teaching, but there are enough holes in my expertise to fill the Albert Hall. Faced with writing a book of this length, I therefore thought it desirable to request some help. In my working life, I'm lucky enough to know a number of fiction writers who also teach Creative Writing and a handful of them have been kind enough to write chapters for *HTWF*. Each of them is a gifted writer and a highly experienced teacher of fiction writing. As you will come to see during the course of studying this book, my guests' contributions add a huge amount to the chapters that surround them.

The book includes four separate kinds of writing task. The first and most basic is what I call a Writing Burst. Writing Bursts are distributed throughout the text and are 10-minute exercises designed to get you writing fit. In other words, they are very similar to playing scales on the piano; they are writing practice. The book's second kind of task is the Writing Exercise. Writing Exercises are in most chapters and have been tailored to the particular content of the chapter in which you find them. You could see Writing Exercises as improvisations for you to do, based on the suggestions about craft which have in each case preceded them. Story Projects are longer writing tasks, designed to stretch you a little more and to allow you to give your growing writer's craft an increasingly extended run-out. Story Projects begin only at the length of a Writing Burst, but increase at incremental stages as the book progresses (and as your craft develops). The bracketed part of the book's title indicates the centrality to *HTWF* of reflective learning. Reflection in this book will take two forms: Self-Evaluations and Reflection Projects. Through the means of both discourses, you will develop the habit of examining not only the creative processes involved in your work, but also your growing understanding of the kind of writer you are and the literary context to which you believe you may belong. Also, as you will see presently, a good reason to write reflectively is that you will become more real to yourself as a writer.

The principle of dramatisation informs much of the thinking in *How To Write Fiction*. Concepts such as immediacy and the use of scenes where characters are shown in a process of change have been prioritised.

The foundational chapters in *Part 1: How A Writer Works* will offer you some insights into how creativity functions and help you acquire the habit of using some of the writer's key disciplines: maintaining notebooks, journals and reading logs. You will learn, too, the invaluable skill of reading as a writer and begin to use it to analyse the ways in which some accomplished contemporary practitioners go about creating their fiction.

In *Part 2: How To Write Short Stories*, you will explore notions of what a short story may be. Alongside that, you will examine some of the major elements of craft involved in writing short stories, from characterisation, through point of view and immediacy, to plot and setting.

Part 3: How To Redraft explores the whole area of refining your first drafts into completed works of fiction and touches on the role of a readership in this vital part of the writing process. Redrafting is central to all creative writing and, consequently, to this book. This is a matter of using your critical faculties and your understanding of craft to evolve and polish first draft work, your raw material. Each piece of work knows its final destination, and if you look at it and listen to it, you will find your way there.

In *Part 4: How To Handle Time*, I've grouped together four chapters which look at the tricky subject of time in fiction.

In *Part 5: How To Write With Style*, you will learn how to express yourself more clearly and explore what to put in and leave out of your sentences as well as how to turn them in terms of their music.

Part 6: How to Broaden Your Canvas introduces you to some subtler elements of craft and looks at how to make your fiction not only broader, but also deeper and longer.

Each part of the whole – theory, contemporary practice, practising yourself, redrafting and reflection – is interdependent.

How To Write Fiction will not teach you everything you need to know about writing fiction – far from it. However, I hope it will introduce you to enough disciplines, skills and techniques to get your fiction-writing career off to a good start. Your future, I can be fairly certain, will consist of years and years of studying other books on craft, of practising the writer's disciplines, of honing your fiction-writing, of continuing to study the craft of other practitioners, of reading and writing, reading and writing, reading and writing.

Writing Bursts

Every class I teach begins with a 10 minute writing exercise which I call a writing burst. I give a stimulus and ask the class to start writing, keep writing for 10 minutes and not to stop to worry for one second about the quality of the work appearing on the paper.

This is good practice. Many of my students' writing bursts end up as the starting point for a short story or become scenes in finished short stories. In course evaluations one of the things students consistently commend is the Writing Burst. It makes you write, it instils the discipline of writing without stopping to criticise and it shows you how much may be achieved only in a short period of time. We all live lives that are too packed with business, so discovering that 10 minutes is a valuable amount of time to spend writing is an eye-opener and an encouragement.

This book is liberally sprinkled with writing bursts. I suggest you just stop what you're doing and write for 10 minutes each time you come to one of these tiny sub-sections of *HTWF*. You may find you want to make it part of your daily routine.

Here's the first one. This sentence might be a first-person narration or you could make it dialogue: your short piece of fiction writing might begin with a character speaking these words to another character.

Writing Burst

I had been feeling like a million dollars.

I
How A Writer Works

1 How A Writer Works

Plenty of expert opinion suggests that our creative practice divides into two categories, however we label those categories. I don't know who it was that claimed that producing great writing was 99% perspiration and 1% inspiration, but this is the division of creativity we're talking about: between the stroke of imagination and labouring at it to produce the finished whole. Oscar Wilde argued that genius was an infinite capacity for detail, which, like the inspiration/perspiration proverb, suggests that the balance lies firmly on the side of effort. Most informed opinion, however, indicates a more even split between inspiration and perspiration, and affirms that creativity involves both stages. The process is one of having an idea and then fashioning it into shape. In writing fiction, the first stage is the imagining. This comes from the same place as your dreams do: the unconscious mind.

Unconscious Mind

Think for a moment: when did you last have a light bulb moment? You know, that feeling when a cartoon light bulb appears above your head because, in a flash, you've just had a great idea? Suddenly it has occurred to you that the new Kings of Leon CD is the perfect birthday present for your brother. Or it comes to you with a shock of recognition how you can afford to go to Australia *and* pay your tuition fees.

Think of a recent light bulb moment of your own and try to remember what you were doing at the time. Most likely you were doing something repetitive and tedious, something hypnotically dull. Driving at a steady 70 mph on a quiet motorway. Ironing shirts. Getting in your daily exercise with a 30-minute walk.

Here's another form of light bulb moment: you wake in the night for the toilet, and while you're there calmly doing your business in the still of the night, it occurs to you with brutal clarity that you should visit your parents more often, and that in fact you weren't that nice to your Dad the last time you did visit them. Or another: you wake up 10 minutes before the alarm, and while you're lying there crawling towards consciousness, you all of a sudden see the solution to the conflict between two of your close co-workers or you see a way out for all of you. Or another: you dream a perfect narrative, what feels like an infinitely more realised, more compelling, more delightful story than you could ever conceive of while awake.

What do these light bulb moments have in common? You've probably got there way before me. Apart from the perfect story in a dream, when you obviously *were* unconscious, in all of these examples, you were either entering or leaving your unconscious mind. Waking in the morning or getting up to go to the toilet in the night, you were obviously just coming out of unconsciousness. In all the other examples, your mind was being nudged towards unconsciousness – put into neutral gear, you might say – by repetitive, tedious conditions. In other words, good ideas emerge from the unconscious mind.

Sometimes they may arrive fully formed. John Lennon differentiated between songs that arrived in a handful of minutes, which he regarded as inspired, and songs that he had to chisel away at over time, which he saw as of inferior quality because he had fashioned them with the craft he had built up over years.

Sometimes the unconscious may throw up an idea ready to go. Many writers eschew plotting, setting off with only a vague idea of where they are heading, they write to discover. According to the novelist Pat Barker, the narrative structure 'is the gift of the unconscious' and Barbara Trapido, whose novels like Barker's have been highly acclaimed, speaks of a story 'lying under the surface, and you're trying to dredge it up.' Guy Claxton, Professor of Psychology at Bath University, corroborates this:

> Even scientists themselves, or at least the more creative of them, admit that their genius comes to them from layers of mind over which they have little or no control (and they may even feel somehow fraudulent for taking personal credit for insights that simply 'occurred to them').[1]

Dorothea Brande, too, is adamant that it isn't by labouring, chiselling, revising, or restructuring 'that an excellent piece of art is born. It takes

shape and has its origin outside the region of the conscious intel-
lect.'[2] You could see the flash of inspiration as a postcard from your
unconscious, inviting you to come and visit and discover the whole
of what that inspired moment intimates.

One way in which you may tap into the fully realised form of the
inspired idea is in the writing itself. Just as inspiration may arrive in
a nano-second when the mind has been stilled by monotonous,
rhythmic activity, I believe first drafts arrive in a similar way. Isn't
the act of writing itself, whether on a keyboard or with pen and
paper, repetitive and monotonous? In both instances – the arrival of
the inspiration and the production of the first draft – aren't you
experiencing something similar to what the hypnotist does to his
subject with a pocket watch swinging back and forth before their
eyes? 'The process of imagination that underlies creative writing,'
says Madison Smartt Bell, 'what happens just as or just before you
are putting the words down on the page, must inevitably involve a
process of autohypnosis.'[3]

Throughout her classic book, *Becoming A Writer*, Dorothea Brande
explains the functions of the unconscious from a variety of angles
and suggests that the unconscious mind is not just where ideas come
from, but also a facility for developing those ideas until they reach
their final, fully realised form:

> Every author, in some way which he has come on by luck or long search, puts himself
> in a very light state of hypnosis ... Far behind the mind's surface, so deep that he is
> seldom aware (unless at last observation of himself has taught him) that any activity
> is going forward, his story is being fused and welded into an integrated work.[4]

Dorothea Brande argues not only that knowing when our unconscious mind is in the ascendant will benefit the writer, but also that
'it is possible to learn to tap it at will, and even to direct it.' At an
advanced stage in a story's gestation, during the work that leads to
completing it, she talks of inducing 'the artistic coma,' of pausing
the mind in order to mine the unconscious. 'Learn to hold your
mind as still as your body,' she tells us[5] and puts forward a model
that amounts, really, to meditation: stilling the mind by focussing
on a word or an object. Brande recommends holding a rubber ball
and focussing on it until the chattering monkey of the conscious
mind is silenced. When we achieve this state – to do so, Brande recommends a walk followed by a bath *and* focussing in a meditative
fashion on a rubber ball – we may escape into the unconscious

mind. Natalie Goldburg, one of the contemporary gurus of Creative Writing, doesn't like this term, though, which she sees as too limiting; for her that creative part of the mind is *wild mind* (which gives one of her books its title). Here in *wild mind*, she writes, we may

> let everything run through us and grab as much as we can of it with pen and paper. Let yourself live in something that is already rightfully yours – your own wild mind... This is all about loss of control... Can you do this? Lose control and let wild mind take over? It is the best way to write.[6]

Writers need solitude and headspace, time in which to idle and daydream. In that respect, being a writer is very time-costly; a frenetic, jam-packed life doesn't lend itself to creative endeavour. You will need the time and the space to stare out of the window, to fart about, to *play*. In learning to maximise your access to your unconscious mind, you could do worse than think of the novelist William Boyd's working day, as he outlined it a few years ago in the British *Sunday Times Magazine*'s 'A Day In The Life' feature. He had a fairly leisurely start to the day with breakfast about nine or nine thirty. After pottering about, looking at the papers and so on, he would leave the house around eleven and walk miles around his neighbourhood, maybe stopping for a coffee in an agreeable café bar or to flip through CDs in his favourite record shop. He would be home for lunch about two, and shortly after that, when he was feeling more like having a nap than working, he would settle at the keyboard and work until around six, when he would stop to cook for himself and his wife, have drinks and dinner, a bit of chat with maybe a few more drinks and then it would be bedtime.

At first glance, not a heavy day's work. But isn't half Boyd's work, possibly the most important half, done during the hours he spends walking?

Conscious Mind

Understanding the unconscious and learning to manage it is something we have to learn (or re-learn) in adult life. Western education prioritises conscious mind functions from the get-go. Schools, colleges and universities depend on order, judging, analysis, logic, rationality. Even before we reach nursery school, the order and logic of language is being imposed on our young, chaotically creative minds. As a university Creative Writing tutor, I see this every autumn when the new first year arrives.

In each workshop there will be an academic student, very diligent, reliable and organised, probably with great A level results, who in an English Literature class can analyse the life out of a text, squeezing every last drop of meaning from it in an accomplished, literate fashion. He may have been the head boy at school and the linchpin of the debating society. He has probably spent the past two years being his local Tesco's most reliable Saturday worker. But this same student won't know where to start with filling a blank page with original writing. In fact, this student lives so much in his conscious mind that he is paralysed by the very idea of having to put so much as one letter on the blank page; he will be worrying about the syntax, the punctuation and whether or not he could ever come up with one original thought of his own. When we move on to reading as a writer, or learning to show rather than tell, this same student will make a pig's ear of it; not only that, but he lives so much in his conscious mind, organising his life, analysing and criticising whatever is put in front of him, that he will find it almost impossible to see *why* he is making a pig's ear of it.

And in the same class, there will be a chaotic freewheeler, the kid with tie-dyed T-shirt and limited personal organisation who attends haphazardly, and this one will fill a page without stopping to think about it, fill it with good stuff, too. Maybe she's doing Drama alongside Creative Writing, so she's used to improvising, I don't know. But she's already got the hardest part under her belt: she knows how to use her unconscious mind and she probably doesn't even know she knows it.

Most of us spend far too much of our lives living in the conscious mind. It's how we get the GCSEs and A Levels that get us into university and on in life. But it isn't, at the core, how we write fiction.

Balancing Unconscious and Conscious

Throughout *Becoming A Writer*, Dorothea Brande puts the case for the existence of these two sides of the mind – the unconscious and the conscious; she goes as far as recommending that we consider them not just as separate functions of the same mind but almost 'as separate personalities' – and argues that, with discipline, we may learn to balance our use of these two distinct personalities. Yes, you have to train yourself to give reign to or hold in check both your inner Tie-Dyed Truant *and* your inner Head Boy. 'The composition of fiction can, at least theoretically, be broken into two stages,' Madison Smartt Bell says. 'First, and most important, comes imagination. Next is rendering.'[7] You need to be able to turn on both your playful, imaginative attributes and your critical, reflective, analytic gifts and you need to be able to switch between the two modes at will. Guy Claxton devotes a good deal of energy in *Hare Brain, Tortoise Mind* to examining how we may move backwards and forwards between unconscious and conscious mind, and how we may close the gap between the two. Here Dorothea Brande proposes a way in which the two parts of the mind may be used to complement one another:

> The unconscious must flow freely and richly, bringing at demand all the treasures of memory, all the emotions, incidents, scenes, intimations of character and relationship which it has stored away in its depths; the conscious mind must control, combine, and discriminate between these materials without hampering the unconscious flow.[8]

This, when the rubber hits the road for writers, has several implications. I've already gone into some detail about how we may tap our unconscious. Conscious mind functions will include reading as a writer (see Chapter 4) and everything we learn about craft, in and out of the workshop, through looking at how published fiction writers achieve their effects. They will include emulating tricks you see your favourite author pull off. Conscious mind functions will cover, too, the theory about certain elements of craft (characterisation, dramatisation or transitions, for instance) that you study in your workshops or in texts like this. All of which presents you with a problem: the more you know from the labours of your conscious mind, the harder it is not feel inhibited from using your unconscious – as Madison Smartt Bell says here:

> So you go home from class with your pumped-up craft consciousness sitting on your shoulder... When you sit down to write, you are stuck in yourself, paralysed by self-consciousness, unable to separate yourself, unable to relax your mind, unable to pass through the auto-hypnotic gate into the realm where the narrative you are working with becomes true and alive to you. Whatever you write falls dead on the page.[9]

What do you do? How do you put pen to paper when you have the whole weight not only of world literature but also of your growing craft consciousness building up over months and years of classes? Well, you turn to your favourite Californian Creative Writing guru, Natalie Goldburg:

Rules of Writing Practice[10]

1. Keep your hand moving
2. Lose control
3. Be specific
4. Don't think
5. Worry about punctuation & grammar later
6. You are free to write the worst junk
7. Go for the jugular.

And you forget about everything except, as Raymond Carver once memorably remarked, getting one word down after the other, one sentence down after the other. After that, you have all the time in the world to worry about whether or not it's any good. And when you turn to that task, you are already an expert in applying your conscious mind to most aspects of life. You will know what to do.

2 Making Notes

Writing Burst

'£1.55.'

Why do 100 metres sprinters train? In part to keep fit, but perhaps mainly so that they are prepared for the events in which they will compete. Same deal with concert pianists: they practise in order to perfect their technique, to keep their fingers supple, to learn to keep in time and it's all preparation for the occasions when they will perform. Every time you sit down to write fiction, you are giving a performance. If you want to perform to the best of your ability, you need to practise, practise, practise – which is certainly part of what writers use notebooks for. John Fowles, author of *The French Lieutenant's Woman*, says, 'I am a great believer in diaries, if only in the sense that bar exercises are good for ballet dancers.'[1]

The Present Moment

Throughout her books for writers, Natalie Goldburg talks about the importance of practice, and she is an enthusiastic advocate of writing in cafés. In the following extract, she recommends one way in which you may use your notebooks to keep writing fit:

There are two tall glass salt-and-pepper shakers on my wooden table, a pottery bowl full of white packages of sugar. Three pats of butter sit in a white dish, and my favourite pen, that one that Pueblo Runner Printing hands out freely and generously, is lying on the table pointing to the big white plate with only one slice of French bread left and a slice of tomato lying on a piece of lettuce. These are the original details. This is what is on the table. Now if you learn this deeply – what is in the present moment – you can transport it.[2]

Writing Exercise: The Present Moment

Take pen and notebook to a café where you know you're not too likely to be disturbed. Begin writing. Describe your surroundings in clean, clear language, working from the tabletop outwards. Stick with what's there. Occupy the moment fully. If you can do this to your own satisfaction, you will have increased your ability to express yourself in writing, to write descriptively and to record the world you live in, which is an important part of what writers do: hold up a mirror to the world which some day others may read and say, *Yes, that was my experience too. That was just how it seemed to me.*

Retaining Your Ideas

Artists maintain sketchbooks, which they carry about their persons so that they may record stimuli as they find them, so that they may break off at various points in the day and, wherever they are, sit down and draw. What's good for Turner and Hockney is good for you, too: it's hard to be a writer, perhaps impossible, if you don't develop the habit of having a notebook on you at all times.

There are several reasons for learning this discipline. For one, without your notebook you run the risk of losing your ideas. Joseph Heller, the author of *Catch 22* once remarked, 'I don't get my best ideas while actually writing.'[3] Your ideas for and about stories will come while you are mooching in shops, while you are unable to sleep in the middle of the night, while you are putting up shelves – mostly at times when you aren't at your keyboard working on your fiction. Carry a notebook.

How It Felt To Be You

Amongst the many further reasons for using notebooks is Joan Didion's in this extract from her essay, 'On Keeping A Notebook':

See enough and write it down, I tell myself, and then some morning when the world seems drained of wonder, some day when I am only going through the motions of doing what I am supposed to do, which is write – on that bankrupt morning I will simply open my notebook and there it will all be, a forgotten account with accumulated interest, paid passage back to the world out there: dialogue overhead in hotels and elevators and at the hatcheck counter…*How it felt to me*: that is getting closer to the truth about a notebook…*Remember what it was to be me*: that is always the point.'[4]

As well as observing the present moment and recording your ideas, your notebook may allow you to make a deposit in some metaphorical bank account, one from which you will withdraw from in the future, and your withdrawal may be more than just the record of what you witnessed, more than just story material; it could be worthwhile as a record of how you were in the moments you were writing up what you saw, a record of how it felt to be you.

Maybe you think you know how it feels to be you. Writing about your observations and experiences in your notebooks would still be a good idea, though, because you may never be in that café, that situation, that city, that country, that moment again.

In any case, maybe you don't know how it feels to be you as much as you think. Look at this, which I came across recently:

We've just come back from a short holiday at Glenwherry. Uncle Billie was cutting, 'tedding,' turning and baling hay while we were there, so I saw plenty of the sun. The weather has been scorching for these last few days and it's just as warm here at the foot of Craigantlet. Jock, needless to say, is running about with his tongue hanging out. (Running is not quite the right word for it, though; slouching would fit better.) All the roses are out at the moment and there is a great variety of shades. One of the nicest is a beautiful maroon colour.

I have a whole stack of short stories, essays, poems, drawings and cartoons home with me which I am trying to edit into next term's school magazine, which we call *OINK*. This is a new idea which a few of us started last term. We have an editorial committee and each member of it takes a turn as editor. David Lloyd was editor of the first issue, which came out last term. I am the editor of issue two, which will come out at the beginning of next term. We sold about 250–300 copies at 6p each of the last one.

I know plenty about how it feels to be me now, but maybe not so much how it feels to be that 16-year-old kid in 1972. All my adult life I've thought of myself as a person who hates rose bushes; here's the evidence that I once admired them. Jock, the West Highland terrier we had in my teens, was killed on a road when I was 20. I haven't had a dog since; I'm no longer somebody who knows about how it is to keep dogs. In 1972 I bought most of the attitudes I had been brought up with wholesale. Nowadays I haven't that many of them left. And so on. By the time you reach mid-life, you have been a lot of people.

Use your notebook to record who you are while you are that person, and how it feels to be that person then. In time, you will become somebody different, and the person you were may be lost.

For Your Own Joy

In a list he made of attitudes and practices necessary to the writer, Jack Kerouac, the beat generation novelist, notes the pleasure of having a place you can go to and write whatever you want. Number one on his list of 30 points was this: 'Scribbled secret notebooks, and wild typewritten pages, for your own joy.'[5]

Writing Exercise: The Joy Of Notebooks

Get yourself a notebook to set aside as your den, your secret place, the snug you go to say everything you want to about everything that matters to you, everything that doesn't matter to anyone and all points in between. Keep this notebook for the sheer pleasure of pouring out your thoughts and feelings about your life, about you. Nobody ever has to see this; it's for you alone. It's your Batcave, your Fortress of Solitude, and what you do there will help you to be the superhero you are when you go back to the real world.

Paying Close Attention

The Greek word *skopos* may mean 'look out for'; it also means 'pay close attention.' In English, we form the words 'telescope' and 'microscope' from *skopos*. This is instructive. We use a telescope to see better things at some distance and we use a microscope in order to see things so small we would otherwise miss. You get the picture.

I went to Glasgow once with a friend and the first thing we did was take an underground train. On the train, I hung on a strap and my friend took the only free seat. She was maybe a couple of metres from me. We were kept apart by other standing passengers hanging on straps along the aisle that separated the banks of seats running along either side of the train. One of these seats contained what seemed to be an old-fashioned hotel commissioner. He was wearing a dark blue uniform generously covered with brass buttons, gold braid and yellow and blue epaulettes. If I remember right, he had that Jimmy Edwards mutton-chops moustache and sideburns look. He was holding an imperious-looking hat.

As I was drinking in every detail of this peacock in our midst, something caught my eye and I noticed that my friend was watching me studying him and grinning her head off. I mouthed *What?* at her and she smiled and shook her head, as much as to say, *Never mind.* I found out later that what she had been laughing at was my characteristic habit of people-watching.

One of the writer's disciplines is paying close attention to the world you live in. My guess is you already study your surroundings. You'll know what it's like then to Hoover up every detail of wherever you happen to be. It's watchfulness. It's being aware of your surroundings, of your fellow travellers on the journey we're all on. It's noticing what goes on, what people look like and sound like. It's paying attention to the ways in which they interact. You're part anthropologist and part spy. Maybe you haven't been conscious until now that this is something you do. Or maybe you have. Either way, it's a tendency you might think of developing; it's a trait that you can easily turn into a discipline.

> **Writing Burst**
>
> *She doesn't live here anymore.*

Watching, Listening

Years ago, when I was in my twenties, insecure and, of course, arrogant as a result, I remember feeling critical of an acquaintance that I considered boring and thinking to myself *I could write a more interesting character*. I was wrong. One thing to get straight as we start to look at the whole business of observing and writing fiction is that life is invariably more interesting and more complex than fiction. Truth, the old saw goes, is stranger than fiction. You bet it is.

The most seemingly uncomplicated person you know is infinitely more multi-faceted than any character you will ever create. Just because it's true it wasn't Wilde that good writing is life with the dull parts left out there's no reason to conclude that life itself is universally dull. Life is richly, abundantly of interest and every time you leave your keyboard and venture into the thick of it, you will be able to harvest all kinds of data, detail, characters, settings and narratives. All you have to do is be alert to what's around you.

Public places are full of stimulus for the writer. As you stand in the checkout queue at Tesco, you'll be able to read people by what they say to the staff scanning their purchases and by the contents of their shopping trolley. Last week as I was looking for a bottle of wine in Morrison's, I witnessed a micro-story. A guy in his late thirties was berating a member of staff, a calm woman who was biting her tongue and offering no resistance to his complaints. His problem was that the price of a pack of Heineken had been confusingly displayed. 'You've done this before,' he was saying. 'It's deceitful, it's a deliberate racket.' The assistant wasn't engaging with him, but was apologising if the signage had been misleading. She said she would report it. The angry guy wasn't satisfied, though, and turned on his heel to leave, shouting behind him that Morrison's had lost a customer.

There are two characters here, each distinct. One is angry for little reason; the other is impressively calm and forbearing. If you were a writer taking all of this in, you would have the makings of a scene here: characters, conflict, setting. You might, as I did, conclude that this guy had had a bad day, that he was transferring anger about something else onto this trivial irritation. Maybe he had been angry since childhood. Maybe he didn't have all that much to put up with – not when you compared him to the assistant, who might be a single mother of three children, living in cramped conditions with a parent suffering from Alzheimer's. And so on.

Watching and listening are part of your job. (And smelling, touching and tasting. What does it smell off in the supermarket fresh produce aisle?) Supermarkets are good places to observe and eavesdrop. So too are railway stations and airports. Why? Because many people gather in these places and they are all interesting and they all are in the middle of the thousands of stories that make up their lives.

Public transport is a gift to the writer. There's nothing like sitting on a bus, a tram or a train and soaking it all up. Mobile phones have made public transport even more of a gift. If, as I was,

you were born in the middle of the last century, you will probably
still be amazed after a decade of mobiles at how naked people are
prepared to allow their phones to leave them when they are travelling.
On crowded trains, I've heard people discussing their sex lives on the
phone. Mobile phones are pure gold for the writer. Join me on the
train from Manchester to London last March and you'll see what I mean.

I'm sitting there, doing a bit of work, and in the course of the
two and a half hours to London, I can't help but overhear the calls
this guy in front of me is making. I can see through the gap between
the two seats before me that he has a laptop, on which he's working
on spreadsheets between calls. From time to time, he scribbles on
the screen of his multifunctional mobile with the little plastic stylus.
He calls his secretary and asks her to book a restaurant for him in
Berlin. His hi-spec gear suggests that he's a corporate high-flyer and
he's definitely a bit of a thruster, very much in control, taking care
of business. But basically he sounds like an okay guy. Once we're
past Watford, he kicks back, puts on headphones and watches a
David Gray concert on DVD.

Then he makes a different kind of call. His tone is defensive now,
not empowered. 'I just want what's best for you,' he's saying. 'I just
want to make a good settlement for you and the kids. That's all.'
He has to do a lot of listening during this call. At one point he refers
to somebody who seems to be his lawyer. Finally, he's talking about
a woman. 'You'd like her,' he says. 'I want you to meet her some
time. I think you'd get on.' Then he makes a lot of short, defensive
replies: 'Yes...Yes...All right...Yes,' and reiterates that he just
wants 'what's best for you and the kids.'

We're on the slow roll into Euston when this guy packs up, puts
his raincoat on and moves diagonally across the carriage to the table
near the sliding doors. He wants to get off the train as soon as it
pulls up at the platform. I can see his face now. He doesn't look like
his high-flying lifestyle is doing him much good. There are shadows
under his eyes. He looks careworn and beaten up – probably by the
conversation he's just had with his estranged wife.

Now I'm not claiming to be good at this kind of stuff, but if you
think about this people-watching anecdote, you may see that a
surface reading of the guy in front of me on the train to London
would have been that he was your average corporate executive,
doing battle in the world of modern business. Doing pretty well at
it, too: the technological paraphernalia, the restaurant booking in
Berlin. But if you were able to hang round long enough, as I was,

and observe closely enough, another tale emerges. Now he's a nice guy whose family has been bust apart, probably by the stresses of his job. On the face of it, a player. Under the surface, a victim.

Writing Exercises: Paying Close Attention

Many novelists have backgrounds in journalism, and one of the things a fiction writer and a reporter have in common is that both are reporting. Your job, like the news reporter's, is to find out about the world and report back on what your research has thrown up. All you need to do is watch and listen. You need to look at the world around you and penetrate the surface of things. Listening will be as important as being watchful. More important than any of these disciplines is the need to record in writing what you pay close attention to; you see and hear the world all your waking hours, but you haven't processed the data until you have passed it through your own thoughts and feelings, until you have written it down.

Eavesdrop as you move from one place to the next. Snippets of dialogue from people who have passed out of earshot before you hear the end of their sentence can be very thought provoking. As I was walking between classes, I once heard one passing student say to another, 'Five pints, right…' which gave me a whole scenario with which to conjure.

Pay attention in lifts. Here you are enclosed in a space with strangers, who if they are alone like you are probably trying to pretend that nobody else in the lift is actually there. If they're with people, they will be talking about something for which you will have to deduce the context. This is fruitful for writers.

When you're watching people, look for the telling physical detail. Everyone's face and body will have a few defining details. Perhaps it's a run of phrase that is characteristic of the person. A friend of mine used to often begin her anecdotes with, And by all accounts…We all have stock phrases that we use too much. As with telling physical detail, look for them and record them.

In his novel, Something Happened, Joseph Heller analyses office politics entertainingly. He does a wry breakdown of the pecking order in the workplace of his protagonist. The way Heller expresses the power struc- ture here is in terms of who has the whammy on whom. Write an analysis of who has the whammy on whom in your workplace and note the difference between official and actual positions.

Research

Be specific comes number three in Natalie Goldburg's Rules of Writing Practice,[6] and just about any book on craft you care to pick up will endorse this advice. For one thing, it's about precision. If I write *I noticed the vase of flowers as soon as I entered the room*, it tells you a little, but not as much as *I noticed the vase of peonies as soon as I entered the room*. In fiction, you are trying to build a believable world in the mind of the reader. Each detail you can specify within that picture becomes a little jewel that decorates the abric and enhances the imagined world. Generalities won't do that, so you should avoid them.

> **Writing Burst**
>
> *I don't know when I last saw the sun.*

The best advice on detail I have come across is in a book on writer's craft by George V. Higgins, the American crime writer:

> Solid reportage is interesting precisely because the reporter has gone to the trouble of acquiring information about his or her subject, and then has carefully organised it, so that the reader completing the text knows something that he or she did not know before. James Reston, reflecting on his long and distinguished career as a reporter and commentator on national politics for *The New York Times*, concluded that any respect he deserved was probably attributable to his early experience as a sportswriter. To cover sports, he said, the reporter soon learns that he must pay attention at all times, because no one ever becomes sufficiently expert to predict unerringly the outcome of every contest...When the reporter is promoted to writing a column about sports, it is usually with the understanding that mere opinions on the topic of the day will not suffice; those opinions will be taken seriously only if they are manifestly grounded in fact...When [sportswriters] get it wrong, there is hell to pay...
>
> The fiction writer owes the same debt of respect to the reader.[7]

What this is all about is a little more than just specifying; it's about doing the necessary research so that you are in a position to specify: the reporter has gone to the trouble of acquiring information about his or her subject, and then has carefully organised it, so that the reader completing the text knows something that he or she did not know before. If you have done the research, you will be able to give your work texture, and so make it credible. It will have the ring of authenticity that your readers require of it.

Recently, the novelist Nicholas Royle came to talk to a group of my students. One of the memorable things he discussed was his predilection for trespassing. He has a fascination with derelict buildings and will regularly enter one, equipped with torch, notebook, camera and camcorder. He risks arrest, attack and, I guess, buildings falling in on him. But his readers benefit because in his work, in novels such as *Antwerp*, buildings are a real presence, lending his fiction genuine atmosphere. Buildings are almost characters (see Chapter 11).

To show you how your writing may benefit from researched data, look at this passage from Carol Shields' novel *Larry's Party*, which won the Orange Prize in 1998. Shields was an academic, and never to my knowledge a coach upholsterer. Yet, as you will see here, she appears to know all she needs to know about this trade.

Stu Weller loves his job. For thirty years now he's worked as an upholsterer for the custom coach company in south Winnipeg…A custom coach is a handmade object, that's something most people don't appreciate. You take a few basic sheets of metal, cut them, bend them, twist them, applying braces and rivets, and there you've got something entirely different. Everything but the motor is built right on the Air-Rider factory floor, even the fuel tanks, even the decorative touches, which is where Stu Weller comes in. It's a fact that some of North America's biggest and brightest names in the entertainment industry have ordered customised vehicles from Air-Rider, wondrous rolling homes and offices with white carpeting on the walls and Italian marble for flooring. A country-and-western singer – after a beer or two Stu Weller will drop the odd hint about who exactly this singer is – customer ordered a model with a bathroom floor that dropped open, bingo, to reveal a hot tub where the luggage compartment generally goes. A cool half-million dollars for that package. This same coach possessed a full kitchen with oak inlay cupboards and a hidden berth for the travelling cook.[8]

In order to write this piece of fiction, Carol Shields had to do some research. That's lesson one. Equally important is to note how she has used this research. Not only has she given us sufficient detail to convince us that Stu Weller is an upholsterer at a custom coach firm, but she also has filtered the researched data through the character. We don't just learn about this arcane world; we learn about it from Stu Weller's perspective. There is a similarity here to what I say about using setting to enhance character (again, in Chapter 11). In just the same way as you may reveal characters by showing them engaging with a particular setting, so too you may reveal characters by the way they engage with a role or a job.

> **Writing Exercise: Research**
>
> Either from a text (a book, television programme or website) or through interviewing somebody, find out about a very particular profession. Piano tuning. Dog training. Car mechanics. Or even, like Larry in *Larry's Party*, floristry.
>
> You will need to generate only one page of notes.
>
> When you have, imagine the character of the person who does this job. Now write about a page of fiction, using not only data, but also some of the other craft you have been studying in Part II of this book, to engage the reader.

Other Purposes For Notebooks

There will be more reasons to maintain the notebook habit than I cover in this chapter, but beyond what I've said so far, here are some further purposes for the writer's vital tool:

- Recording overheard conversations.

- Collecting interesting words you come across.

- Noting down dreams.

- Capturing thoughts, impressions, reflections, feelings – everything that passes through your head.

- Making observations, in the manner of an anthropologist: look at human behaviour like a clinical psychologist. Chekhov brought a physician's perspective to his characters, whom he almost diagnosed like the doctor he was. Somehow if you are studying the world to record it, you notice a great deal more.

- Making sketches in words of settings for your fiction. There's a spirit or a character to every place you go, and creating a sense of place in fiction is crucial.

- Put these last two together: how do people behave in particular places? At the airport or in a café. At motorway services or in the bank.

- You might like to collect your research in a notebook. This may mean taking notes from a book, a film on DVD or a TV programme

- Make notes on your reading from the novels and writing about writing that you study (see the section on The Reading Log in Chapter 4).

Writing Exercise: Test Drive A Writer's Notebook

Buy yourself a notebook that will fit in your pocket and carry it with you at all times for one whole week. As a bare minimum, set aside 10 minutes to write in your notebook between getting up and lunchtime and a second 10 minutes between lunchtime and bedtime. (You may well end up taking the notebook out and writing more than twice a day, but keep to the commitment of at least two 10-minute slots.)

In these short slots, take yourself away from the people around you, find a quiet spot and either observe and record your surroundings or reflect on something interesting that has occurred in the previous few hours. Maybe you will write down interesting conversations you have overheard. Maybe you will have an insight about some issue or relationship in your life. Perhaps you will describe a billboard that strikes you as entertaining or resonant. You might have to express your frustration about something you've just experienced.

Maintain this twice a day habit for a week. At the end of the week, summarise the kinds of writing that have appeared in your notebook and assess the worth of this writer's discipline.

500-word Story Project: Person, Place, Problem

Throughout this book you will find Story Projects, assignments to get you practising what you have been studying.

Your first Story Project is to attempt a very short story, one of only 500 words. While we're here at your first (slightly) extended fiction assignment, let me defend the discipline of word limitations. Being asked to write to a given length is very good for your development. Having limitations placed on the length of the story you write will concentrate your mind and teach you how to use language and your developing craft economically and efficiently.

As a stimulus, here's a table.

Person	Place	Problem
Nurse	Starbucks	Man she was meeting hasn't turned up
Fresher	Campus finance office	Loan hasn't come through
Shop assistant	Department store	Colleague is stealing from till

Each of these has the makings of a story, but I don't want you to do the obvious and select horizontally. Instead, take the Person from one row, but take the Place from a different row and the Problem from yet another row. In other words, if you select 'Nurse,' you can't select 'Starbucks' and 'Man she was meeting hasn't turned up.' You could select 'Nurse,' 'Department store' and 'Loan hasn't come through.' In selecting, you can hop around as you like, but no two items may come from the same row.

Your story doesn't need a beginning, middle and ending, but it must have a change of some kind. If you haven't been, now is the time to get used to writing with a word-processor, so produce this Story Project on your computer. You'll learn more about page design later in the book, but for the moment, your only design consideration is making sure you have double-spaced your work.

3 Keeping Journals

The habit of keeping a writer's journal is one of the key disciplines of writing fiction. Apart from anything else, it is where you assemble the resources that will become your fiction. In *Words Fail Me*, Patricia T. O'Connor argues that

> a writer with good material is one who never lets a useful nugget slip away... A titbit doesn't have to be earth shattering to be worth saving. It only has to be useful.[1]

Faced with beginning to keep a writer's journal, you may feel squeezed in and inhibited by a flurry of questions the answers to which seem elusive. Questions like: what does a writer's journal look like? Where do you keep it? How do you use it? How is it different from using a notebook? Before starting, though, let's get one thing out of the way: your journal and your notebook are not two separate things. Inevitably, your notebook may form part of your journal.

> **Writing Burst**
>
> *We'll never know for sure.*

The Theory

Looking back on notes I made on the first book I ever read on the subject of journals, Tristine Rainer's *The New Diary*, I would say the most appealing concepts of journal writing I derived there are that it may be:

- a repository for thoughts, feelings and ideas which would otherwise be lost
- a creative project journal

- a diary (record of daily events etc.)
- a place to paste in photo, clippings, letters, quotes, drawings, doodles, dried flowers, business cards, labels
- a place for the writer to work out.

On that last topic, Natalie Goldburg promotes the idea of *writing practice* (see Chapter 1), a discipline writers need in the same way as musicians need to practise their instrument or athletes to train each day. The journaling habit is a way to keep ourselves writing fit. In a related aspect of the subject, Dorothea Brande's *Becoming A Writer* suggests writing each day to develop the habit of opening up a channel to the unconscious mind, harvesting our own creativity (again, see Chapter 1). Jennifer Moon's *Learning Journals*[2] introduces other attributes of journaling – that it can enable learning from experience and increase critical reflection and, most notably, that writing is a method of thinking, and thus the journal is a place to think, and that thinking in written words slows the pace of thinking and creates time and space for reflection. Moon also suggests that the habit of keeping a journal as a place to reflect will develop self-awareness and self-confidence.

Less well known than Rainer *et al.* is Daniel Price's *How To Make A Journal of Your Life*, a left-field little book with a handmade feel, which includes advice that is often liberating:

> When there are no more rules about how much time you're supposed to be spending with your journal, and when you feel light-hearted and buoyant about what you want to put in, you'll find yourself enjoying the time and doing good work. Not just making it another addition to your already busy schedule.[3]

In other words, it will be liberating to bear in mind that journaling, rather than being a chore to feel bad about when you're not keeping to some imagined schedule, is best seen as an opportunity to work enjoyably, to play even.

Price has come to see journaling as at least as much a visual record of his perspective on life as a written one, so his book may introduce you to new ways of recording your life, beyond what you write. 'Always remember,' he says, 'that your voice and anything you create is uniquely yours. No one else in the entire world can say things quite the way you do.'[4]

Amongst the approaches he recommends are:

- sketching what you observe alongside what you write about it
- photocopying paragraphs from books, newspapers or magazines and pasting them into your journal
- collecting flowers and seeds in the journal by attaching them to the page with clear adhesive tape
- taking a camera everywhere with you and attaching the resulting photographs to the pages of your journal. (Some or all of your journal may be on a computer so saving digital photographs within a digital journal makes this final technique easy.)

My Writer's Journal

When I look it square in the eye, I see that for almost as long as I have been trying to be a writer – certainly for as long as I have been trying to teach Creative Writing – I have had an unconscious view that a writer's journal looks like something, that it is something, *one* thing. I have to admit, though, that I don't really believe this. I don't think that there really is such a thing as 'the writer's journal.' If I'm honest, I've never kept one.

Does this mean that I have never practised any of what I preach? No. What I'm trying to get off my chest here is that I have been labouring under the illusion that I always maintain two physical items in my writer's armoury, a notebook and a journal. I don't. I certainly have at least one and usually two or three notebooks on the go at any time, but when it comes down to it, I have never had a physical object that could be described as a writer's journal. It's much more diffuse than that.

My writer's journal isn't ever in any one place; it's spread through several places, through quite a few physical locations. In electronic form, it's either inside the Mac I'm writing this chapter on or on scores of floppy discs and CDs stored just by it. Here I can find the following:

- research notes and draft chapters for my last novel and for my next one
- short stories, in various stages of completion

- a daily spiritual journal I've been keeping for almost 20 years now
- a folder of song lyrics, both work in progress and completed work
- research, planning, reflection, drafts and completed scripts for the youth arts group I've been working with these past seven years
- drafts and competed chapters for books like this one – including, in five minutes when I stop for lunch, this draft of this chapter.

Note that one of the possible uses of your journal mentioned twice in the bullet points above is *research*. Often in your fiction you will need to find out about an aspect of your story or novel of which you have inadequate prior knowledge. This is one of the functions of your journal: as a repository for research notes. And speaking of research, bear in mind that research isn't only what you find; it's also what finds you, as Bernard Mac Laverty explains here:

> I attended an advertised composer's workshop at the BBC, with the Chinese composer Tan Dun. He worked on a stage with about ten music students. There were no musical instruments and he used breath and voice to compose – along with mouth pops and hand claps. He talked about pre-hearing and inner hearing. I was sitting rapt on the edge of my seat in a lecture on composition listening to people breathing. Tan Dun became the basis for the composer Huang Xiao Gang in *Grace Notes*.[5]

If I step a metre to my left, I come to a second desk in which I have stashed letters, postcards and mementoes from quite a few friends over the past 30 years, going back as far as this 1975 letter from my girlfriend then, telling me about her Christmas vacation job delivering mail in North London:

> I made the acquaintance of a dog and a few cats – which are so cold sometimes that I ring the bell hoping they will let their cat in again.

If I move beyond the desk with the letters a further metre to the left, I come to a section of the bookshelves in the study where I stash old notebooks. In a spiral notebook with a faded cover, which at a guess comes from 1990, I find a heading, 'SHORT STORIES,' and two shorthand ideas:

> John & Picasso on the beach at the Isle of Wight.
> Paul B. stuck in Belfast harbour trying to rescue a dog from some trees. Nothing on but his underpants. A bunch of residents looking on.

Helen Newall (see 'Characters') recently told me that she recommends assiduous journal keeping because, as she said:

> When I'm having a black writing day, and can't come up with a single word, I put on some music and go trawling through old notebooks and journals and look for a starting point. I flip through old journals and if I'm lucky I may come across something where I'm excited by, for instance, a certain rhythm. Since I no longer know why I wrote the original piece, I am liberated from the original intention. Not so long ago, I managed to use this technique to produce a story which *Mslexia* published.

And by the way, in the same conversation, Helen told me that her writer's journal, unlike mine, is always a physical object, an attractively bound book with unlined pages. 'I like to have at least one journal for each writing project,' she said. 'For one thing, it means you have more chance of finding what you're looking for when you want to turn up the crucial notes you made on, say, eighteenth century Highland crofts.'

Your Writer's Journal

Let's try to summarise some of the key points of this chapter. Arguably, the most important uses you can put your journal to are:

- recording your experiences and perceptions
- as a place to work out, to practise writing
- as a creative nursery, a place to nurture your ideas for stories, poems, scripts, memoirs
- reflecting about your reading and writing, about your intentions as well as your achievements.

What I have been at pains, I think, to say here is that it doesn't matter whether what you call your journal is a single physical object, a stylish artefact from Paperchase, or a collection of writing spread through computer files, notebooks, letters, desk drawers, shelves, cupboards (and, if you're like me, over the carpet). Your writer's journal may take the form that suits you best. What matters most is, first and foremost, that you are writing on a daily basis. If you acquire this habit, what you are doing, according to Dorothea Brande, is:

training yourself…simply to write. It makes no difference to the success of this practice if your paragraphs are amorphous, the thought vague or extravagant, the ideas hazy.[6]

If you're not writing every day, you won't be as able as you need to be when you sit down to compose something you hope to polish and publish. I can't help thinking here of the cellist Julian Lloyd Webber, who once claimed in a magazine feature that if he didn't practise three hours a day he would notice an impaired performance at his next concert; if he practised only two hours a day, his fellow musicians would notice; and if he practised only one hour a day, the public would notice.

Of the things which matter most about acquiring the journaling habit, perhaps second on the list is that in keeping a journal you are storing up your small precious items. As Patricia T. O'Connor has it:

> an idea in your head is merely an idle notion. But an idea written down, that's the beginning of something! Stripped to its briefs, a piece of writing is nothing more than a handful of ideas, put into words and arranged to do a job. We all get ideas – try *not* thinking in the shower. The trick is to write them down.[7]

You could think of your journal as the storehouse for all the grapes you pick at harvest time: you're collecting the resources you will need to make your very own Shiraz Cabernet (quaffable, and who knows, maybe even transcendent).

Writing Exercise: A Week With Your Journal

This is an exercise for which you should commit one week. This way, you may experience some of the virtues of maintaining a journaling habit.

What You Will Need

Whether you use a bound book with 80 gm paper or files on your computer you will need to create three repositories for your writing:

1. a place to practice

2. a place to record

3. a place to reflect.

You will also need to put your writer's notebook to work during the course of each day, recording anything interesting that you think of, witness or experience. (See the end of Chapter 3, *The Writer's Notebook*.) For this initial exercise, I'd suggest aiming to make just three entries in your notebook each day. The idea throughout this exercise is to make all of this as feasible for yourself as you can.

What You Do

First of all, *practising*. Choose a point in the day when you can spare 10 minutes. Because you are closest to your unconscious when you wake, early in the morning is best, but you will have to decide yourself what is actually achievable. All you're committing to for those brief 10 minutes is sitting down and writing the first thing that comes into your head – writing without stopping. All you have to do is keep your pen moving over the page, your fingers over the keyboard. If you find getting started difficult, why not select a Writing Burst from this book to help you begin each day?

Next, *recording*. Decide on a point in the evening when you can spare another 10 minutes and copy your three notebook entries into the recording section of whatever you're using for your journal.

Finally, *reflecting*. Once you have reached the end of a week in which you have practised and recorded each day, set aside half an hour to look at what you've amassed. As Helen Newall suggests above, put on some music that will help to create a relaxed mood. Have a glass of wine, a beer, or some peppermint tea – whatever your poison. Do all you can to make the experience chilled and pleasurable. Having spent half an hour looking over your writing and your notes, contemplating anything that seems to have some promise, spend another half hour expressing your thoughts about what you see before you now and about the experience of this week long exercise. Here you might surprise yourself with what you have discovered – either in the habit of writing each morning, or in the potential in some of the notes you have made.

Finally, you might like to tot up how much of your time this exercise has cost you. Not much, I think you will find.

4 How To Read As A Writer

According to the novelist Joyce Carol Oates, 'For the writer, reading is part of the process of writing.' For Oates, reading is an essential part of any writer's apprenticeship:

> Even before we know we will be writers, our reading is a part of our preparation for writing…Every book, every story, every sentence we read is a part of our preparation for our own writing.[1]

This is corroborated by research into how we read. The American novelist Jonathan Franzen interviewed an expert in the subject, Shirley Brice Heath, Professor of English and Linguistics at Stanford University.

> There's a second kind of reader. There's the social isolate – the child who from an early age felt very different from everyone around him…What happens is you take that sense of being different into an imaginary world. But that world, then, is a world you can't share with the people around you – because it's imaginary. And so the important dialogue in your life is with the *authors* of the books you read. Though they aren't present, they become your community.[2]

John Gardner gives a less positive inflexion to the case for reading: 'No ignoramus – no writer who has kept himself innocent of education – has ever produced great art.'[3] You already know you are a writer, and you empathise with anyone who advocates reading as much as you can, reading like your life depended on it. (I was at a Reader's Day last year where the English novelist Lesley Glaister expressed her passion for reading by saying that if it came to a choice between reading and eating, as long there was no question of dying from the decision, she would always opt for reading.)

> **Writing Burst**
>
> *Was the glass half-full or half-empty?*

As a writer, of course, you will want not only to read as much as you can, but also to read work that challenges your views about what is good fiction. In other words, when it comes to reading, quality counts as much as quantity. Your reading is what shapes your writing; it is your diet. Good nutrition makes for a healthy writer. I remember once hearing the notion expounded, in another context, that what you focus on is what you image – or more simply, what you concentrate on is what you will come to resemble. This is one of the reasons why Stephen King insists that 'reading is the creative centre of the writer's life.'[4]

Why Read As A Writer?

'My purpose in reading,' the distinguished American novelist John Updike has stated, 'has ever secretly been not to come and judge but to come and steal.'[5] This, frankly, is what artists do. Artistic practice is a matter of consumption that leads to production. Artists in any field consume their preferred examples of good practice and synthesise them into something new. David Byrne, the main songwriter in the 1980s band Talking Heads, talks about the process in his song 'The Good Thing,' where he alludes to adapting things and making them his own. In fiction, Graham Swift modelled the structure of his Booker Prize winning novel *Last Orders* on that of William Faulkner's *As I Lay Dying*. At the time, Swift drew a good deal of flack in the media, just as Zadie Smith has done with her new novel *On Beauty* which is informed by the work of E.M. Forster. However, to anyone who ever tried to write fiction, to anyone who has engaged in any kind of artistic practice, these accusations of plagiarism must have seemed wide of the mark. If we can't base what we create on previous models, how can we be expected to come up with anything at all? There's nothing new under the sun. 'All great writing is in a sense imitation of great writing,' John Gardner argues.

> Writing a novel, however innovative that novel may be, the writer struggles to achieve one specific large effect, what can only be called the effect we are used to getting from good novels.[6]

This is how artists work. We look at the models of good practice we admire, several of them at once, and we synthesise the techniques we see here to make something new, something the world has never seen before. Why is it new? Because each of us has different tastes and selects his or her own range of influences. Here's the American writer Rick Bass discussing one of his influences:

> I used to model a lot of stories after [Richard Ford's] *Rock Springs* collection. It's a very powerful book. I remember the end of the title story, 'Rock Springs,' where the narrator asks the reader all these questions beginning, 'Would you think...' I never heard of such a thing. We're always told it's bad to put rhetoric in a story. To put it at the *end* of a story, what kind of stunt is that? All of a sudden, five or six stories in a row, and he's ending them with questions. There was an opening of boundaries. Also, I like his roundabout way of telling a story, that air of relaxation mixed with immediacy. It's a fine tension, a fine ambivalence.[7]

How To Read As A Writer

Heather Leach talks about learning 'to look beneath the surface of the print for traces of the *making* process, the writer at work.'[8] This is at the heart of reading as a writer. If you study Literature at university, you will be trained in the disciplines of literary criticism, taught to interpret, to look at themes, to examine meaning and literary context and often to do so with an implicit understanding of some literary theory or other. None of these things trains you to read as a writer. When you read as a writer, as Heather Leach intimates, you are trying *to find out how it was done*. Rather than interpreting the fiction, you are dismantling it to see how the end result has been achieved. As a writer, you read each short story, each novel, to see what you can take away from it, adapt and make your own.

In studying the art of writing fiction, I would argue, you are learning a craft or, to use Joyce Carol Oates' term, serving a writer's apprenticeship. Thus, reading as a writer will involve you in discussing specific elements of craft. Some of the following, for example, will be relevant to your work in this regard:

- point of view
- characterisation
- narrative structure
- plot

- setting
- use of dialogue
- description
- plant and pay-off
- transitions
- voice
- flashback.

Over the years, the method I've evolved with students preparing reading as a writer assignments has been to combine a response to the text they are dismantling with an understanding of some of the relevant works that theorise the specific element of craft they happen to be considering. So, if you happen to be looking at Margaret Atwood's use of dialogue to try and see how and why it succeeds, you will not only analyse her use of it in context, but also relate her approaches to dialogue writing to some of the work that has considered the art – work by, for example, Lewis Turco, Kate Grenville or James N. Frey. Thus you might summarise some contemporary theories about what makes for good dialogue and then relate that to the actual use of dialogue you are examining. This might well lead you to attempt an analysis of the effect on the reader of this particular piece of dialogue, which brings me on to the relationship between writer and reader.

Much of the focus of reading as a writer is on the reader's response to the text. (Indeed, much of the focus of the fiction writer will inevitably be on how his or her work affects the reader.) The notion of affecting the reader, of putting the reader's mind and heart to work is crucial for the fiction writer. And it might be worth saying in passing that while most people come to university to exercise their minds more than their hearts, you as a learning writer are going to be more occupied in learning to create emotional effects than intellectual ones. If your fiction doesn't at all times engage either the mind or the heart of your reader, and ideally both, you are wasting your time. Much of your efforts as a fiction writer will be devoted to intriguing your readers, to creating questions in their minds – questions such as *Who did it? What is going to happen to this beleaguered protagonist? Is this character going to get away with it? Are this man and this woman going to end up together*? Finding out how the text affects the heart and mind of the reader is most of what you are doing when you read as a writer.

Let's practise reading as a writer on an extract from Elizabeth McCracken's *The Giant's House*. The novel is about the relationship between Peggy Cort, a spinster librarian, and James Sweatt, a giant she befriends while he is a child and has an affair with when he is in his teens. Late in the narrative, after the affair is over, Peggy encounters the father who had abandoned James years before. Just prior to the point where we enter the scene, Sweatt Senior requests some photographs of his son from Peggy, the narrator-protagonist of the novel.

I could give him a picture, a small one.

'I'll bring some to the library Monday,' I said.

'No good. I'm leaving Sunday. Can't I come over?'

Why not, I thought. 'Okay. So. Why did you leave?'

He grabbed his coat. 'Let's go,' he said.

'What? Not now.' I looked at my watch. 'I have to go back to work.'

'After work?' he said. 'I'll pick you up.' He took out his wallet to get money for the check. A snapshot fell out, a pretty girl in a dress.

'Who's this?' I picked it up. 'A girlfriend?'

'Girlfriend emeritus,' he said. 'Gina. Retired as a girlfriend some time ago, but still retains some rights and privileges of the position.'

'Like her picture in your wallet.'

He shrugged and reached further into the slot of his wallet. He extracted a small stack of pictures, then dealt them onto the table like a hand of solitaire. The last two were of Mrs Sweatt, one alone, one holding a baby James.

'I keep 'em all,' said Mr Sweatt. He stacked his pile of pictures, his neat exosomatic memory, and put it away.

'You haven't answered my question,' I said. 'Why did you leave?'

He smiled. 'Boy, you *are* feisty. Okay. I left because my wife asked me impossible questions, and she never let me get away without answering. And if you want a better answer than that, you're going to have to wait until – what, five o'clock?'

I sighed. 'Five o'clock,' I said. 'Sure.'

Writing Exercise: Reading As A Writer

Tom Bailey refers to 'a sort of demon-driven reading...at the heart of learning for a writer.'[9] If you're going to learn from fiction you want to read as a writer, you need to be to some extent like a dog with a bone.

So here's your first reading as a writer exercise.

Since I used it to illustrate what an element of craft might be just now, let's begin with dialogue.

Most pundits agree that good dialogue will create and maintain tension. How does the dialogue in this passage achieve that?

Next, dialogue is a particularly potent means of revealing character. From this very short excerpt, you ought to be able to tell a few things about the personalities involved. What can you deduce about the characters of Peggy and Sweatt Senior and how has Elizabeth McCracken conveyed this information to you?

I alluded earlier to intriguing the reader. This is a formidable device for creating narrative tension. Intrigue usually boils down to creating questions in the mind of the reader. What questions does this passage raise for you?

It's quite likely you will have some hint of how these questions might be answered later in the narrative. What do you think will happen next?

If you're going to be any good at reading as a writer, you'd better practise it, and if you're going to practise it, you need a place to do it, you need a way of getting in the habit of reading as a writer. How about making notes on what you read and storing your notes somewhere you will easily find them?

Writing Exercise: The Reading Log

You're not going to benefit as much as you might from your reading if you don't create a means of digesting your intake. A reading log is one way to do it. Buy yourself a notebook that you will enjoy writing in, something that looks attractive and feels agreeable. Now keep it adjacent to wherever you do most of your reading: on the bedside table if you read in bed, on an occasional table if you read on the sofa in your living room. The kinds of entries you make in your reading log are up to you, but here, to get you started, are a few suggestions:

■ Make notes on passages you especially admire. Here's an example: I've just been reading Colm Toibin's *The Master*, a novel about Henry James. In my reading log, I've made some notes on how Toibin suggests and implies, how he very often communicates between the lines.

- Reading fiction will inspire you. Art often inspires further art, in ways that have nothing to do with plagiarism or *homage*; you just get excited by the imagination of the writer you're reading and that fires your own imagination. Have your reading log ready for such occasions.

- Sometimes your entries will be variations of the previous Writing Exercise: you will be looking at the use of a particular technique in the novel or story you're reading and making notes in your reading log.

- Then, when you finish what you're reading, you will want to see what you thought of it, which will be more fruitful if you write some concluding notes on it in your Reading Log. You'll be saying why this novel or story worked for you, or, to the extent that it didn't, saying why this was so.

Of course, keeping a Reading Log isn't a writing exercise at all; it's a way of life.

Two things writers need to remember about reading. First, that you read fiction in a different way when you are intending to write it. Second, that you can never read too much. You write because you read and you read because you write. If, in years to come, you can emulate the breadth of Hemingway's influences, you won't be doing badly.

Mark Twain, Flaubert, Stendhal, Bach, Turgenev, Tolstoy, Dostoevsky, Chekhov, Andrew Marvell, John Donne, Maupassant, the good Kipling, Thoreau, Captain Marryat, Shakespeare, Mozart, Quevedo, Dante, Virgil, Tintoretto, Hieronymus Bosch, Brueghel, Patinir, Goya, Giotto, Cezanne, van Gogh, Gauguin, San Juan de la Cruz, Gongora – it would take a day to remember everyone. Then it would sound as though I were claiming an erudition I did not possess instead of trying to remember all the people who have been an influence on my life and work.[10]

Reflection Project 1: The Writer Reading

I wanted you to think about your making at this stage in the novel, but you may find it helps here to refer to Chapter 13. A good reason to write reflections is that you will become more real to yourself as a writer. Writers are isolated in a way that perhaps only other artists – painters, composers, sculptors – are. We spend our lives doing work that for a long time nobody ever sees, and, it often feels like, nobody cares about. Teachers, car mechanics and landscape gardeners all get to discuss their work with others on a regular basis. While you're on the road – which may be long – to the agent and literary editor and readership you seek, writing reflectively means that you get to discuss your work with somebody. At worst, this may be with yourself, although if you're studying Creative Writing at university, you will at least be able to discuss your work with your fellow students and your tutors. I say 'at worst' your reflection will be a dialogue with yourself, but of course the dialogue you have with yourself is crucial. It is in this dialogue with yourself, which may only come about through reflective writing, that you will discover your identity as a writer.

As I hope this book continually suggests, what you read forms a great part of what you are as a writer, so examining yourself as a reader will lead you to a greater understanding of your identity as a writer. Francis Spufford has written a memoir about his reading, a reading autobiography. In *The Child That Books Built*, he explores his childhood reading and comes to a greater understanding of the adult he became – as the title suggests, the adult that his reading made him. Look at this self-portrait in books:

I began my reading in kind of hopeful springtime for children's writing. I was born in 1964, so I grew up in a golden age comparable to the present heyday of

38

J.K. Rowling and Philip Pullman, or to the great Edwardian decade when E. Nesbit, Kipling and Kenneth Grahame were all publishing at once. An equally amazing generation of talent was at work as the 1960s ended and the 1970s began. William Mayne was making dialogue sing; Peter Dickinson was writing the *Changes* trilogy; Alan Garner was reintroducing myth into the bloodstream of daily life; Jill Paton Walsh was showing that children's perceptions could be just as angular and uncompromising as those of adults; Joan Aiken had begun her Dido Twite series of comic fantasies; Penelope Farmer was being unearthly with *Charlotte Sometimes*; Diana Wynne Jones's gift for wild invention was hitting its stride; Rosemary Sutcliffe was just adding the final uprights to her colonnade of Romano-British historical novels; Leon Garfield was reinventing the eighteenth century as a scene for inky Gothic intrigue. The list went on, and on, and on. There was activity everywhere, a new potential classic every few months.[1]

Francis Spufford is reflecting on his childhood reading and coming to some conclusions about the adult it made him. Your catalogue of reading that has affected you could be just as detailed as his. However, you are going to reflect from the perspective of a writer, so you will be thinking not only of the authors who were important to you, but also of the way in which they may have influenced you. At the very least, you will be reflecting on what you learned from these authors, as Clare Boylan does here:

The novelist and short story writer William Trevor helped me to understand the difference between long and short fiction forms...Another eminent author helped me out when I was having trouble with my first novel which was too episodic. 'Try taking the last sentence of each chapter and making it the first sentence of the next,' he surprisingly suggested. Surprisingly often, it worked.[2]

Reflection Project 2: Reading As A Writer

For your second Reflection Project, write 1000 words on the books that may have formed you as a writer and try to articulate what you may have learned from them. As before, include a bibliography.

Jotting down answers to the following questions may help you get started.

- What were your earliest encounters with books?
- Did they have any lasting effect on you?
- Do you have a favourite book?
- Why do you like it so much?
- How do you think it may have influenced you?
- Write a list of 10 ways in which reading aids and nourishes the writer.
- Did a book ever change your life?
- In which ways?

II
How To Write Short Stories

5 A Brief Tour Around The Short Story

The term 'short story' did not appear in an English dictionary until 1933. The form is difficult to define. The short story comes in many shapes and sizes. Short stories are usually restricted in time, place and number of characters. Some stories move towards a single ascending dramatic scene or revelation which is generated by conflict. Joyce Carol Oates's definition of the short story is a useful one:

> It represents a concentration of imagination and not an expansion; it is no more than 10,000 words; and no matter its mysteries or experimental properties, it achieves closure – meaning that when it ends, the attentive reader understands why.[1]

It's safe to say that the short story is not a brief novel. According to Valerie Shaw, 'the novel and the short story are separate entities which share the same prose medium but not the same artistic methods.'[2] The short story is a distinct literary form, as different from a novel, perhaps, as a novel is different from a play. Neither is the short story a brief novel. (Mark Twain once apologised for writing a long letter; if he had had more time, he said, he would have written a shorter one.) A short story may have more in common with a poem: Valerie Shaw describes the form as 'short but resonant; written in prose, but gaining the intensity of poetry.' She also draws the comparison with photography: a short story has certain things in common with a snapshot. It may well be a moment revealed, and may deal with only a single incident, or even a single perception. Edgar Allan Poe, one of the earliest theorists of the form argued that composition begins with the conception of 'a certain unique or single *effect* to be wrought out.'

All of this suggests that the story is a distillation. Anton Chekhov observed that 'in short stories it is better to say not enough than to say too much,' and D.H. Lawrence's view was that 'the great thing to do in a short story is to select the salient details – a few striking details to make a sudden swift impression.'

Superficially, novel and story look the same; they are both fiction. But that may be where the similarity ends. You might already have noticed that many short story practitioners are unable to succeed with the novel – V.S. Pritchett, for instance, or, arguably, William Trevor – while some, such as Alice Munro and Grace Paley, are sensible enough not even to attempt it. Equally, you will come across the accomplished novelist who dabbles in short fiction without ever really shining in the medium.

John Lennon once remarked that before Elvis there was nothing. What Elvis Presley is to rock'n'roll, Anton Chekhov (1860–1904) is to the short story. Almost. Prior to Anton Chekhov, short stories were typified by the well-made plot, often with a sting in the tale. Chekhov marks the point where the nineteenth-century short story ends and the twentieth-century short story begins. His stories are a revelation of character and situation that dispense with the need for a traditional plot. Chekhov famously spoke of writing stories with a beginning, middle and end, and then removing the beginning and the end. The American novelist and short story writer Richard Ford is emphatic about the long shadow that Chekhov continues to cast:

> To twentieth century writers, his presence has affected all of our assumptions about what's a fit subject for imaginative writing; about which moments in life are too crucial or precious to relegate to conventional language; about how stories should begin, and the variety of ways a writer may choose to end them.

From Sean O'Faolain in Ireland through Flannery O'Connor in the United States to Alice Munro in Canada, just about anyone writing short stories in the past hundred years has been influenced by Chekhov.

Chekhov is responsible for instigating the partial or complete removal of the author-narrator within his stories. Another trait of his work which has become almost a given of contemporary fictional discourse is the absence of a message or moral. The traditions of fiction writers avoiding explanation, moralising, or inserting a twist in the tale could all be said to have originated with Chekhov. Not to mention the primacy of dramatisation over exposition or the tendency of short stories to use few characters and not many scenes. And finally, there's the notion that the short story is something compressed, a distillation of its chosen reality.

After Chekhov, in my short story hall of fame, comes Ernest Hemingway. His fiction often featured characters outside mainstream society, and, like Chekhov, Hemingway's work conveyed more about characters and situations implicitly than explicitly. Ann Charters in *The Story And Its Writer* calls Hemingway 'probably the most influential writer of English prose in the first half of the 20th century.' This influence can be seen first of all in detective fiction – what's known as 'the hard-boiled' style – in the work of writers such as Dashiel Hammett, Raymond Chandler and Elmore Leonard, but the shadow of Hemingway can also be seen in the minimalist style of late twentieth-century writers such as Raymond Carver and Donald Barthelme.

In the last two decades of the twentieth century, perhaps the two most influential short story writers in the English language have been Ann Beattie and Raymond Carver. In their different ways, both are proponents of domestic realism and both major in the snapshot approach to narrative. Jay McInerney writes of Beattie's 'habit of trailing off into thin air that seemed tremendously mimetic and apt to many young readers and writers but must have frustrated many *New Yorker* readers looking for epiphany.'[3] What Carver and Beattie have in common is perhaps characters who are unable to do much about their situations; maybe with both authors the emphasis is on revealing character rather than resolving conflict. Carver's work is usually minimalist, flat, stripped to the bone and somewhat – to use his own term – *concrete*. In Beattie's fiction, there is more texture, more surface detail. Her prose is arguably more lush and sensual than Carver's anorexic sentences. Both authors work under the influence of Chekhov in that they leave endings that are open; which, if we see Carver and Beattie as dominant influences on the short story form this past 20 years, suggests that Chekhov looks set to continue shaping the way people write short fiction in the twenty-first century.

From now on, I suggest you add to your knowledge of what people have been up to in the short story for the past century or so. Here are a few more short story writers you might like to try: Jorge Luis Borges, Elizabeth Bowen, Angela Carter, André Dubus, F. Scott Fitzgerald, Richard Ford, Janice Galloway, Nadine Gordimer, Shena Mackay, Bernard MacLaverty, Carson McCullers,

Bobbie Anne Mason, Lorrie Moore, Edna O'Brien, J.D. Salinger, Helen Simpson, Isaac Bashevis Singer, Elizabeth Taylor, Fay Weldon and Eudora Welty.

Being a creature of limited attention span, I've always preferred reading anthologies of short stories to single-author collections. Here are a few anthologies that I'd particularly recommend.

Malcolm Bradbury (ed.) *The Penguin Book of Modern British Short Stories* (Penguin, 1985).

Anne Charters (ed.) *The Story and Its Writer* (New York: St. Martin's Press, 1995).

Richard Ford (ed.) *Granta Book of the American Short Story* (Granta, 1992).

Hermione Lee (ed.) *The Secret Self: A Century of Short Stories by Women.*

John Updike (ed.) *The Best American Short Stories of the Century* (Houghton-Mifflin, 1999).

Tobias Wolff (ed.) *The Picador Book of American Short Stories* (Picador, 1993).

6 The Distance Between: Author, Narrator, Reader And Point Of View

Every work of fiction has a viewpoint character. The viewpoint character is your host, the person from whose perspective – perhaps even from within whom – we access the story.

Because point of view may be confused with opinion, which it isn't, Janet Burroway in *Writing Fiction: A Guide to Narrative Craft* suggests 'vantage point' as a more precise term. The viewpoint is the vantage point from which we experience the story. Burroway goes on to suggest that

> it might be better to think of viewpoint as being about speaking: 'Who speaks? To whom? In what form? At what distance from the action? With what limitations?' All of these issues go into the determination of the point of view.[1]

Perhaps, then, in beginning a piece of fiction writing, the first decision to make is: who is speaking?

Who Speaks?

From the earliest literature all the way through to the end of the nineteenth century, the author speaking, the author acting as an omniscient narrator, was standard practice. The narrator of George Eliot's *Silas Marner* (1861) is a good example of the omniscient point of view:

> In the days when the spinning-wheels hummed busily in the farmhouses – and even great ladies, clothed in silk and thread lace, had their toy spinning-wheels of polished oak – there might be seen in districts far away among the lanes, or deep in the bosom of the hills, certain pallid undersized men, who, by the side of the brawny country-folk, looked like the remnants of a disinherited race.[2]

Since Chekhov, omniscient narrators have largely fallen from favour. Throughout most of the twentieth century, the idea that there is one truth has been as much disputed as the existence of God. For this reason – but also because readers don't particularly take to being *told* things – for some time now, omniscient narrators have not been greatly esteemed. This means that although the answer to the question 'Who speaks?' will sometimes be the author, readers will not generally take to the author's narrative voice coming in omniscient form. However, the author speaking through the persona of the point-of-view character works for contemporary readers.

Your next narrative choice is deciding from whose point of view the fiction should be written. It may be the protagonist. In Dickens' *David Copperfield*, for instance, as in Saul Bellow's *The Adventures of Augie March* about a century later, the authors have gone for the protagonist-narrator. This means that for the duration of the narrative your reader is trapped inside one character's consciousness – and neither of these novels is short. An alternative is to have a narrator who is not the protagonist, as in the Sherlock Holmes stories, where Dr. Watson, the great detective's sidekick, narrates. F. Scott Fitzgerald's *The Great Gatsby* adopts the same strategy. Nick Carraway, the narrator, is a quiet observer and reporter of life rather than a proactive character, and is the confidant not only of Jay Gatsby but also of Daisy Buchanan, with whom Gatsby has an affair. Many novels use this choice of narrator, the narrator-reporter, if you like. Perhaps the reason the narrator-reporter is popular is that most writers tend to be people who observe more than they act?

To Whom?

Mostly the person being addressed in a piece of fiction is you, the reader – Hi! – and Janet Burroway stresses taking care in the way we go about this: 'The one relationship in which there must not be a distance, however, is between author and reader.'[3] When we write fiction, most of us assume the reader is somebody we can confide in, someone who shares our education and culture and will understand our references. Our narrators usually speak to somebody we

> **Writing Burst**
>
> *'I wish you had told me this before.'*

assume is somewhat like us. Usually. Sometimes you will come across fiction where the explicit audience is not the reader, though, fiction where the narrator speaks to another character.

In Richard Burns' highly emotive story 'Perfect Strangers,' the narrator is an adult looking back on a childhood holiday he took with his divorced father. The whole story is addressed to another character – his father, who, we learn during the story, has since died.

> You took me straight home to Mum, the clumsy caravan still fastened to the back of your Maxi. 'I'll not come inside,' you said. 'Your Mum might have visitors.'
> This didn't seem likely but I wasn't going to argue. 'Thanks then,' I said.
> 'I'm glad you enjoyed it.'
> 'Oh Dad, I did. Really. The best holiday ever.'
> And you drove off, as you always drove off, alone.[4]

The emotional impact is amplified through the narrator's direct address to his father and further enhanced by son and father being largely separated by divorce and later death. If you can emulate it, having your narrator address the narrative to another character within it may achieve a wonderfully resonant emotional effect.

In Which Person?

You've decided which of the available characters narrates your story and you have an audience in mind. The next decision facing you is the form or *person* this narrator will take.

First person offers the possibility of an intimate bond between narrator and reader and this of course is desirable. Fiction is primarily about people, and as readers we all decide, as we do in life when making friends, whom we get on with and whom we don't. First person opens up the inner world of the narrator and if readers empathise with what they experience there, a relationship may be formed. This is what we're all hoping for when we create a fictional world. First person is highly appealing to beginner writers. Perhaps this is because first person appears to be the form in which it is easiest to create a character; becoming your character may seem less of a leap when you are doing it using the 'I' form.

One of the great advantages of first person is that the narrator may address readers directly, which is friendly, and may also confide in them, as Amy Hempel does here in her story 'In the Cemetery Where Al Jolson is Buried':

> She introduces me to a nurse as 'the Best Friend.' The impersonal article is more intimate. It tells me that *they* are intimate, my friend and her nurse.
> 'I was telling her we used to drink Canada Dry Ginger Ale and pretend we were in Canada.'
> 'That's how dumb *we* were,' I say.
> 'You could be sisters,' the nurse says.
> So how come, I'll bet they are wondering, it took me so long to get to such a glamorous place? But do they ask?
> They do not ask.
> Two months, and how long is the drive?
> The best I can explain is this — I have a friend who worked one summer in a mortuary. He used to tell me stories. The one that really got me was not the grisliest, but it's the one that did. A man wrecked his car on 101 going south. He did not lose consciousness. But his arm was taken down to the wet bone — and when he looked at it — it scared him to death. I mean, he died.
> So I didn't dare look any closer. But now I'm doing it — and hoping I won't be scared to death.[5]

Writing Exercise: Make Friends With The Reader

In the extract we've just looked at, Amy Hempel uses two techniques to win the reader's confidence. The first seven lines are all immediate fiction — action and dialogue. In the following four lines (from 'So how come...' to 'and how long is the drive?'), Hempel's narrator expresses her anxieties about the situation to the reader: 'So how come, I'll bet they are wondering, it took me so long to get to such a glamorous place? Etc.' She then tells a micro-story — the narrative strategy that lends the story its distinctive nature — which is a metaphor for her anxiety about visiting her terminally ill best friend. Two slightly different forms of discourse, both variants of addressing readers, both designed to make friends with them.

Think of a situation where you found it difficult to do what you knew you really ought to do and write a 250-word piece of fiction. Your narrator's brief is to use all four forms of discourse Amy Hempel uses in this passage:

action

dialogue

expressing the narrator's feelings to the reader

telling the reader a micro-story to illustrate these feelings.

First-person narration has shortcomings too, as Orson Scott Card observes:

> The main limitation on first-person narrative is that your narrator has to be present at the key scenes. A first-person narrator who merely hears about the major events of the story is no good to you at all.[6]

Also, it's far too easy in first person to go into claustrophobic internal monologue mode; I can't be the only reader in the world to lose the will to live during protracted internal monologues, can I? It's like getting trapped at a party by somebody who loves the sound of their own voice.

More flexible and more potent than first-person narration is what often gets referred to as *third-person limited*. John Gardner here suggests why this particular point of view is preferable:

> First person locks us in one character's mind, locks us to one kind of diction throughout, locks out possibilities of going deeply into various characters' minds, and so forth. Third-person-limited or third person subjective is the same as first person except the 'I' is changed to 'she.'[7]

Note Gardner's reference to 'third-person subjective.' Part of the flexibility, the fluidity, that third person offers is that it may be subjective or objective – in other words the author may inhabit the consciousness of the character or remain on the surface of that character. Thus you (and, of course, the reader) may be privy to his or her thoughts and feelings, or not. One advantage of third-person limited is what Jenny Newman refers to as its 'tight focus.'[8] As we will see in a moment, the use of third person also offers you the facility of adjusting the focus – or, if you like, zooming in and zooming out again – which first person does not.

The table following summarises the advantages and disadvantages of the various viewpoints just explored, plus a couple of rarities I haven't so far examined.

	First-Person Singular ('I')	Second-Person ('You')	Third-Person ('He' or 'She')	First-Person Plural ('We')
For	Immerses reader in narrator's heart and mind and may thus create an intimacy between narrator and reader which will help you hold onto the latter. If you wish your narrator to be unreliable – and one of the advantages of unreliable narrators is that they make for active readers: the reader has to form views of the characters and situations different from those of the narrator – first person would be the obvious choice.	See First-Person Singular. It also appears to make the narrator and the reader one – not a bad trick if the latter buys it.	Whereas first-person singular only permits you to adjust the distance between the narration and the story being narrated, third person allows you to adjust the distance between narrator and reader. Stories told in this person can stay *outside* the point-of-view character.	Ultra rare. Jeffrey Eugenides' *The Virgin Suicides* is narrated by a bunch of neighbourhood boys. Shares the advantages of ordinary first-person singular and its disadvantages, plus the disadvantages of second-person narration.

| Against | Excludes reader from entering the minds of other characters; can be claustrophobic; your narrator cannot be everywhere and so will inevitably miss key action. | Because this is a rare narrative perspective – you can find it, for example, in Jay McInerney's *Bright Lights, Big City* – readers may find it mannered. Because the author is assigning responses and emotions to the reader, the reader may find this presumptuous. | There are no major disadvantages to third person. It may be as intimate as first person. Although most of us start out thinking first person is easier and more comfortable, it probably isn't. Henry James described first-person narration as 'barbaric.' | Lacks one particular character with whom readers may empathise. Shares the disadvantage of second person – may seem mannered. |

At What Distance From the Action?

John Gardner talks of 'psychic distance,' which he defines as 'the distance the reader feels between himself and the events in the story.' This is something you can control in a couple of ways.

First of all, you may adjust the position of Burroway's vantage point. You could, for example, shift from third-person omniscient to third-person limited. William Trevor's story 'The Ballroom of Romance' opens in the former:

> On Sundays, or on Mondays if he couldn't make it and he often couldn't, Sunday being his busy day, Canon O'Connell arrived at the farm in order to hold a private service for Bridie's father, who couldn't get about any more, having had a leg amputated after gangrene had set in. They'd had a pony and cart then and Bridie's mother had been alive: it hadn't been difficult for the two of them to help her father on to the cart in order to make the journey to Mass.

Within two paragraphs, the focus has narrowed and the camera has zoomed in, as we enter third-person limited:

> As she cycled back to the hills on a Friday, Bridie often felt that [some of the girls she'd been at school with] truly envied her her life, and she found it surprising that they should do so. If it hadn't been for her father she'd have wanted to work in the town also, in the tinned meat factory maybe, or in a shop.[9]

These two short passages illustrate part of John Gardner's suggestion that

> the beginning of [a] story find[s] the writer using either long or medium shots. He moves in a little for scenes of high intensity, draws back for transitions, moves in still closer for the story's climax.[10]

Here you can see that the distance between both character and action affects reader's emotional response to the fiction. The first passage from 'The Ballroom of Romance' sets the scene; the second focuses on a character within that scene ('As she cycled back to the hills on a Friday, Bridie...') before moving the vantage point inside the consciousness of the character ('If it hadn't been for her father she'd have wanted to work in the town also'). To my mind, the movement from third-person omniscient to third-person limited represents a much greater change in the reader's perception than could the differences between opting for first- or third-person narration. It's in adjusting the distances between character, story and reader, not in choosing between, say, first-person and third-person narration, that you make decisions about viewpoint that offer you greatest control and flexibility. In the end, such decisions help you control the reader's responses – which is your overriding goal as a fiction writer.

You can control the distance between the reader and the events of the story in a couple of ways. The first, which we have just seen in action, is adjusting the position of your vantage point – by, for instance, moving from third-person omniscient to third-person limited. The second way is by adjusting the position of the narrator in relation to the events of the story and to the reader. Put simply, your point-of-view character may be within the action, as Christopher Boone is here, in Mark Haddon's *The Curious Incident of The Dog In The Night*

> I put my liquorice laces and my Milky Bar in my special food box on the shelf which Father is not allowed to touch because it is mine.
> Then Father said, 'And what have you been up to, young man?'
> And I said, 'I went to the shop to get some liquorice laces and a Milky Bar.'
> And he said, 'You were a long time.'
> And I said, 'I talked to Mrs Alexander's dog outside the shop. And I stroked him and he sniffed my trousers.'[11]

But flick through to another point in the same novel and you will find Christopher in a different position with regard to the reader:

> When you put something down somewhere, like a protractor or a biscuit, you can have a map in your head to tell you where you have left it, but even if you don't have a map it will still be there because a map is a *representation* of things that actually exist so you can find a protractor or the biscuit again.[12]

Christopher has moved and changed role. In the second passage, rather than being a character within the action, he is addressing the reader directly; he is conducting a one-sided conversation with the reader.

With What Limitations?

The other significant adjustments you may make to your use of viewpoint have to do with the limitations you place on your narrator. Let's start where there are scarcely any limitations.

Omniscient Narrator

Here the narrator speaks as though he or she were God. John Gardner
says of the omniscient narrator:

> He sees into all his characters' hearts and minds, presents all positions with justice
> and detachment, occasionally dips into the third person subjective to give the
> reader an immediate sense of why the character feels as he does, but reserves the
> right to judge (a right he uses sparingly).[13]

If you're going to use an omniscient narrator in the twenty-first
century, chances are you will not want to wear your omniscience on
your sleeve; nobody likes a show-off. This may well mean keeping it
fairly quiet that there is an omniscient narrator in the house, as
Flannery O'Connor does here, in 'Everything That Rises Must
Converge': 'Behind the newspaper Julian was withdrawing into the
inner compartment of his mind where he spent most of his time.'[14]
The narration is omniscient, but O'Connor can pass it off as third-
person limited; at a casual reading, the viewpoint may seem to be
Julian's. Alternatively, you need to use a tone so arch, so dripping in
irony, that the reader is bound to realise you know fully well the
omniscient narrator went out of fashion in 1899. See how Joyce
Carol Oates does so in her story 'Is Laughter Contagious':

> Christine Delahunt. Thirty-nine years old. Wife, mother. Recently returned to
> work – a 'career.' A woman of moral scruples, but not prim, puritanical, dog-
> matic. Isn't that how Mrs. D. has defined herself to herself? Isn't Mrs D., in so
> defining herself, one of us?[15]

Whichever way the whims of fashion may blow, the thing to
remember about omniscient narration is to use it as a means of pulling back, of giving the bigger picture, and to do it subtly, sparingly.

First-Person and Third-Person Limited

If you opt for one of these, you are either narrating submerged in
the viewpoint character's consciousness, thinking and feeling what
she is thinking and feeling, or staying on the surface, following her
around like a reality TV crew, recording her every word and deed,
but leaving readers to deduce from these what she is thinking and

feeling. In first person, the reader is stuck with the consciousness of your narrator, but, as I've already mentioned, if you adopt third-person limited you have the option of pulling back for a spot of omniscient narration. This will allow the reader room to breathe. Imagine a film entirely shot in medium close-up and close-up: that's what first-person narration means for readers – fine in a 5000-word short story; harder going for readers in a 150,000-word novel.

Dual Viewpoint

In a story, dual viewpoint, alternating between the viewpoints of two characters, is appealing because it lends the fiction some variety – it gives the reader a temporary holiday from one viewpoint character when you move to another. It also means that you get two perspectives on the story and these will often benefit from being conflicting perspectives. The two viewpoints may also represent separate narratives which only converge at the end.

Writing Exercise: Dual Viewpoint With Jack and Meg

It can be both appealing and dramatic to look at a relationship from the perspectives of the two characters in it. Jack and Meg have been on tour for two months now. Jack is having a terrific time, but is unaware that Meg is tired of playing second fiddle to him. Only at the end of the story does it emerge that Meg has been rehearsing with Rocky the sound engineer and that the pair of them have secured a recording deal with Huge Records. Imagine Jack's surprise!

Making this a dual viewpoint story might well work better than single viewpoint. For one thing, narratives are in large part about movement, and changing viewpoints is a form of movement, one which keeps readers interested.

Begin a dual viewpoint story based on the tongue-in-cheek Jack and Meg scenario.

Multiple Viewpoint

Many recent novels use multiple viewpoint. The earliest example of the multiple viewpoint novel that I'm aware of is William

Faulkner's *As I Lay Dying*. This approach has been emulated many, many times – in America, for instance, by authors such as Amy Tan and Louise Erdrich, whose novels tend to be made up of chapters with a rota of narrators. Tan's *The Joy Luck Club* has four different viewpoint characters, Erdrich's *Love Medicine* more than twice that.

Multiple viewpoint is fun for the writer and for the reader; both of you get to spend quality time with several characters. When using it, it's helpful to establish a pattern. *The Joy Luck Club* is made up of four sections, and within each section, four daughters each tell stories that relate to their mothers. The pattern doesn't have to be so rigid: Anne Tyler's *Dinner At The Homesick Restaurant* has six viewpoint characters, some of whom have one chapter each, and some of whom have more. As a reader, the structure that perhaps unifies the narratives is the relationship between the characters; they are three generations of one family.

If you want to see a fresh spin on multiple viewpoint, you might like to look at the closing chapters of Anita Shreve's *Sea Glass*, where, at the climax of a mill-workers' strike, multiple viewpoint is used to stop time. The violent conclusion to the strike is seen from the perspective of several of the viewpoint characters, which involves Shreve stopping time, ending one chapter at point D in the chronology and beginning the next a few moments earlier at point C. This is highly effective in making the incident which concludes the strike multi-dimensional and therefore richer for the reader.

Floating Viewpoint

You don't have to begin a new scene or section or a new chapter to change viewpoint, though. If you're skilful enough – and if you establish a clear pattern for the reader – you may shift viewpoint several times in a page. In this excerpt from Alice Hoffman's *Here On Earth*, Gwen has called on Judge Justice and his wife Louise, who have just invited her to stay for dinner.

> She'd have first and then second helpings, with apple pie for dessert, then she'd go upstairs and sleep in the guest room, on clean white sheets, with the dog curled up beside her. The problem is her attachments, as if devotion were a downfall.
> 'I'd better get back,' Gwen says.
> Louise Justice can't help but think of that windy night, all those years ago, when she saw the bruises on Belinda's arm.

'Well, you're not walking,' Louise decides.

'Really it's not far,' Gwen insists, but the Judge, who's come in for dinner, has seen the stubborn expression on Louise's face. He won't get dinner for another hour, that much is sure.

'I'll drive you.' The Judge has made up his mind.[16]

Trace the viewpoint changes here from Gwen's to Louise Justice's, to the Judge's. This is fancy footwork. If I were you, I'd master the nursery slopes of viewpoint before you attempt slaloming of this order.

Of course, it's possible to destroy in a flash the reader's engagement with your narrative by falling into inadvertent multiple viewpoint. Your first-person viewpoint character is film director Orson Welsh, who is growing increasingly frustrated with his female lead Rita Hayseed. The story is trucking along nicely, the reader is enjoying being immersed inside the head of this genius of filmmaking and then on page 2 line 3 runs into this little landmine: 'On the twenty second take, Rita thought she might faint.' Bye-bye, reader.

Point of view is perhaps the most significant element of your fiction writing and so is something that will repay further study.

7 Characters
Helen Newall

Writing is a laboratory in which writers, like mad midnight scientists, create creatures, and having created them, toy with them, plunging them into terrible situations to watch and describe their behaviour. If you've ever played *The Sims*, or watched *Big Brother*, you might note disturbing similarities.

In the twenty-first century, character and characterisation is big business: celebrities spend time and money honing, surgically stitching and hawking versions of themselves to sell films, CDs, TV shows, magazine. And the gossip columns and the paparazzi spend time and money prying for scandalous alternative versions to undermine the official stories. All this because we are a species that revels in people watching, listening to stories about people and vicariously living other people's lives.

A Life In Edited Highlights

From this you should gather that characters are never real; they're constructions, even when presented as being reality, as in biography, or autobiography. The contestants in *Big Brother* are often heard to exclaim that they've been misrepresented in the way the 'story' has been edited: they're probably right.

In fiction too, characters are edited: detailing every single second of a life would make for very dull reading. The writer makes selections, which are determined by the distorting lens of an authorial point of view (as opposed to the narrative's point of view). Put Jane Austen and Irvine Welsh in the same sentence: both are creators of great characters but they look through very different lenses. Nothing is neutral: everything has spin. Two people describing the same person might offer similar accounts, but there'll be things on which they disagree – 'That's ridiculous: I've never seen that side of her,' 'She's always been extremely rude to me' – especially if one is a good friend, and the other is the neighbour who lives on the other side of the Leylandii hedge. And when you hear a bit of gossip, do you trust the person telling you? Are they a reliable witness? Perhaps they have an axe to grind. Perhaps it's to their advantage for you to believe something about the person described, even if it's not true.

In other words, we love characters, even if they are unreliable and lie to us. We can't get enough of them. We deal with them everyday, whether we're writers or not. The characters in your fiction are therefore vital. They *are* the story. But don't just take my word for it: if you're crazy enough not to have done so already, read John Gardner's *The Art of Fiction*:

> However odd, however wildly unfamiliar the fictional world...we must be drawn into the characters' world as if we were born to it.[1]

Keeping It Real

However fictitious characters are (and some are more fictitious than others), you need the semblance of reality. Ernest Hemingway's advice to John Dos Passos is worth writing out and sticking onto your morning mirror:

> Don't let yourself slip and get any perfect characters in...Keep them people, people, people, and don't let them get to be symbols.[2]

Perfect characters are, frankly, tedious: the meteoric rise of a beautiful person who already lives in a beautiful apartment and, through beautiful luck and unimpeded beautiful business success, rises from riches to even more riches and more beauty etc etc...rapidly gets mind-numbing.

So, how do we keep it real? The big news is that you already instinctively know, because writers use the same everyday cues to present character as we use to read the people around us. Rightly or wrongly, we judge people on:

- Appearance
- Actions

- Speech – what they say, and how they say it
- Opinion – what others tell us about them.

A writer, being a mad scientist, also has a character's thoughts to add to the arsenal.

Writing Exercise: Reading People

Look at photographs. Documentary pictures, in books, or Sunday colour supplements are a good source of action shots. That you don't necessarily know the names of the people depicted is immaterial, in fact it can be advantageous.

- What are your initial impressions of character?
- Suggest names
- Explain the expressions on faces (and no face is ever truly blank)
- Think about people in terms of appearance and actions
- Add speech bubbles – what are people saying to each other? (The temptation here is to win the comedy caption competition – have fun, yes, but try to work out a series of realistic exchanges as well.)

You can go on to write mini-narratives using the pictures as starting points.

Just as some theorists tell us that there are only so many plots to go round, others tell us about archetypal characters and their narrative functions. There are only so many goodies and baddies. Good characterisation is therefore in the detail, and yet again, another old maxim comes into play: it's not what you say, but the way that you say it.

Character Building: The Nature Versus Nurture Debate

Where do characters come from? For some writers, they spring fully fleshed out into narratives with miraculous ease. No work needed. No pencil chewing required. For others, however, character creation is tortuous and laborious and lasts months longer than bringing a real baby into the world.

So, are the best characters the product of nature, or careful months of thoughtful nurture? The debate is as complex as the one the psychologists are having in the real world about human nature. The answer for writers and writing is that it depends on the writer: no method is any better than any other; as long as you know your characters, it doesn't matter how you find them.

In all probability, there's a blend of both nature and nurture going on, for the simple truth is that characters are born out of the story, and the story is born out of the characters; the two are inextricably linked. And remember, too, that writing is a process: just as your perception of people changes as you get to know them, so it is for writers with characters. Over the course of the weeks, months, years you spend with your cast, you will learn more about them, however fully formed they were when they first arrived in your head. So, knowing everything about a character before you begin is impossible: be patient; accept that there's a process to undergo that takes time.

In any case, some writers prefer not to know their characters too well at the outset, finding that if characters are too worked out in advance, they become too fixed to go with the flow of a narrative in a state of developmental flux. Horses for courses: find out how it works best for you.

Shifting And Changing Is The Story

Consider also a finished product: a short story, a novel perhaps. These rarely have characters who remain the same throughout. Just as people change in response to things that happen to them over time (so the nurture debate has it), so it is with characters; and narratives often centre on just such character developments.

Leo, in L.P. Hartley's *The Go Between*, is an old man irrevocably shaped by the events of a long-ago summer. Self-reflection is triggered by the discovery of a diary detailing a visit to a school friend's country house: his re-assessment of the past helps him, and us, understand its impact on his character:

> If Brandham Hall had been Southdown Hill School, I should have known how to deal with it. I understood my schoolfellows; they were no larger than life to me. I did not understand the world of Brandham Hall; the people there were much larger than life; their meaning was obscure to me...they had zodiacal properties and proportions. They were in fact the substance of my dreams.[3]

This will be, then, a narrative *about* character, and the divergence between who we think they are, and who they really are, and why they are as they are. It employs the archetypal situation of a protagonist being out of his depth in a strange world. This allows not only Leo to observe the world and explain it to us, but also us to observe him because the tests he has to undergo in this strange world throw his character into sharp relief.

Knowing And Understanding

You'll see it again and again, *ad infinitum*: Know Your Characters. I've said it myself above. It stands to reason that if you know a character well, you'll know what makes them laugh, what brings them joy or causes them grief, and you'll be able to exploit that information as you weave a credible narrative. But how you get to know them is often what troubles some people.

Questionnaires generate character information, and they can provide very valuable information, but unless you process the information, it can remain as frozen as a list of attributes for a sign of the zodiac, at which point Leo's downfall will be yours too. Consider John Gardner's advice:

> The writer's characters must stand before us with a wonderful clarity, such continuous clarity that nothing they do strikes us as improbable behaviour for just that character, even when the character's action is, as sometimes happens, something that came as a surprise to the writer himself. We must understand, and the writer before us must understand, more then we *know* about the character.[4]

You could now spend a few moments jotting down what the differences between knowing and understanding a character might be.

Writing Exercise: The Questionnaire

It's a popular character development technique, so let's see how it works for you. Use a character from an ongoing project, or generated in a previous exercise, or invent someone new. Spend a moment daydreaming: consider a seat on a train. Imagine your character walking in and sitting down.

What's your character's name? What shoes are they wearing? Any jewellery?
What's their favourite item of clothing? What's in their pocket? Colour of hair?
Favourite drink? Favourite book? Favourite song? Birthday? Star sign? etc.

This gives you a starting point for further character development. It's the equivalent of an actor 'hot seating' a character: the actor becomes the character; the others ask questions. If you're feeling fearless, try this, too. Be your character. Answer all questions as your character. Don't take anything personally. Get someone to scribe your character's answers.

If you're in a writing class, invent weird, wild card questions, write them on slips of paper and pass them to someone elected to be the question reader – it might be your lucky writing tutor. Scribble an answer for each question. Keep your hand moving; don't question the question; write down the first response whether you understand the question or not. You never know, you might find a diamond.

Active Development

Think back to John Gardner's distinction between knowing and understanding, and consider the notion that knowing, however extensive it might be, might sometimes be merely offering you surface detail; understanding comes with the deeper sense of character that emerges when characters start doing things.

You'll read accounts of writers being mysteriously possessed by characters, and having to write till dawn to take down their stories à la dictation. Ha! Hot news: since they're constructions, characters can't really do this, but perhaps what is being articulated is that the subconscious mind has understood a character so well that it seems as if this ink-and-paper creation has taken over the narrative and is leading the way through the stony path that is storytelling.

Characters *can* haunt you. Like insistent ghosts, they demand their stories be told, and it can feel as if these stories are waiting to be discovered, or excavated, rather than invented. But not everybody gets this oceanic feeling, so if you never experience it, fine. It doesn't make you any less of a writer. But to understand your character, you must start making them act.

Writing Exercise: Action Sketches

Take a character from a previous exercise. Write them into a scene. Don't worry too much about how the scene comes about; write excerpts from imaginary bigger bodies of work, and get straight into the immediate action. The following are situations you could use.

■ Your character is late for a train when an old man asks for help to carry a case in the opposite direction…

■ At dusk, your character sees a gang of children about to throw some kittens off a canal bridge into the water…

■ Your character wants to ask another person to go out for a drink, but the other person seems uninterested…

You might now see that your characters really start breathing when they want something. Badly. Madly. Deeply. What do your characters want?

Life Drawing

Some writers have allegedly exacted revenge on sworn enemies in their fiction. Characters can be incendiary devices if mishandled. Words and swords have much in common: they can both pierce hearts and sever friendships irrevocably. So, while it's possible to use the character traits of people you know, it's a technique not to be taken lightly. People won't necessarily recognise themselves, but if they do, they won't always thank you, and heap you with wonder, love and praise. They might feel flattered, but they might feel embarrassed and hurt. And beware: it isn't enough to disguise an identity by changing a name but then using the salient details of someone's life. If a person is sufficiently recognisable from the way in which you've described them, and you then depict them doing something that they didn't actually do (rob a bank, have an affair, give up a child for adoption and so on) then tempers can flare and lawyers can get involved, however fictional a context you give the work. Remember the angels who fear to tread where fools rush in.

There's nothing to stop you, however, using the character traits or mannerisms of several people and amalgamating them in your laboratory into one monster. In all probability, this is what we do anyway since writing expresses our experiences of life.

Writing Exercise: Street Scene

While you're doing all the other observation exercises in this book that require you to sit watching people in busy cafés or train stations, then write brief character sketches based on Appearance; Actions; Speech – if you hear any, and now is also the time to jot down those weird little bits of conversation you might catch.

Playing thought games such as this in crowded places trains your eye and offers you raw material and telling detail that can tighten up your characterisation and thus your writing.

Assumptions

Observation asks the fledgling writer to put aside all that healthy stuff about not judging by appearances: what it doesn't ask you to do is make value judgements. Every life is worth examining. Everybody has something good and bad about them. Everybody has a secret. But remember that the assumptions you make are just that: assumptions which, in all probability, are very wrong, which is why you should be discreet when observing strangers. But you'll find that making assumptions is a game you can play with your readers: ask them to think something about a character and then demonstrate that character to be different. The mysterious Boo Radley in Harper Lee's *To Kill a Mocking Bird* is mythologised by the neighbourhood: he is an absence whose story is filled in by gossip and hearsay, and whose actions when he does make an appearance confound expectation.

Writing Exercise: Tiny Tales That Say So Much...

Think of something simple like making a coffee and being interrupted by a phone call from someone wanting to sell you a caravan. That's all you need. If you have no tale of your own, use the coffee story.

Now list some characters. Include characters from previous exercises, current writing projects, stereotypes such as Angry Man, Bored Teenager, Fairy Tale Princess and so on.

How would each one tell the coffee story? You shouldn't need to embellish too much, but show character by *how* they tell the tale. Keep moving on through as many versions as you can. If you're working in a writing class, swap work and see if others can glean the traits you wanted to demonstrate. There's more than one way to skin a cat, and it's not what you say, it's the way that you say it.

Raymond Queneau used this pattern of writing in *Exercises in Style*. Borrow a copy from your library (make an inter-library loan if it's not on the shelves) and study his amazing techniques! It may not be the greatest art, but the point is clear; there's more than one way.

Extras

Beyond the main characters, there are the waitresses, taxi drivers, portly uncles, and messengers who people your fictional world. They might need to be convincing too, but the truth is there isn't time for everyone, otherwise films would last for days, and books would be bigger than houses.

Deft writers – Charles Dickens springs to mind – have coloured bit-part players with brilliant flashes of miniature characterisation. Other writers merely offer the bare minimum and acknowledge a presence: a waitress pours a cup of coffee and is gone. But while these characters are glimpsed for only a moment, they sometimes have a vital function: they might offer your questing protagonist a vital clue as to the next destination in the journey; they might reveal someone's true identity, or obstruct the action.

The trick is not to spend too long on them in case they seem more important than they actually are and turn into frustrating red herrings ('The writer is lavishing so much attention on this waitress that I know she'll prove to be very, very significant later.' Said waitress then disappears, never to be seen again).

The other end of the scale is bit-part characters who are so thin that narrative function is protruding through their skin like rib cages, and their presence, especially if they deliver vital plot information, feels like a clunky structural necessity. So flesh them out a little if things are sticking out, but not too much: it's a fine balance.

Blocking The Way

While some writers find fixing things too early is constricting, others find that the grindingly awful lack of inspiration that screws up many a white page is really insufficient background work on character, structure, or setting, and sometimes all three. The important thing is to experiment and find out how *your* mind works best (and remember that your mind may change its mind about how you work best; so don't fix your narrative of how you work best too soon!).

If you ever get the feeling that things are forced and everything feels wrong, then you're probably right: go back to basics; run your characters through some of the exercises here and see if working on a few details doesn't shift something and move you forward.

Think of these writing exercises not as producing parts of a finished narrative, but as preliminary sketches; the preparatory work that artists do before they start the finished piece. Use them to limber up before the main work begins, and use them to keep going when everything seems to be falling apart.

8 Living Elsewhere: Plot

Maybe there are some writers around who give birth to plots like Mother Hubbard did children, but I haven't met one of them. Most of us struggle immensely with the whole business of constructing a storyline that will ensnare, retain and move – not to say change the whole life of – the reader. Plotting is hard, but let's see if we can't make it a little easier.

As you know, all genuinely creative art originates in the unconscious and you will be best able to tap that most fertile part of your mind when you are closest to a state of unconsciousness. A corollary of this is that too much planning will not benefit your fiction. Here's British novelist Henry Green on the subject:

> As to plotting or thinking ahead, I don't in a novel. I let it come page by page, one a day...try and write out a scheme or a plan and you will only depart from it. My way you have a chance of something living.[1]

What's wrong with too much planning? Well, you will almost certainly plan with your conscious mind; it is after all partly for ordering and structuring. Rather than putting a lot of energy into planning, you might be better to concentrate on maximising your access to the unconscious. Your unconscious knows what it is doing. You might find it helpful to think of your story as something which already exists somewhere on the far shore of consciousness. Your job is to tap into the appropriate part of your mind so that you can go and live there. Then, over as much time as the length of your story dictates, slowly collect all the pieces of it on a computer file. Like Raymond Carver:

> I made the story just as I'd make a poem; one line and then the next, and the next. Pretty soon I could see a story, and I knew it was my story, the one I'd been wanting to write.[2]

When you have your fiction safely home from the other side, all assembled there on your computer, your conscious mind comes into its own, analysing, judging, editing, ordering and re-ordering. But that's much later. Your initial task is to go and live where your story, mysteriously, already exists. 'Plot,' says Ashley Stokes,

is part of the process of writing. It is something we find in the activity itself. More importantly, it comes to us in the amorphous work of notebooks, long walks, versions, false turns, hard decisions, insomnia and staring out the window.[3]

For professional novelists, living where the story already exists means that their daytime social circle consists of their characters. If you read Colm Toibin's *The Master*, a biographical novel about Henry James, you will gain some idea of the kind of monastic servitude to literature to which those who go all the way are called. If you are going to make your fiction authentic, life-like, to some extent you will have to emulate Henry James; instead of rubbing shoulders with colleagues, engaging in the challenges of the workplace, you will be living your life elsewhere, in your imagination, and living your life vicariously through your characters. In a recent interview in *The Daily Telegraph*, the English novelist Rupert Thomson enthused about just this, saying that he found the experience of living day after day in his mind so exhilarating that he couldn't imagine not doing it. Anne Tyler, the *doyenne* of American women's fiction, concurs:

For many years, my writing had to work itself in around the rest of my life – first because I had a 9 to 5 job, then later because I had small children. I don't think I gave my fiction proper attention, which may be why my first four novels are so much weaker than the later ones. But along about the time I started *Celestial Navigation*, I began to see how deeply absorbing and fulfilling it could be to sink completely into an imaginary character's world.[4]

Finding this other world has to do with tuning in to the part of your mind where it exists, as Michèle Roberts explains,

The unconscious is part of yourself: it's like this big country which sends you messages if you tune in and do your work.[5]

Now, unless you're somebody who thrives on solitude, this may not appeal; it will involve sacrifice. But the more time you can spend living elsewhere, the better you will be able to bring your fiction back and exhibit it for the world to admire.

So relax. In one sense, you don't really have to think up a plot. It's more a case of positioning yourself where you are most likely to discover and then bring it home with you.

What Is Plot?

Here's a useful definition of plot, from Ansen Dibell's book on the subject:

> Plot is built of significant events in a given story — significant because they have important consequences... Plot is the things characters do, feel, think, or say, that make a difference to what comes afterward.[6]

Two things are worth noting here, right away. First of all, the events aren't any old events; they are *significant*. The King has indigestion. The Queen has a corn on the little toe of her left foot. Insignificant. You'll have heard that drama is life with the dull parts left out. Keep it in mind. Like every other writer on the planet you will all too often produce fiction which includes the dull parts. That's okay. Just remember to take them out afterwards. The second thing to note is that these significant events have consequences — they alter what ensues. In this regard, analyses of author's craft often speak of *causality*. Because *this* happened (the King died) *that* resulted (the Queen died of a broken heart). The King dies and then the Queen dies could be regarded as two random events, but stories are never random. One thing, as they say, leads to another. The King died and the Queen died of a broken heart.

Writing Burst
'Five pints, right...'

At this stage, it would be timely to wheel in James N. Frey again. The one part of his *How To Write A Damned Good Novel* that has always stayed with me is the notion of three kinds of conflict. He speaks of static, jumping and steadily rising conflict and advises that only one of these three variants will work.

Scene One: Molly tells Harvey that he is lazy and useless; he won't ever help with the dishwashing.

Scene Two: Molly tells Harvey that he is lazy and useless; he never does any cleaning round the house.

Static conflict. Readers want news, not history. They already know she thinks he's no help to her.

> Scene One: Molly tells Harvey that he is lazy and useless; he won't ever help with the dishwashing.
>
> Scene Two: Molly arrives home with her solicitor friend Rose, who declares Molly's intention to divorce Harvey.

Jumping conflict. This has gone from a skirmish to the Battle of Trafalgar.

> Scene One: Molly tells Harvey that he is lazy and useless; he won't ever help with the dishwashing.
>
> Scene Two: While Harvey is sitting in a deck chair in the front garden picking fluff from his belly button, their hunky new neighbour Bill offers to relieve Molly of the four bursting bags of shopping she is straining to carry in from the car. Molly gives Harvey a significant look.

Steadily rising conflict.

What's At Stake?

It's generally thought to be a good idea to place your characters in a situation which involves some conflict (see also Chapter 30). 'What's at stake?' is one of my most common comments on student work. If you want your reader to read on, there has to be something at stake – right from the start. This means that you will need to raise a question in readers' minds in the first paragraph of your story, ideally in the first line. Then, having hooked readers with some initial intrigue, you will either have to develop that reader-question or introduce further ones.

Your first sentence establishes that Amy, your protagonist, has awoken in a strange bed with a thundering headache. She doesn't know where she is. Your reader is hooked and wants to read on – to find out, with Amy, where she is and what she got up to last night. In the second sentence, Amy hears the sound of water running in the bathroom down the corridor and realises she is not alone in this strange flat. She looks at the walls, where the framed art prints indicate nothing much about the owner of this room. Her head still hurts and she is having trouble waking up. She realises she is naked. You are now reeling your reader in very nicely. Amy hears the shower go off and, presently, footsteps coming down the corridor towards her. A young woman wrapped in a towel comes into the room, drying her air with another towel. She seems not to notice Amy. As she moves to the dresser, the glance of the woman in the towel falls on Amy, and she nods a silent greeting. At the dresser, she turns on a radio and John Humphreys and James Naughtie are bantering about something as they move towards the news headlines.

'I must have put some drink away last night,' Amy says.

The woman in the towel hums 'Uptown Girl' and fidgets with her hair. Your reader, like Amy, is deeply intrigued about what's going on here. You have been thickening the plot quite effectively. More footsteps coming down the corridor. What now? Amy wonders. A naked man carrying a towel walks into the bedroom and chucks the towel he is carrying at the woman by the dresser, who goes '*James!*' and indicates Amy under the duvet. 'Woops,' says James.

Reader questions abound. What did Amy do last night? Who are these strangers? What is their relationship to Amy? To each other? What will happen next?

I don't know the answer to any of these questions, but I do know that creating those questions in readers' minds is essential to fiction writing. If you don't generate similar questions on page one of your story, you will be, in F. Scott Fitzgerald's phrase, *chewing with no gum*. You can have the most deathless prose in the world, but unless you create and sustain narrative tension, readers will desert you in droves. Picture them stampeding away from your beautifully crafted sentences, a vast herd of buffaloes, careering across the prairies.

Writing Exercise: 1. Intrigue 2. Thicken the Plot

Write the first two or three paragraphs of a story in which you

1. Keep your protagonist and your reader in the dark about what's going on and
2. Keep building on the initial intrigue by quickly creating new reader questions.

I'm trying to make plotting your work feel easier to you, but every writer knows it's a struggle. It may help to think of plot in the following, terribly basic way. Order exists before the story begins. (It's safe to swim at a particular New England beach.) The start of the story is a disruption of that order, which is often known as the inciting incident. (A shark attacks and kills an attractive woman in a bikini.) No matter how much the protagonists fight against the forces of disorder (the shark, in this instance), things go from bad to worse. Eventually when everything has got about as bad as it can possibly be, the protagonists snatch victory from the jaws – sorry – of defeat. (The shark is killed.) Order is restored. (Okay to go swimming on that beach again.)

The American writer Anne Lamott came up with my favourite description of the way fiction writers wrestle with plots; she speaks of 'flail[ing] around, *kvetching* and growing despondent, on the way to finding a plot and structure that work.'[7] That's pretty much the way I've felt about making stories for as long as I've been trying to do it. For me, one of the most helpful explanations of plot is Michael Baldwin's breakdown (in *The Way To Write Short Stories*[8]) of what he calls the simple linear plot. As he claims, this plot structure covers most of the stories in the world.

The Simple Linear Plot

A character has a goal. It could be that he wants to win the Tour de France. Maybe he's been smitten by this gorgeous woman who has started to work at the desk opposite him. Or he and his two companions have crashed their light aircraft into a snowdrift in the Himalayas and they have to find their way back to safety. The goal could be anything. Now ask yourself this: if this character pursues his goal and gets it just like that, is it a story? You're right; it isn't. Character pursues goal and achieves it right away is okay as an anti-narrative joke in those ads they used to run for the new Mini – you know, Martians invade the earth...new Minis thwarts invasion...The End...It's a Mini adventure. But as a story you want to engage and retain readers with this won't wash.

The simple linear plot is your way through. Here, the protagonist's goal meets one obstacle after another, right from the start. I often use *Roadrunner* cartoons to illustrate this. What is Wile E. Coyote's goal? To kill Roadrunner. What are the obstacles he encounters in pursuit of this goal? You name it, really. Roadrunner is faster, smarter and luckier than Wile E. The other side of which is that Wile E. is probably the stupidest, slowest, unluckiest creature on the planet. Added to which he gets all his supplies from the Acme Corporation, probably the shoddiest manufacturer in the field of munitions. That's your simple linear.

How does it end? In Wile E's case, always badly. He never achieves his goal, but the effect of that is always humorous. It's in not achieving his goal that the laughs are raised. In most examples of the simple linear, the protagonist is likely to achieve his goal. Rocky, against all the odds, becomes heavyweight champion of the world. Nemo's Dad overcomes every obstacle the story throws at him and rescues his boy. Catastrophe, in the simple linear, is almost always averted. Usually many times – check the number of obstacles overcome in *Finding Nemo* – and, in the normal run of things, each of these obstacles may be a little greater than its predecessors with the final obstacle being the greatest of all. But don't forget Ansen Dibell and causality:

> Each set-piece (after the first) should be set in motion, at least in part, by what happened in the previous one. This present scene should dramatize and arise from the effects created by what's gone before, and in turn have effects played out in the story thereafter. Cause sparks effect, which in turn becomes cause, right up to your story's end.[9]

In all of the above, the kind of story implied has the three-stage structure that goes all the way back to Aristotle in Ancient Greece. However, in the kind of short story which has dominated the form in world literature in English ever since Chekhov, plot has become secondary to character. Vladimir Nabokov said of Chekhov's best-known story 'The Lady with the Dog':

> All the traditional rules of storytelling have been broken in this wonderful short story…There is no problem, no regular climax, no point at the end. And it is one of the greatest stories ever written.

Character Revealed

So. Not all fiction, especially short fiction, is plot-driven. In Chekhov, there is rarely any sense of conflict and resolution, or rising action. There is certainly no nineteenth-century sting in the tail. Instead, he focuses on character, which is slowly revealed, distilled to its essence. Perhaps the key to Chekhov's approach to characters is his compassion for them, his empathy. Eudora Welty observed that 'The depth of Chekhov's feeling for man is the very element out of which his stories spring.'

What I admire most about Chekhov is this compassion, his graciousness towards his characters, the way in which he regards them more kindly than they deserve. Chekhov looks at characters with a fresh eye and with considerable generosity of spirit. We see this demonstrated in his story 'Lady With Lapdog.' Gurov is a tawdry character, a seasoned, cynical philanderer, who in middle age has grown jaded. He might be unsympathetic in many respects, but Chekhov treats him better than he deserves. And the result for the reader is that we sympathise, possibly even empathise, with somebody we might normally look down on or not look twice at. It's the Tony Soprano effect. This instructive approach to characterisation is illustrated in an 1891 letter of Chekhov's to another writer, which proposes the importance for the fiction writer of seeing the value in everyone:

> Noah had three sons, Shem, Ham and Japhet. Ham noticed only that his father was a drunkard, and completely lost sight of the fact that he was a genius, that he had built an ark and saved the world. Writers must not imitate Ham, bear that in mind.

We are all flawed human beings, and if you can show the good side of a character who isn't obviously virtuous, the effect can be affecting for readers. 'Chekhov's wish,' says Richard Ford, 'is to complicate and compromise our view of characters we might mistakenly suppose we could understand with only a glance.'

To return to my earlier metaphor, living elsewhere may just mean living inside your chosen character, walking a mile in his shoes, and showing us what he's like. Sometimes your short story may be an exploration of two or three characters and their particular situation, by the end of which they or the reader or all of them have realised something. Characters and situations have been revealed.

Writing Exercise: The Tony Soprano Effect

Think of the most difficult person you know. Somebody who not only annoys you and makes your life hard, but ideally somebody who you also suspect is plain nasty.

Write a piece of fiction for 15 minutes in which you show both the unsympathetic and the sympathetic side of this person. Before you start, take another look at Chekhov's Noah letter above.

9 Scenes

The screenwriter William Goldman has this advice about beginnings: 'We must enter all scenes as late as possible. We must enter our story as late as possible.'[1] While it's true that cinema is a less patient medium than, for instance, the novel, my view is that fiction readers are impatient enough. I regularly receive student work in which the story doesn't actually begin until late on page 1, 2, or 3. Sometimes this is because the authors don't discover what the story is about until they have warmed up their engines. Sometimes it's because they aren't fully aware of the reader's need to commit to the story.

How often have you set aside a story or a novel because you have not been able to do that? Isn't it nearly always because you haven't been hooked? The bottom line is that your reader will not commit until you have established the story, until you have shown that something is at stake.

A couple of thousand years ago, the Roman lyric poet Horace suggested that epics ought to begin in the middle of the action and coined the phrase *in medias res*, which literally means in the middle of things. Nothing has changed. Your story begins with the clock on the terrorist bomb counting out the final 10 seconds before Big Ben blows up – not with the terrorist's trip to Bombs R Us to buy supplies, not with his difficulty attaching the timer to the explosives, not with the five-mile tailback on the M25 on the way into London. As Goldman says, enter your scene as late as possible. Why? Because it dramatises, raises the narrative tension and ups the stakes. These are good steps to take if you want to grab a hold of your readers. Here's a little checklist for your story, scene, chapter, novel beginning:

- Have you started *in medias res*, in the middle of the action?

- Ask yourself what the hook is. How soon does the hook appear?

- Have you spent half a page, a page, or even two warming up your engines? If your reader hasn't been snared by the end of page 1, it's unlikely that they will remain with you for much of page 2. When you revise, and discover that the hook comes in the fifth paragraph of the story, it's easily fixed: cut the first four paragraphs. Some of what's in there may seem to you like essential information about, say, character and setting. Okay. Chop it up and distribute it through the first few pages of your story. If you give it to the reader in dainty morsels, if you offer it on the hoof, while action and dialogue are moving the story on, you will get away with it. If your story opens with a page of scene-setting or character description, you can forget readers and go back to the day job.

- Remember the lessons of page design (see Chapter 15). The notion that shorter paragraphs are more desirable than longer ones is never truer than at the beginning of your fiction and an excellent place to locate a very short paragraph is right slam at the start of the first page.

Writing Exercise: Beginnings

Here are five films you may know: The Incredibles, Home Alone, The Titanic, Manhattan and The Sound of Music.

Imagine you've been given the job of writing the novelisation of one of them. Write an intriguing and compelling first paragraph.

Dramatisation

Which would you prefer: seeing, say, *Sideways* in a state-of-the-art multiplex theatre, widescreen, in full Technicolor and Dolby, or sitting there as I recount the story of the film to you? Nobody wants to hear about a movie; we want to *experience* it. The same is true of fiction. Readers will barely register what you tell them, but they will take what you dramatise to heart and, if you're doing your job well enough, they will join your characters on the emotional journey you send them on. Rather than summarising, explaining, recounting, telling the readers about what your characters are going through, the idea is to let them see for themselves. Flannery O'Connor got it in one when she said, 'Readers aren't going to believe something just because you tell them.'

Showing

A good starting point in learning how to show is to think of your story as a piece of theatre. Picture a hologram theatre in front of you right now. Imagine yourself, the author, sitting in your office chair in the wings. It's a comfortable chair with its own wheels, so you can slide around in your hologram theatre. The most potent elements of your story, though, are those that happen onstage. In fiction, you are creating an imitation of life, and if you can imagine this hologram theatre now, it's what goes on between your characters onstage, on the set, that will impact the reader. Should you shunt yourself in your office chair onto the stage to address the audience, to explain something, you will disrupt their suspension of disbelief. If you're doing it right, your audience has been emotionally involved by your characters, swept along with the quest of your protagonist, Angus, whose son has died from a spiked drink in a club, to track down the dealers who put drugs on the streets of this town. *Point 1: ideally, you will not, most of the time, be telling readers anything; rather, you will be using your skill with words to create a drama in their heads.*

Concentrate on what your characters do and what they say. Action – what they do – will always be showing. Dialogue – what they say – will also always be showing. Why? Because both constitute the story's reality unfolding. 'In a scene,' James N. Frey says, 'the narrator describes actions as they happened.'[2] *Point 2: remaining on the surface, sticking to what the characters say and do, is one way to ensure that you are showing.*

Oftentimes, showing a reader something means what it says: the way your characters behave will show us how they feel. When the blood rises to Kath's face, it shows us that she is embarrassed. Your telling us so would not have nearly as much effect. Why? Because when you show, the reader has to do the detective work; you have made your readers active and readers like being active. Readers who are forced by bad writing to become passive soon weary of the fiction they are reading. *Point 3: when you want to convey a character's feelings, resist the urge to explain them.* ('The writer should especially avoid comment on what his characters are feeling'[3] is John Gardner's advice.) Instead, become a student of human behaviour and show us how your characters' actions, gestures and facial expressions demonstrate what they are feeling.

Telling

The Geiger counter for telling in fiction is to look out for that author in the office chair, wheeling himself onstage. It's when the author addresses the reader that you will find telling in its purest form. Maybe instead of presenting characters in dramatic situations the author in question delivers notes on character. If you find yourself describing a character, you are telling.

> Sue had always been sharp as a pencil and thin as a rake; until now, she had never had a problem with her weight.

If, however, you use action and dialogue to show a character in a dramatic situation, you will be showing.

> Sue held her old summer dress against herself and studied her reflection in the mirror. Her body extended beyond the edges of the dress by a good six centimetres on either side. She sighed and threw the dress onto her bed.

Telling crops up in fictional discourse when authors try to give the readers information they think important. The irony is, readers only regard as important information they deduce for themselves (see Flannery O'Connor above.), which brings us to exposition: background information. Jo, your protagonist, is now a respected primary school Head, but you want readers to know that, to pay her way through teacher training, she worked for an escort agency. The last thing you should do with significant data like that is deliver it on a plate as a piece of exposition. Readers don't want much on a plate, but they definitely won't thank you for conveying dramatic back-story in this way. As John Gardner says, 'A good writer can get anything at all across through action and dialogue ... he should probably leave explanation to his reviewers and critics.'[4]

Exposition is easy to spot: it's usually in the pluperfect tense.

> Boris had always been a buffoon. On his first day at Kings, he had nearly caused a riot by cycling into a party of Korean tourists.

The pluperfect is the 'had been' tense and, because it's so far removed from the immediate, it's lethal. The pluperfect feels as if it didn't happen today, or even yesterday. It feels as though it took place weeks, months or years ago. Avoid the pluperfect like the plague.

Telling, then, is when you try to give your readers information on a plate. It's when you explain, lecture, summarise, recount. It's second or third, not first-hand information. No good for you, Fictionist. The kind of writing you are aspiring to produce is, in Ansen Dibell's words, 'dramatised, *shown*, rather than summarised or talked about.'[5] Clearly there isn't a novel in the history of literature that doesn't feature a fair amount of telling, so as a narrative mode it does have a place. Many of the most memorable openings to novels consist of an author addressing the reader. Think, for instance, of that in Tolstoy's *Anna Karenina*: 'Happy families are all alike; every unhappy family is unhappy in its own way,' or this from L.P. Hartley's *The Go-Between*: 'The past is a foreign country. They do things differently there.'

> **Writing Burst**
>
> *That was the moment I wished I could remember what we had been taught.*

If telling is a valid option, how do you know when to use it? A good rule of thumb might be to avoid telling the reader any part of your story that has dramatic substance. 'Many unimportant parts of a story may be *told* rather than shown,' Barnaby Conrad advises, 'but the reader will feel cheated if not "present" at the important ones.'[6]

Learning writers are often blind to the difference between telling and ordinary description of action. They can think that this is telling: *Mhairi tuned her mandolin*. Yes, it does tell you something, but it isn't *telling*. It's action.

Another problem is that sometimes the difference between showing and telling is too fine to spot. That's okay. There are grey areas in anything. And sometimes what you write may be interpreted as both showing and telling – simultaneously. That's fine, too. But learning the difference between telling and showing in their purest forms is one of the most important steps a fiction writer can take.

Your job is to make readers forget that they are reading and give them the illusion of being in the story, seeing and hearing and smelling and feeling what's happening to your characters. Your job is to create scenes.

The Scene

Scenes are where the reader sees your characters live in person, speaking and acting. The word 'scene' makes you think of films or

plays, which is only right, as a scene should be *dramatic*. Something
is dramatic when it has been dramatised. You dramatise when you
use conflict to reveal character. If the author tells the reader about
it, it has not been dramatised. Dramatising is *showing*.
Apart from revealing characters in conflict, what is the function
of a scene? Simple: it moves the action forward. 'A *scene* is one connected and sequential action,' according to Dibell. 'It's built on talk
and action. It arises for a reason, and it's going somewhere. It has
meaning. It has a point: at least one thing that needs to be shown or
established at that spot in a story.'[7] At the end of a scene, things are
no longer as they were at the beginning. The way a scene moves the
action forward is by having characters *act* and *speak*. It explores and
reveals character and motivation. By the end of each scene the
reader should know more about the characters. Also, the scene
makes clear where and when the action is taking place. And,
because it has a mood or atmosphere – funny or tragic, hopeful or
desperate – a scene will affect the reader's emotions.

How To Make A Scene

A scene will always be immediate. 'It seems to happen,' Ansen
Dibell says, 'just as if a reader were watching and listening to it
happen.'[8] The point of writing immediate fiction is to put the reader
right inside the action, experiencing it vicariously. How do you do
this? Well, an approach that seems to work for me is a writer's bread
and butter: imagining that you the author are this character in this
situation and trying to convey the experience in words so direct that
the reader will share the experience with you. Writing fiction is not
so different from method acting. You need to immerse yourself in
character and situation, *become* the character, as De Niro does in
Raging Bull.
A scene, especially if it is an opening scene, may well have a hook
to snare the reader. Sometimes this will be terribly dramatic: 'As he
neared the top, Ben wondered how much weight this old drainpipe
could hold.' But sometimes the hook will simply be a matter of
intrigue: 'I swore I was never going to do this again.'
A scene will often have a reversal. Lester who wanted to send
Dennis to the gallows ends up being hung himself. Nina, who had
seemed so sympathetic to begin with, turns out to be an obnoxious
character.

A scene often builds up to some kind of climax that will conclude it. Maybe this will be a nail-biting moment where readers will wonder whether or not Ann is going to get the sack. It may be the moment where Poppy announces that she has to go to Rio De Janeiro, and we will want to move swiftly to the next scene so that we can find out why.

You ought to be able to learn a few things about writing scenes by looking at the following extract from Denis Johnson's story 'Emergency.' First of all, the opening maximises reader engagement. It may seem like stating the obvious, but if you can write down why this opening is engaging, it may help you to emulate it in the exercise that follows. (And you will have noticed that it could not be more *in medias res*.) Next, see how much is told (very little), how much shown and what, in this case, showing involves. You might say that in this scene, rather than tension rising – it's pretty high from the start – the plot thickens. Note down how this is done. And note how quickly the scene is over after the climax – immediately.

Around 3.30 a.m. a guy with a knife in his eye came in, led by Georgie.

'I hope you didn't do that to him,' Nurse said.

'Me?' Georgie said. 'No. He was like this.'

'My wife did it,' the man said. The blade was buried to the hilt in the outside corner of his left eye. It was a hunting knife kind of thing.

'Who brought you in?' Nurse said.

'Nobody. I just walked. It's only three blocks,' the man said.

Nurse peered at him. 'We'd better get you lying down.'

'O.K., I'm certainly ready for something like that,' the man said.

She peered a bit longer into his face. 'Is your other eye,' she said, 'a glass eye?'

'It's plastic, or something artificial like that,' he said.

'And you can see out of *this* eye?' she asked, meaning the wounded one.

'I can see. But I can't make a fist out of my left hand because this knife is doing something to my brain.'

'My God,' Nurse said.

'I guess I'd better get the doctor,' I said.

'There you go,' Nurse agreed.

They got him lying down, and Georgie says to the patient, 'Name?'

'Terrence Weber.'

'Your face is dark. I can't see what you're saying.'

'Georgie,' I said.

'What are you saying, man? I can't see.'

Nurse came over, and Georgie said to her, 'His face is dark.'

She leaned over the patient. 'How long ago did this happen, Terry?' she shouted down into his face.

'Just a while ago. My wife did it. I was asleep,' the patient said.

'Do you want the police?'

He thought about it and finally said, 'Not unless I die.'

Nurse went to the wall intercom and buzzed the doctor on duty, the Family Service person. 'Got a surprise for you,' she said over the intercom. He took his time getting down the hall to her, because he knew she hated Family Service and her happy tone of voice could only mean something beyond his competence and potentially humiliating.

He peeked into the trauma room and saw the situation: the clerk – that is, me – standing next to the orderly, Georgie, both of us on drugs, looking down at a patient with a knife sticking up out of his face.

'What seems to be the trouble?' he said.[9]

Writing Exercise: Making A Scene

Divide a page in two. On the left side, list five different kinds of journey. On the right, make a list of five things a person might take on a journey. Now write a scene structured around one of the journeys on the left of your page, and use in it two of the items on the right side of your page.

You need a minimum of two major characters. Don't forget to use dialogue. Follow this chapter's advice on scenes as well as you can.

Spend 25 minutes on this.

Endings

Stories don't just stop, not if they're dramatic. They have to end. Finding your way to the appropriate ending is, as William Goldman admits, 'just a bitch. (Tattoo that behind your eyelids.)'[10] Because pulling off a story that works all the way through is a challenge that not many people often pull of, the world is littered with flawed endings. There are two major ways to fluff an ending. One is to write past it. This is frighteningly common. To snatch three examples out of the air, I had packed up and gone home well before the end of two movies I can think of and one novel. In Quentin Tarantino's *Jackie Brown*, I was thinking that my toenails needed cutting about half an hour before the ending, which is unbelievably drawn out. The film was taking so long to end I lost the will to live, and when you lose the will to live, it's pretty hard to care what's happening on-screen. In *The Bourne Identity*, when Matt Damon defeats the bad guy in a gritty car-chase and then leaves Germany to tidy up some other bits of stray business in Russia, I'm afraid I didn't go with him. We had found out before the Berlin car-chase who the traitor was and in the car-chase Damon's nemesis had been killed. There wasn't a good enough reason to move onto Russia at this stage. The screenwriter (or the novelist – it was a novel first) had written past the ending. In Anne Tyler's *Back When We Were Grown-Ups*, Rebecca Davitch, a widowed grandmother, spends much of the novel attempting a reunion with a college boyfriend, Will. Whether or not things will work out with Will isn't the only thing at stake in this novel, but it is the major source of narrative tension. Thus when this particular question is resolved fifty pages before the end of the novel, there isn't a huge amount to hang around for. I'd give my eyeteeth to have written a novel even half as good, but the fact remains, Tyler wrote past the end. Here's a little checklist for your endings:

- Bear in mind that more is riding on your ending than on any other bit of your story. You do no want to screw it up.

- Have you written past the ending? If you have resolved the major conflict, answered the major questions, your story is over and you should exit stage left pronto.

- Has your ending gone on forever, or have you failed to end the story in one decisive action? Bad endings can be like a stuck CD. You think it's over, but no, here comes the ending again, and again and – you get the picture. Think of Glenn Close coming back from the dead in the bath at the end of *Fatal Attraction*: an ending too far.

- Is your ending clear? It will need, obviously, to be shown not told. If it's told, you've completely banjaxed your ending. But beyond that, it will need to be clear. A deliberately ambiguous ending is one thing, but watch out for one that is accidentally ambiguous. Readers won't be happy.

- Is your ending appropriate? Have your characters got what they deserved? Have your readers been given what they were fervently hoping for? The 1960s TV serial *The Fugitive* is legendary in my family; it put my mother off long drama serials for life. The show had run for years and was all about the protagonist finding and bringing to justice the one-armed man who had framed him for the murder of his wife. The ending was so full of holes, inconsistencies and coincidences and, apart from anything else, lacked the complete vindication that the previous four seasons of drama had called for, that my mother vowed never to watch another long TV serial. Readers want to see poetic justice; they want to see characters get what they deserve.

Perhaps the one thing to remember about endings is this: when you reach the end, stop. If your story begins with the blue touch-paper burning, it ends with the largest rocket exploding in the sky, not with the dishwashing after the firework party guests have gone home.

10 Dialogue

Stories move forward most efficiently through characters acting and speaking, so lesson one on dialogue is that it is a terrific way of keeping your story moving forward. Most of what I hope you will learn in this chapter can be found in this edited passage from Sarah Waters' first novel, *Affinity*.

In this scene, one of the novel's viewpoint characters is visiting the other in prison for the first time. The novel takes place in London in the 1870s.

> When Miss Craven had fastened the gate on us and moved away I said, 'Your name is Dawes, I think. How do you do, Dawes?'
>
> She did not answer, only stared at me...[Her] hands are slender, but rough and red. The nails are split, and have spots of white upon them.
>
> Still she did not speak. Her pose was so still, her gaze so unflinching, I wondered for a moment if she might not after all be simple, or dumb. I said I hoped she would be glad to talk with me a little; that I had come to Millbank to make friends of all the women...I gestured to the light that glanced from her white bonnet and from the crooked star upon her sleeve. I said, 'You like to have the sun upon you.'
>
> 'I may work,' she answered quickly then, 'and feel the sunlight too, I hope? I may have my bit of sunshine? God knows, there is little enough of it!'
>
> ...I moved to her folded hammock and placed my hand upon it. She said then, that if I was only handling that for curiosity's sake, she would rather I handled something else, perhaps her trencher or her mug. They must keep the bed and blankets in prison folds. She said she wouldn't like to have to fold them all again, after I had left her.
>
> I drew my hand away at once. 'Of course,' I said again. And: 'I am sorry.' She lowered her eyes to her wooden needles. When I asked, what was she working at? She showed me, listlessly, the putty coloured knitting on her lap. 'Stockings for soldiers,' she said....
>
> I said next, 'You have been here a year, I think? — You may stop your knitting when you talk to me, you know: Miss Haxby has allowed it.' She let the wool fall, but still gently teased it. 'You have been here a year. What do you make of it?'
>
> 'What do I make of it?' The tilt of her lips grew steeper. She gazed about her a second, and then she said: 'What would *you* make of it, do you think?'[1]

Let's look at seven attributes of dialogue in this passage.

1. Dialogue creates and builds narrative tension, which, you will notice, rises steadily

For starters, there is tension, and a hook, in the fact that Dawes does not initially respond to the narrator, Margaret Prior's greeting. When she does finally respond to one of the narrator's remarks, it is to dispute it: 'I may work and feel the sunlight too, I hope?' When Margaret Prior touches her bedding, Selina Dawes challenges her, flouting the prison visitor's authority by asking her to handle something else instead. Finally, and climactically for this movement of the scene, in response to Prior's query about what she makes of prison, Dawes asks her, 'What would *you* make of it, do you think?'

2. Dialogue reveals character

' "I may work and feel the sunlight too, I hope? I may have my bit of sunshine? God knows, there is little enough of it!" ' Clearly, Selina Dawes is aggressive, angry and embittered and not what you would call welcoming. Two lines of dialogue showed us that.

' "What do I make of it? What would *you* make of it, do you think?" ' Dawes resents her visitor's presence, isn't at all happy about being incarcerated and doesn't suffer fools gladly.

Margaret Prior's response to Dawes saying she would prefer her to handle something else is, ' "Of course. I am sorry." ' So, now we know that our narrator is gracious, polite and kindly disposed towards Dawes. This is conveyed in five simple words. Because these words are in dialogue and *shown*, from a reader's point of view they are as potent as they could be.

> **Writing Burst**
>
> *Should I? No. Should I? No.*
> *Should I? No.*

3. Dialogue is usually at its most effective when it comes in short speeches

In all of the dialogue quoted in my points above, no speech is longer than two lines. I would say it's unusual in good dialogue to extend speeches beyond one or two lines. Why? Short=snappy, so your pace is enhanced, but also you've a better chance of keeping things clear. The longer the speech, the greater your chances of writing flaccid dialogue – so, beware of monologues.

4. Dialogue is often indirect

In other words, characters say one thing and mean another. This is most authentic – we spend our lives saying one thing and meaning another – but authenticity apart, indirect dialogue is desirable because it will involve readers in some thinking: they will have to deduce what it is the character really means. Making the reader think is always a good idea.

> 'I may work and feel the sunlight too, I hope? I may have my bit of sunshine? God knows, there is little enough of it!'

What Selina really means is she is very hard done by, something she wants Margaret Prior to understand. When Dawes says she is knitting 'Stockings for soldiers,' the brevity of her answer indicates that she is reluctant to engage in this conversation – something the rest of what she says here corroborates. Then, when Selina says 'What do I make of it? What would *you* make of it, do you think?' what's going on between the lines is the clear implication that Dawes thinks the question very stupid, is angry at being asked it and is in so many words telling Prior to clear off.

5. Dialogue is characteristic of the person speaking it

' "What do I make of it? What would *you* make of it, do you think?" ' From what Sarah Waters has established about Selina so far in this scene, her saying this seems entirely characteristic. Similarly, even with the little knowledge of her character which this short passage affords, it would seem uncharacteristic for Margaret Prior to say something like this. So it's always a good idea when redrafting dialogue to check that you've got the right character saying the particular line. If it sounds exactly in character, readers' understanding of the character is confirmed and they feel good about themselves.

6. Dialogue is multipurpose

John Singleton suggests that 'The key to good dialogue and successful scenes is that more than one thing should be going on at the same time.'[2] You may have noticed that I have used the same snippets of dialogue from the Sarah Waters passage to make different points here.

7. People don't listen

The artist Whistler on what he and his friend Oscar Wilde spoke about when they got together: 'Oh we always talk about me.' To which Wilde responded, 'We always talk about you, but I'm always thinking about me.' For this reason, characters shouldn't always respond to what has been said to them. Non-sequiturs make for good dialogue:

'I've had a terrible day. You wouldn't believe it.'
'Do you know how to set this timer?'

Apart from anything else, they make the reader work.

Further Dialogue Writing Guidelines

■ In laying out dialogue, make it easy on the reader: take a new paragraph for each new speaker.

■ Anything the narrative attributes to the speaker may be contained in the same paragraph. *She paced the wings, getting more anxious by the minute. Finally she strode onto the little stage. 'I've got something you should all hear.'*

■ Avoid using speech tags (*he said*) if you can possibly manage without them.

■ Don't let your speech tags draw attention to themselves – *he expostulated.*

■ Make them as plain as possible – *he said, she asked.*

■ Don't use adverbs on speech tags – *she cried distressingly.*

■ Speech tags – and remember you're trying to avoid them – can be before, during or after what is said. And sometimes the rhythm of what is said will require it to go in the middle – *'There is no question in my mind,' Henry said. 'She is dead.'*

■ Use a statement instead of a speech tag. (*Jenny caught his eye. 'Hello.'*)

■ Weed out unnecessary dialogue when you redraft.

■ There should nearly always be some tension in dialogue. If there isn't, it will be flaccid.

■ Phonetically rendered dialect such as *There's yin or twa lambs on thonder hillside yet* is very hard to get away with in dialogue. Because you don't want your story to grind to a halt while readers work out syllable by syllable just exactly what has been said, you should use dialect words very sparingly. As in almost everything, less really is more.

- For the same reason that you would try to avoid telling the reader things (because Flannery O'Connor told you not to, right?), avoid using dialogue as a vehicle for exposition.

- There are those who fly in the face of this – Roddy Doyle and Haruki Murakami – but too much dialogue will tend to make your fiction feel loose and diluted. A balance between dialogue and narrative passage is widely thought to be a good thing.

Writing Exercise: Dialogue

See how much of this chapter has stuck: write a short scene in which an unfortunate passenger in a non-smoking train carriage confronts the only other passenger on board – who is smoking.

---

11 Setting

Seagoon: What are you doing down here?
Eccles: Everybody's got to be somewhere.

The Goon Show

As in the legendary Spike Milligan exchange above, everybody has to be somewhere and this is true in your fiction of the characters and their situations. Internal monologue, authorial summary and exposition might be included in a list of exceptions, but as far as scenes in fiction go, you will have to set them somewhere.

Earlier in this book, I suggested thinking of your fiction as taking place onstage. Well, sets are an important element of theatre. A good set should complement character and plot. Setting in fiction serves several purposes. It contributes to the solidarity of your fictional world and so makes it more convincing. Setting is a means by which you can make the world your readers imagine when they read your fiction more vivid, more real. Setting, in fact, is nearly as important as character and plot and can almost be a character in its own right.

In the following passage, from David Park's novel *Swallowing The Sun*, the setting is the Ulster Museum in Belfast, where the novel's central character, Martin, works. One of the things uppermost in his mind is the fact that his daughter, Rachel, has recently gained ten A* GCSEs.

> He takes a detailed interest in everything he has to watch over, knows each exhibit with an intimacy that is prompted by respect and mostly with affection. But it's driven also by self-interest because now he understands the value of knowledge and so he stores it all away as an investment that will one day pay dividend, and just maybe that dividend will be to stay within the orbit of his daughter...
>
> It irritates him to see those of his colleagues who parade their indifference, or even disdain, for what is all around them, and thinks they don't have the vocation. Because he considers it to be a vocation – preserving the best things of the past, keeping them safe for the future. Safe for people to look at. He believes, too, that

looking is what a museum should be based on – looking and learning. There used to be a children's magazine called *Look and Learn* but it belonged in the distant world of encyclopaedias and train sets, of games like Monopoly and Scalextric. But there's still time to learn, to make up for what was missed in the past.

But looking isn't good enough anymore. Participation, touch, full sensory experience – these are the fashion now, the words they use, as if they think things can be understood like Braille with the tips of the fingers. His unvoiced opinion is that it's a gimmick, a cheap card trick that results only in disrespect and in the young a belief that everything must fall inside the entitlement of reach, and so he is fearful of where it will end.[1]

You may notice in this passage that there is a constant dynamic between Martin and his workplace. He has a relationship with the building, with the institution, and this relationship, the tension between character and setting not only creates character, it advances the plot.

Here we get to know Martin better because we are learning about something important to him: his job, and specifically his workplace. The setting characterises. In the first paragraph, the way he feels about the knowledge housed in the museum is used to show how Rachel's outstanding GCSE results have affected him. The setting advances the plot. In the second paragraph, the way he responds to his less committed colleagues shows us how committed to his work he is, how important it is to his sense of self. In the third paragraph, his attitude to the new emphasis in exhibitions on full sensory experience reveals how at odds he feels to the contemporary museum world. In three paragraphs we have learned that his job means a great deal to Martin, and that he is an older man, looking slightly askance at the modern world; each of which has been expressed as a facet of the setting. Setting has been used to characterise.

> **Writing Burst**
>
> *Imposter.*

What have we learned from David Park so far? That setting may be used to create character and advance plot. Let's move close to the end of the novel and find out a couple more wheezes that skilful use of setting permits.

In the climax of *Swallowing The Sun*, Martin traces Jaunty, with whom in his youth he was a Loyalist paramilitary, to a private health club. Jaunty is now a prosperous drugs baron, one of whose dealers sold Martin's daughter the Ecstasy tab that killed her. Jaunty and three of his men are in the club's Jacuzzi, where Martin suddenly appears and stands over them.

'Well, look what the cat dragged in,' Jaunty says. 'Didn't think you had the money for this sort of place, Marty.' ...

'I have something belonging to you,' he says.

'And what's that, Marty?'

'This,' he says, taking the plastic bag of drugs out of his pocket and sprinkling the contents into the water with a shake of his hand as if he's sowing seed.

'For fuck's sake, Marty, are you off your head?' Jaunty asks.

More tense dialogue follows, leading to Martin taking out a handgun and shaping up to shoot Jaunty. At what seems like the climax of the scene, Martin backs off and turns to leave. As he does so, one of the men in the Jacuzzi shouts abuse after him and Jaunty, recovered and now standing up in the water, joins in, shouting, 'Respect, Marty, you need to learn some fuckin' respect!' Martin turns, and approaches the men again, raising the gun, which makes Jaunty cower down in the water again.

Then he steps on to the rim and sprays his piss into the water. They squirm and shudder away from its gush, their eyes blinking and hands pawing at the water.[2]

In the first passage we looked at, the one in the museum, we saw how Martin was in part characterised through being at odds with the setting: he was irritated by colleagues who were indifferent to their work and he disapproved of the new emphasis on touch in museum exhibitions. In this Jacuzzi scene, the fact that the protagonist (Martin) is at odds with the setting does more than characterise; it dramatises the situation, in more ways than one. Jaunty reminds him that he is a poor man, who could never afford to join a club like this. Choosing a Jacuzzi as the setting enhances the confrontation. For one thing, it means that the hero can tower over the villain: Martin stands on the rim while the hoods are sunk beneath him in the water. Also, Martin is fully dressed while the villains are vulnerable in their swimming trunks. In addition, chucking a bag of Ecstasy tabs into a pool of water in which the man who brought them onto the streets is sitting seems to me a notch or two more vivid and dramatic than, say, throwing them on the ground, if this were set in, say, a pub. For one thing, the reader may picture the tablets floating on the surface of the water around Jaunty, confronting him for that little bit longer with what he has done. Finally, the choice of setting enables the hero to piss not only on the villain – from above, which is more dramatic – but also into the water in which the villain sits, which extends the moment: he is left in a bath of urine, which increases the poetic justice of this resolution.

All of which means that you now have a few ideas about how setting may be used to create character, advance plot, dramatise, and enhance narrative tension.

Writing Exercise: Setting

Pick a workplace you are familiar with: a supermarket, a college, a restaurant, or a newsagent's. Think of somebody you know well who would both fit in and be at odds with the place.

Now write for 20 minutes using this character in this setting.

Your task is to see if you can manage to deploy three of the setting-related skills that we have just observed in David Park's work:

creating character

advancing plot

dramatising

enhancing narrative tension.

12 Epiphany

The moment when the three wise men have the revelation that the baby Jesus is God's messiah is the first use of the term 'epiphany.' James Joyce appropriated the term for literary applications, but it has never lost its original characteristics: it has to do with revelation and it has a spiritual dimension. The critic Valerie Shaw explains that

> By an epiphany [Joyce] meant a sudden spiritual manifestation, whether in the vulgarity of speech or of gesture or in a memorable expression of the mind itself. He believed that it was for the man of letters to record these epiphanies with extreme care, seeing that they themselves are the most delicate and evanescent of moments.[1]

Epiphany has similarities with the Zen Buddhist term *satori*, which is central to Jack Kerouac's novella, *Satori in Paris*. It roughly translates as a moment of enlightenment, or a flash of sudden awareness.

Put simply, an epiphany is when a character in fiction comes to a significant, emotional or spiritual realisation. This will usually be self-realisation, but may also be about another character, or about a situation. Joyce, influenced by Chekhov, uses this climactic moment of self-realisation in at least three of the stories in his 1914 collection *Dubliners*. In the Joycean epiphany, it isn't just a character who has the moment of revelation. According to Daniel J. Schwarz,

> Joyce expected the reader to have her/his own revelatory moment of awareness that went beyond the character's and to see the plight of the central character from a larger and often ironic perspective. The reader's epiphany is an awareness of the limitations of the character's epiphany.[2]

In 'The Dead,' the point-of-view character is Gabriel, who, as the party they have been attending draws to a close, begins to have a prolonged epiphany about his wife Gretta. In the earlier parts of the story, Gabriel has been portrayed as a man of letters and an able public speaker, prominent within his social circle, and, despite a couple of flashes of self-doubt, rather proud of his social position.

> He was in a dark part of the hall gazing up the staircase. A woman was standing near the top of the first flight, in the shadow also. He could not see her face but he could see the terra-cotta and salmon-pink panels of her skirt which the shadow made appear black and white. It was his wife...he could hear little save the noise of laughter and dispute on the front steps, a few chords on the piano and a few notes of a man's voice singing.
>
> He stood still into the gloom of the hall, trying to catch the air that the voice was singing and gazing up at his wife. There was grace and mystery in her attitude as if she were a symbol of something. He asked himself what is a woman standing on the stairs in the shadow, listening to distant music, a symbol of. If he were a painter he would paint her in that attitude. Her blue felt hat would show off the bronze of her hair against the darkness and the dark panels of her skirt would show off the lights ones. *Distant Music* he would call the picture if he were a painter.[3]

In this passage, Gabriel's view of his wife seems to be altered in an epiphanic way: because he has stumbled on her in an unfamiliar situation, cast in an unusual light, she is newly illuminated to him. This voyeuristic moment is the catalyst for warm emotions and strong sexual feelings in Gabriel as he and his wife travel back to their hotel. But as 'his riot of emotions' has been intensifying, it turns out that Gretta was, during the latter part of the evening, having nostalgic thoughts about Michael Furey, a young man who loved her and died, perhaps because of his passion for her. The song they heard earlier at the party has provoked these memories, so, ironically, while Gabriel was having his *Distant Music* epiphany, Gretta was listening to distant music of her own. As the story ends, with Gretta asleep, Gabriel reflects on what she has told him about Michael Furey.

> It hardly pained him now to think how poor a part he, her husband, had played in her life. He watched her while she slept, as though he and she had never lived together as man and wife....
>
> The air of the room chilled his shoulders. He stretched himself cautiously alone under the sheets and lay down beside his wife. One by one, they were all becoming shades. Better pass boldly into that other world, in the full glory of some passion, than fade and wither dismally with age. He thought of how she who lay beside him had locked in her heart for so many years that image of her lover's eyes when he had told her that he did not wish to live.

> Generous tears filled Gabriel's eyes. He had never felt like that himself towards any woman, but he knew that such a feeling must be love…
>
> A few light taps upon the pane made him turn to the window. It had begun to snow again… His soul swooned slowly as he heard the snow falling faintly through the universe and faintly falling, like the descent of their last end, upon all the living and the dead.[4]

As you may deduce from these two edited passages, there is more than one epiphany in this story. That in the first passage, as I've said, is Gabriel's, but the epiphany of the second passage is shared between Gabriel and the reader. During it, Gabriel's previous position as the alpha male in his circle – at this and previous parties at this house, he is asked to carve the goose and to make the after-dinner speech – is undermined, both in his own eyes and in the understanding of the reader. In the course of the story, our knowledge of Gabriel has been deepened through three stages:

1. He starts off seeming competent and perhaps slightly full of himself.

2. When he is enraptured by the vision of her he has been studying his wife in secret while desultory music plays, we see another, more sensitive and emotional side of him.

3. When we leave him, he appears despairing and, almost, emasculated by his second revelation: that Michael Furey and not he is the love of his wife's life. Furthermore, he has the sudden insight that Michael Furey must have loved his wife in a way that he never had.

James Joyce wrote of epiphany:

> First, we recognise that the object is *one* integral thing, then we recognise that it is an organised composite structure, a *thing* in fact: finally, when the relation of the parts is exquisite, when the parts are adjusted to the special point, we recognise that it is that *thing* which it is.

This is more than a tad opaque, but after a reading of 'The Dead' you can see, at least in the second half of the statement, what he means. Joyce has adjusted the parts of the story – Gabriel's view of himself and of his wife, his wife's view of him, our view of, in particular, Gabriel – until they become exquisite. In other words, this adjusting of the parts amounts to simultaneously altering the reader's view of the character and the character's view of himself. In this example of epiphany, the central character has, over the space of almost 40 pages, been brought increasingly into focus. It begins with a one-dimensional view ('we recognise that the object is *one* integral thing'). At this stage of our understanding, we see Gabriel in the mainly positive light that he mostly sees himself. Next that simplistic view is complicated ('we recognise that it is an organised composite structure'). Now we see that Gabriel is more than a peacock. He is, in the *Distant Music* passage, a man of strong and subtle emotions and when Gretta's nostalgic reverie is revealed, he becomes more multi-dimensional. Finally, the complication of our view of him shows us all of Gabriel's sides, including his weakest ('when the parts are adjusted to the special point, we recognise that it is that *thing* which it is').

Writing Burst
McJob.

In all of this, Joyce is writing in the shadow of Chekhov who revealed the strengths as well as the weaknesses of his characters, who regarded his characters graciously. What Joyce does here seems to me very close to Richard Ford's analysis of Joyce's mentor: 'Chekhov's wish is to complicate and compromise our view of characters we might mistakenly suppose we could understand with only a glance.'

And that is how, it seems to me, you might go about creating an epiphany in your own fiction. Although some of its definitions suggest that epiphany is sudden, if it is to be genuine it is the work of a whole story or chapter. Picture a puppet theatre where the puppeteer moves the mannequins and adjusts both set and lighting until the optimum moment, when all sides of the character and situation have been revealed. This is first of all a cumulative process, one that cannot be achieved in one final scene. The final scene may include the revelations that illuminate everything that has preceded it, but all that leads up to this final revelation is a necessary part of it. As Tom Bailey says, 'Pat endings or simplistic moralisations, summaries of emotion, and quick fixes may be termed epiphanies, but they will never punctuate good stories with meaning.'[5]

The epiphany comes about as a result of an altered view of things for the main character, an emotional journey, and, if you can provoke the requisite empathy, also for the reader. It involves us seeing different, perhaps conflicting, aspects of the character, ideally at the same time as he or she sees some or all of what we see. In 'The Dead,' Gabriel's epiphany has been at the cost of illusions he has harboured, so it's possible that in your fiction, an epiphany may be something that is costly to the character having it.

Writing Exercise: Epiphany

Nazia and Brendan have recently been married. She's a British-Asian Muslim; he's a Catholic, the son of Irish immigrants. Both families have opposed their marriage and this opposition has united the couple. Nazia is an accountant, Brendan a solicitor. They are educated professionals, both highly competent.

The story is from Nazia's point of view. She has been in flight from her father's patriarchal attitudes. The epiphany in this story is going to come as it dawns on the reader and on Nazia that Brendan is more like her father than she had believed.

Study the way Joyce orchestrates his epiphanies in 'The Dead' – reading the whole story in Dubliners would help – and see if you can create some for your protagonist and your readers. Introduce and adjust all the parts to that special point where the readers and Nazia are confronted with the difference between their perceptions and reality.

1000-word Story Project: Family Plot

As your stimulus this time, I want you to think of one of those occasions when your family has got together. The obvious ones are the calendar's holidays: Christmas, New Year, Easter, Eid, Passover, Diwali. You may well no longer go on a summer holiday with your family, but this story doesn't have to be set in the here and now. It may be inspired by experiences you had when you were a child or a teenager. Maybe you are more drawn to another kind of family gathering – a wedding, a birthday party, a funeral or an anniversary of some kind.

Once you have the setting – Christmas Day 1986 or your cousin's *bar mitzvah* – settle on a relationship. You and your father. You and your big brother. Your father and his mother-in-law. You and your younger sister, the usurper who simply by being born bumped you out of pole position in the universe. Within the relationship you have opted for, choose your viewpoint character. A fictional version of yourself at the age of 10. Your mother. Your precocious only-child cousin.

Next, focus on an habitual perspective your point-of-view character has on the other person in this relationship. The view that has hardened in you over the years that your big brother is only concerned with himself and, worse, that your existence barely matters to him; in fact, it's an irritation. Here's a mocked-up illustration:

Family Gathering Your grandparents' golden wedding anniversary.
Family Relationship You, aged 14, and the cousin who has always bullied and tormented you. (When you were both seven he would always greet you by wrestling you to the ground. When you were 11, he would taunt you with how useless you were at soccer, or how uncool your tastes in TV programmes were.)
Viewpoint Character Your 14-year-old self.

Habitual Perspective That this cousin is ridiculously competitive, a sadist whose role in life is to make people feel worse about themselves.

Your challenge is to come up with a story in which, during the course of the family gathering, at least one of your characters arrives at a new understanding of the other.

Remember, this is a very short story. All you should aspire to do is reveal the situation between these two characters and show how the understanding of one of them is altered by something that happens to them. Finally, a further challenge: you may only include what the characters say (dialogue) and what they do (action).

13 Reflection: How To Think About Your Writing

The title of this book gives a clue to the thinking behind it, and in particular the part in brackets will hopefully suggest the importance of reflection in learning to write fiction. The ethos and methodology of the whole book have to do with thinking about the way you read and write, all with the intention of helping you become a better writer of fiction. It's a good idea to acquire the habit of doing this not just in your head but also on paper – thinking about your writing in writing. (If you don't write down your thoughts, they are never more than half-formed.) You will benefit from habitually examining not only the creative processes involved in your work, but also your growing understanding of the kind of writer you are. You need to learn to be both self-aware and self-critical. Also, you will develop faster as a writer if you are able to articulate your creative processes. As well as reflecting on your own developing craft, you need to be able to analyse the craft of those you aspire to emulate. It's hard to overstate the importance of this: you will grow much faster as a writer if you regularly examine your own and others' work. You also need to begin to be able to analyse the literary context you wish to be a part of and to articulate your own intentions.

Fundamental to the discipline of keeping notebooks and journals is the notion that if you do not record them, your ideas will be lost. A similar rationale underlines the equally essential discipline of reflection: just as you will always be having ideas for your work, so you will always be having thoughts about your work. You will, for instance, be thinking about how to develop the piece of fiction you are working on. If you don't record it, you will lose it. Reflection is a way of thinking on paper. In reflecting, you can see your thoughts, organise them and decide what you want to do with them. Seen in one light, reflection is simply a particular mode of journal writing.

Seeing What You Say

Let's make this more concrete. I'm writing a novel about a comedy double act at work in 1960s and 1970s British television. In the past week, I've had a couple of ideas about the characters in it. One was that I might like to try using the epistolary form with Barbara, one of the principal characters. If I record this in my journal, it has the status of, I suppose, a note to self, a reminder of a development of the novel I might make. But as I am making this entry in my journal – *Maybe use epistolary form with Barbara?* – perhaps I get caught up with the idea and begin to tease it out:

> At the moment, Barbara is very important to the novel's central character, Eddie, but so far we always see her from the point of view of another character – Eddie's or Peter's. However, the more time I live with this novel, the more intrigued and charmed by Barbara I am. Also, the few people who have read extracts from it have commented favourably on Barbara. If I were to give her the status of viewpoint character, it would extend the range of the novel. It would for instance become multiple viewpoint rather than dual viewpoint. But if the chapters that are from her viewpoint were to be in the form of letters, it would lend the novel greater variety of narrative technique. It would also give the readers a direct insight into the consciousness of Barbara, one which they are not afforded with either Eddie or Peter.

Here I am doing more than recording an idea; I am thinking about it, putting my thoughts into writing, and as they appear before me on the page, they are in a very real sense given birth. Unless and until I try to articulate these thoughts in writing, they are vague and unformed; they are only embryonic. But when I put them in writing, I find out what I am thinking. Thoughts are of limited use until they have been articulated. As E.M. Forster famously said, 'How do I know what I think until I see what I say'. Thoughts, perhaps, are to dough what articulation is to bread; in other words, thoughts are half-baked. Lesson one in reflection: your thinking about your work has little or no value until you have made it concrete in the form of words on a page.

For all of the reasons mentioned so far and more, I recommend that you start to acquire the habit of reflection by writing a short evaluation of each piece of fiction you complete. You will reap the benefits.

How To Evaluate Your Own Work

In a self-evaluation, you may discuss the influences you had for a piece of creative work: any fiction that has fed into your fiction. Were you trying to learn from the way Rose Tremain uses flashback in *The Way I Found Her*? You might examine how she does it and then look at your own attempts.

In self-evaluations, you might also consider the elements of craft you have used in this story. Transitions? Fragmented narrative? Which books on craft had you been looking at? Which particular theories about, say, characterisation, were you picking up on? How successfully? In a self-evaluation, you might want to say something about your developing philosophy of writing. Are you a naturalist or a dirty realist? What are your priorities when you sit down to write a story: the style, the plot or the emotional experience you want your readers to have?

In evaluating your work, you might deal with problems encountered and the ways in which they have been overcome (or not). When you came to a dead end with your plot and could see no way out, what were your strategies for overcoming this obstacle?

Your self-evaluations will contribute to changing the story before finishing it – in other words, it will be a redrafting tool. However, the major benefit of writing self-evaluations is that it will make you a self-conscious, self-critical writer, somebody who knows what you're doing, and if you can train yourself always to know what you're doing it's inevitable that you will learn to do it better.

To summarise: an important function of the self-evaluation is to produce writers who are more self-conscious, more self-critical, and have a better understanding of the kind of writing they are attempting.

What Students Write About In Self-Evaluations

I thought it might be helpful to give you some examples of self-evaluation. Two students currently on the BA Creative Writing at MMU Cheshire have kindly agreed to have their work cited. Angi Holden and Jo Selley are at the time of writing early in Year 2 of their studies, but the self-evaluations from which I'm quoting here were written to complement creative work they did during Year 1. I've organised the quotations to try and illustrate the range of subject matter that may occur in a self-evaluation. They come in no particular order and the sub-headings are mine.

Inspiration

My inspiration for the piece initially came from two delivery men who delivered a lounge suite to me a couple of weeks ago. It was very obvious that one was the boss, a bit of a wide-boy, and did all the talking and I got to wondering about their relationship and what conflict could follow these two throughout the day.

Working Methods

Instead of starting with the story, this time I started with the characters. This was as a result of reading 'How I Wrote The Moth Essay' by Annie Dillard in which she says start by describing something, be precise about things. So I drew up a character sketch for each person and from this various other ideas flowed.

Redrafting

During the redrafting process I decided to delete a few large scenes which took place with the people they were delivering to. By incorporating a few more lines into the main character's dialogue it was possible to exclude these scenes altogether without losing the fact that they had made the deliveries.

Process Log

When I had finished the first draft of the story, I considered rewriting it to include direct speech. In the end I felt that this would be a mistake; the tone is one of reminiscence and the introduction of dialogue would be artificial.

Genesis of the Work

When I was a teenager growing up in West London, there was a significant level of racial prejudice and homeowners expressed concern that the property values would plummet if a non-white family moved in nearby. Southall was held up as an example; experiencing an influx of Indian and Pakistani families, it had acquired the nickname Little Asia. This became the background for my story.

Reading which Informed the Work

Around this time I picked up a book by Preethi Nair in my local library, a romantic novel with a plot pretty typical of the genre – boy meets girl, boy loses girl, boy wins girl back again. What made it a particularly enjoyable read was the setting of New Delhi and the expatriate Indian community in Cairo.

Reflecting about Craft

Sharples, in *Writing as Design*, mentions a 'primary generator' which is something that sets an idea off and that for it to be effective it should 'provoke rather than answer questions.'

Examining the Creative Process

Dorothea Brande, in *Becoming a Writer*, recommends writing as soon as you wake up, while the 'unconscious is in the ascendant.' In 'Deconstructing Creativity' Debbie Taylor quotes writers who talk about submitting to their unconscious, allowing the structure to develop while they write. My unconscious mind obviously takes over at some stage, as I never have any preconceived idea of how the story will end.

Discussing Intention

I tried to create an impending sense of foreboding by using the weather to build tension which I think adds to the overall feel of the story:

'Cold wind blew down the back of her neck, icy fingers dancing down her spine.'

Thinking about Literary Context

I'm also starting to discover what style of writing I prefer: MacLaverty's straightforwardness and simplicity to Virginia Woolf's stream of consciousness and Faulks's emotion and realism to Carver's minimalism. This will help me develop my own voice.

I hope that will help you as you begin to develop the habit of self-evaluation. A self-evaluation forms the next Writing Exercise, but this is only the beginning: from this point on, I would like you to write a 250-word evaluation of each Story Project that follows (they're distributed throughout the book). It will help your work develop much more quickly and it will give you an understanding of your craft that is priceless as well as a strong sense of yourself as a fiction writer.

Writing Exercise: A Self-Evaluation

Write a 250-word self-evaluation of your 1000-word story project (p. 102). Here are some areas you may include in it:

■ Discuss the influences you had in writing this story.

■ Examine any techniques you've been trying to emulate. Look at the way a favourite author has used, say, dialogue, and then look at how you have tried to learn from this.

■ Consider any theories about writing fiction you may have studied to produce this particular piece of creative work. (You can make it easy on yourself for now and perhaps discuss your attempt to apply some of the suggestions about craft in this book. For instance, was there anything in 'Living Elsewhere: Plot' that influenced your writing in this story?)

■ What kind of writing is this? For example, has your story been an attempt to write dramatic fiction? Or have you, like Chekhov, been aiming to reveal character?

■ What kinds of effect were you aiming to have on the reader?

■ Specify which effect at which particular point in the story.

■ Which problems have you encountered in writing this piece?

■ What were your strategies for overcoming these problems?

You should include (with this and all your self-evaluations) a bibliography of any texts that have informed the creative work.

Broader Reflection

Whereas we have just been looking at reflection about a particular piece of work, if you are to understand the kind of writer you are and thus continue to develop, you will need to acquire the habit of reflection in a broader sense of the term. This kind of reflection is something I think we all do at regular intervals in life. When you go away for the weekend, because of the perspective standing apart from the thick of your day-to-day life permits, don't you often find yourself contemplating what you're doing with your life? The same is true, perhaps to an even greater extent, when you take a week's or a fortnight's holiday. Being away from your routine existence allows you to stop and consider where you're up to now and where you might perhaps be going. This kind of self-examination involves you in putting some distance between yourself and the woods so that you can see the trees. Let's try to turn that into some useful advice. Reflection involves the perspective that distance from your work offers. It will sometimes mean looking back and looking at where you are now so that you can make some decisions about where you want to go next. Note also that the purpose implicit in this examination of your work is to improve it, and, more than that, to grow as a writer. Reflection for writers is about self-development.

You should by now have acquired the habit of reflection in a few different forms. You know the value of keeping a journal and using it, for instance, as a nursery for your creative work. This involves reflective thinking. (*What if, in the middle of their wedding preparations, Sarah's Dad is rushed to hospital for a heart bypass operation? How will Jacob – whose own father died of a heart attack when he was 12 and who has come to regard Sarah's Dad as a father – deal with this?*) You are also aware of how keeping a reading log may enhance your growth as a writer and you have begun to learn how to self-evaluate your own work. In other words, you are already becoming familiar with reflective writing in a number of different forms.

The idea of writing self-evaluations for story projects in *HTWF* is to encourage you in the habit of reflective writing. This will inevitably lead, at points when you stand back from your work as whole for instance, to writing longer pieces of reflection. These can be about your writing in general. You can reflect about the kind of writer you think you are and the kind of writer you would like to be. You can look at what you are able to do well and what you struggle to do in your writing. You can examine your intentions for a piece of work and the differences between the intention and result. You can discuss inspiration, technique, drafting, where characters come from. You can endlessly discuss why you write. (Jonathan Coe's reason, hard to beat, is that he is unhappy when he doesn't.) Or why you *keep* writing, as Thom Jones does here, at a time when he was feeling like giving up:

Then one day, watching television, I saw Wile E. Coyote chasing the Road Runner across a cartoon desert. Cartoon New Mexico, I figure. I was hoping that he would catch the stupid annoying bird and rip its head off. But then, in the middle of the chase, the coyote came to a screeching halt, stepped out of the cartoon, and walked toward the audience with a wry, self-satisfied grin on his face. His footfalls ka-flop ka-flop ka-flop, cartoon style. No big hurry here. He acted like he had all the time in the world. When he was finally in place, he pulled his shoulders back, looked into the camera, and said, just as cool as you please, 'Allow me to introduce myself. Wile E. Coyote ... *genius*.'

'Genius,' he said. Genniiee-us. *Genieuz*. Maybe that's just another word for perseverance. Wile E. Coyote, no matter what else you might say about him, was not a quitter. I mean, if you keep plugging at it, you *might* get it. If you quit – pow, it's over.[1]

Eventually, the practice of reflecting about your work before you begin it, while you're doing it and after you have completed it should become second nature to you. That's the way writers work. Like icebergs, the work the reading public sees represents only the tip of what we write.

III
How To Redraft

14 Redrafting 1: Editing

Redrafting is where you get down to the nitty-gritty. Your first draft is only the raw material from which you are going to sculpt a thing of beauty and truth. In a sense, with a first draft you have assembled the resources from which you are going to build the finished item. You probably won't need all these resources, and many of them won't initially be up to the task they need to perform. As Tom Wolfe says, 'You go to bed every night thinking that you've written the most brilliant passage ever done which somehow the next day you realise is sheer drivel.'[1] But that's okay. You can make the resources you've assembled better, and if you can't, you can get rid of them and generate some new resources in their place.

Flaubert, who redrafted his writing obsessively, wrote, 'It's never finished; there is always something to do over,'[2] and both Tolstoy and Joyce kept reworking right through until the printing presses were rolling. More recently, Raymond Carver claimed to go up as far as 30 drafts and never to do less than 10. The probability is you're going to spend an awful lot more time redrafting than you are writing. 'Occasionally you can hit it right the first time,' said John Dos Passos. 'More often, you don't.'

What Is Redrafting?

For a start, redrafting is about looking at your work and seeing what it says to you. It involves revising and improving at the level, for instance, of story and character, developing the fiction, but it is also a matter of correcting and editing, tinkering with the details. Thus at the deep structural level, redrafting may be about the protagonist you originally thought would return home ending up in Australia, while at the surface level you may be honing, polishing and refining, moving a conjunction, avoiding vocabulary repetition, wondering how the introduction of a present participle *here* might alter the emotional effect.

I suppose the essence of what you're trying to do is to finish off what you've started, complete the work. In this sense, you are clearly trying to perfect something. But doomed as you are to spend your life trying to perfect what you have created, you never will. Each finished work will always in the end fall far short of the form you imagined it taking when you first conceived it. So it's worth bearing in mind that there's only so much you ought to do in the way of perfecting each piece of fiction you write; you might as well recognise that each new work you begin offers you a further opportunity to develop your craft, to complete your masterpiece. There comes a point in the redrafting of everything you write when you will benefit from stopping and moving on to your next story or novel.

When Do You Redraft?

Before you set in to redraft, you need something to work on – a first draft. To get as far as that, follow the spirit of Natalie Goldburg's 'Rules of Writing Practice' and worry about what you write later – much later. If you start to criticise what you are writing while you are writing it, you are unlikely to get far. Cut yourself some slack. Trust yourself in two ways. First, you are a good writer and can produce a first draft with the potential to be excellent. Secondly, you are a good re-writer and can make your first draft fulfil its potential – once it's on the page. You need distance and perspective to redraft and you cannot have that while you are drafting for the first time. So leave it alone until your first draft is complete. Otherwise you may never get as far as a first draft.

When you have a holiday, you take a break from your life and move both physically and metaphorically some distance from it. Distance lends perspective. When you're in the forest you can't see the wood for the trees, but if you leave the woods and stand on a hill far enough away, you may be able to see the full picture. This is the essence of redrafting. You need distance to gain perspective and distance will always involve time. Many writers suggest putting your work away and leaving it alone for weeks or months.

Partly this is a matter of distancing yourself from your project, but it's also to do with leaving the unconscious mind to go to work on what you have produced. Creative Writing involves composing and redrafting which leads in turn to more composing and to more redrafting. It's a cycle of tapping the unconscious and moving what it comes up with on through using the conscious mind. In other words, if you can leave your draft alone for some time, your unconscious will be mulling it over even if you scarcely ever think of it.

In short, the time to redraft is not when you are producing the first draft, nor when you have finished the first draft, but rather some time, weeks or months afterwards.

Spelling, Punctuation And Grammar

If you're using Microsoft Word, the Grammar and Spelling checker will highlight most of your spelling and grammar mistakes and should most of the time indicate to you when your sentences aren't sentences. However, to get a real understanding of what is and what is not grammatical in sentence construction, there is no better way than immersing yourself in good writing – reading your head off.

Do be aware that Grammar and Spelling checker in Microsoft Word is by no means 100% reliable. It has a limited vocabulary and there are quite a few reasonably common English words that it will not recognise. And although the checker often makes helpful grammatical suggestions – such as making passive phrases active – it will often suggest bizarre alterations or highlight grammar errors that are perfectly fine, idiomatic English. So you will have to supplement the spelling checks your computer offers with dictionary use and you will have to take quite a bit of the grammatical advice it offers with a pinch of salt.

Nobody has perfect spelling or punctuation, but correcting the former is much easier than correcting the latter. I've spent my whole working life marking written work – half of it in 11–16 schools and half of it in universities – and my experience is that an awful lot of writers cannot punctuate to save their lives. If you have a problem with punctuation, I recommend that you study it. There are quite a few simple primers around and it won't take you long to find out how to use apostrophes, colons and semi-colons and how to punctuate direct speech. The bottom line is this: using, for instance, the apostrophe correctly is as important as any other aspect of fiction writing. Punctuation is fundamental and poor use of it undermines your credibility as a writer.

Writing Exercise: Get The Basics Right

Find a first draft of some fiction you have been working on – between 500 and 1000 words long would be ideal. Now, using the last two sections of this chapter as your guide, tidy it up so that it is properly laid out and grammatical.

Your challenge is to produce a second draft that has been accurately spelt, correctly punctuated and which has the same standards of presentation as the latest piece of literary fiction Amazon is discounting this very minute (for which, see 'Page Design').

Editing

'Every word is there for a reason,' according to Jerzy Kosinski, author of *Being There*, 'and if not, I cut it out.' Like Kosinski, when you edit you may well be stripping the clutter from your sentences so that the information you are communicating can go directly from your mind to the readers. An awful lot of what you do when you edit is remove the extraneous – words, phrases, sentences, passages. You will have done some of this when you reworked your spelling, grammar and punctuation; some, but by no means all. In my own work, the lion's share of editing has to do with cutting flab. In first drafts, I have a tendency to go all around the houses to make my point. If you do, too, your job as editor of your own work is to find these rambles and remove them.

Another perennial problem for me is almost the opposite: telescoping in on detail that doesn't warrant it. Being a film buff, it helps me to see this in cinematic terms: what I'm talking about is the close-up on something insufficiently significant. Every good writer is born with or develops the gift of noticing the world in its tiniest details – of paying close attention. But in my own work and in a lot of the student work I see, the author sometimes zooms in on details that just don't require it. When you edit, you will need to remove any focus on the superfluous.

Refining

Some editing tasks have to do with refining, with honing the language so that the meaning is clearer. Jonathan Swift's definition – 'Proper words in proper places make the true definition of style' – implies that style is simply a matter of fitness for purpose: if you redraft as Hemingway claimed to, 'to get the words right,' the result, in a very functional fashion, will be style (see Part V).

Apart from accurate usage, in editing you also shape your sentences for rhythm, music and *feel*. We absorb the beauty language is capable of in everything we read and hear, and we emulate this when we write. What you take in is inextricably linked with what you put out. All artistic endeavour has to do with absorbing influences, synthesising them and making them your own. Because of this, when you refine your work to make it beautiful, the stylistic flourishes and tics you have admired in your reading (and in your listening, if like me, the cadences of lyrics in pop music have influenced your writing) will emerge. What you focus on is what you will reflect.

Writers have, in their feel for language, an ear for a tune. If you want to develop this ear, read more and read better. What goes in comes out. So, read ambitiously as well as voraciously. Beyond that, write poetry. In any kind of verse writing – almost all of mine these days is in the form of song lyrics – language has to be distilled and, yes, *refined*. In a sonnet, you have 14 lines to say what you need to say. Speaking of sonnets reminds me of this, which makes my point for me: 'Delmore Schwartz wrote a sonnet every day. He didn't really like sonnets, but he wrote them for discipline.'[3]

Sharpening

Another task you will perform in editing is sharpening your vocabulary so that it performs more effectively. Sometimes this will mean replacing one word with another that is more accurate, sharper, more direct. If it wasn't Flaubert who first spoke of seeking *le mot just* (the right word), it should probably have been. You're re-reading a draft and you suddenly realise that your comic character Vladimir was not looking *vacant*; he was in fact looking *oblivious*. English has the largest vocabulary of any language. This means that you, as a writer in English, have more flexibility, more opportunity to be fluid and accurate, than writers in any other tongue.

One hoary old piece of writer's wisdom, which has found its way on to the Spelling and Grammar Checker in Microsoft Word, is making your verbs active and not passive. Watch and I'll show you it in action. If I now write *The French were defeated by Nelson at Tra-falgar* and use the Word checker, it will suggest alter-

ing it thus: *Nelson defeated the French at Trafalgar.* Somebody doing something is more dynamic than somebody having something done to them. Active verbs will give your prose more zip, more vim, more strength.

A related wheeze for sharpening your use of language is choosing your verbs carefully for their dynamism. Rita Mae Brown suggests that your choice of verb can dictate the pace of your fiction: 'Any action verb will accelerate a sentence. Run, jump, shoot, ride, and so on.' Once you digest this piece of wisdom, it's not hard to propel your sentences through your choice of verb – when you want to propel them, that is. Sometimes you will also want to slow down, to pause, to be gentle. Brown also recommends your choice of verb as a means of creating motion where there is none:

> If you've got characters sitting in a formal dining room, your verbs better reflect some inner motion or the reader will be bored by the characters' physical inactivity. So you might have a character steaming, seething, writhing.[4]

Writing Exercise: Edit, Refine And Sharpen

In the last exercise you took a first draft of 500–1000 words, checked that its layout conformed to contemporary conventions and redrafted the spelling, grammar and punctuation.

Now, see, if you can't use the preceding three sub-sections of this chapter to edit, refine and sharpen this same piece of writing.

In redrafting you will sometimes replace words with better ones. You will sometimes remove words that are surplus to requirements. But there will be occasions, all too many of them, when you will need to cut perfectly concise, even exquisite, writing. Some of the time editing is going to mean chucking out work that is beautifully expressed and artfully realised: Samuel Johnson, G.K. Chesterton and Kurt Vonnegut have all in their time suggested that you will need to cut parts of your work that you think are particularly fine. If it's possible to draw a line, I think we are now moving from editing to revising. We are no longer tinkering with the details; we are on to more major reconstruction, which I'm going to leave for a later chapter.

15 Page Design

Your page should be double-spaced (1.5 line spacing is also fine) and you should format your page with a clear font (Arial and Times New Roman are the most commonly used) and a font-size that will be easily read (for instance, 11 in Arial, 12 in Times New Roman). Up at the top of the first page, the titles of stories and chapters are usually in bold. When you mention them, you will need italics for the titles of books, films, CDs, magazines and newspapers. The convention for a long time has been to put the titles of articles, short stories and songs in single speech marks, but the music press has begun to italicise song titles in recent years, so you'll have to play that one by ear.

Page design amounts largely to the use of white space and is a crucial element in the reader's perception of your fiction. White space can be used to make the page accessible and inviting to the reader. With this in mind, both at the composing and the revising stages, it may be helpful to use short paragraphs and, in dialogue, speeches that are generally no longer than a line or two.

In its day, Fay Weldon's use of the page, in novels such as *Puffball*, was innovative. She was influenced in this by her background in advertising, where the most effective work carries a minimal amount of text (see, for instance, almost any print advertisement for Volkswagen cars). The logic behind this awareness of white space is that we live in a visual society. Just as description in nearly all contemporary fiction acknowledges the fact that most readers will know what most things look like, so intelligent use of white space works on the understanding that contemporary readers aren't nearly as text-friendly as their nineteenth-century forebears. Fay Weldon theorises this approach here:

Designers and topographers actually teach you to look upon the page. Words are given resonance by their positions, they must be displayed properly. If you wish to give something emphasis, you surround it by space.[1]

Some basic strategies will maximise white space on a page. Here are a few suggestions.

Dialogue

When you use dialogue, the length of the speeches is a factor too. A good rule of thumb is that longer speeches are harder to pull off. If you look you will find that, in most contemporary fiction, speeches are often one or two lines long. In the Michael Chabon passage below, only one speech is longer than that – and it's just three lines long. Once a speech rises above five or six lines, it becomes a bit of a monologue and, to my mind, monologues are not conducive to good dramatic fiction.

Paragraphs

One-paragraph pages might have been accessible in the nineteenth century, even in the first half of the twentieth century. However, today's reader is unlikely to find such a monolith of text inviting. On a page without dialogue, two to three paragraphs will admit a little white space, but I would go as far as to say that more than three paragraphs a page will make your fiction easier on the eye and more engaging for the reader. If you want to increase the pace of a passage in your fiction, short paragraphs will do the trick. Michael Chabon's *The Amazing Adventures of Kavalier & Clay* won the Pulitzer Prize in 2000 and his work is not only critically acclaimed but also popular with readers. I would suggest that his approach to paragraphing is typical of contemporary fiction writers. Look at this extract.

'They're all gone,' Ruth said, sounding surprised to see them. 'You missed them.'

'These men are not suspects,' Fellowes's agent said. 'They're merely witnesses.'

'We need to interrogate them further,' said Agent Wyche, not bothering to disguise his amusement at his own implicit meaning. 'Thank you ma'am. We have our own vehicle.'

Sammy managed to raise his head and saw that Ruth was looking at him curiously, with the same faint air of pity he thought he had spotted there earlier that afternoon.

'I just want to know this,' she said. 'How does it feel, Mr Clay, to make your living preying off the weak-minded? That's the only thing I want to know.'

Sammy sensed that he ought to know what she was talking about, and he was sure that under ordinary circumstances he would have. 'I'm sorry, ma'am, I have no idea what – '

'A boy jumped off a building, I heard,' she said. 'Tied a tablecloth around his neck and – '

A telephone rang in a nearby room, and she stopped. She turned and went to answer it. Agent Wyche yanked Sammy's collar and dragged him to the door, and they went out into the burning cold night.

'Just a minute,' came the housekeeper's voice from within. 'There's a call for a Mr. Klayman. That *him*?'[2]

This is fast-paced, and not just because of the action. It's a quick read and in its short speeches and paragraphs it is representative of contemporary fiction. Is all fiction published today like this? No. Is the whole of Chabon's book like this? Again, no. But if you flick through this or almost any other twenty-first century novel, you will find that less than three paragraphs a page is rare and that scenes will often resemble the shape on the page of this extract. If you design your page differently, you may have very good reasons for it, but you won't make your work as accessible as it might be for the reader.

Section Breaks

Just as the use of shorter speeches and paragraphs in today's fiction recognises how much more impatient we now are as readers, similar thinking lies behind the development over the past two or three decades of chapters and short stories that are broken up through the use of section breaks. The first chapter of Rose Tremain's novel, *The Colour* (2003), is 18-pages long and has been broken down into seven sub-sections, giving each section an average length of less than three pages. The rest of *The Colour* is similarly structured. A typical section in David Mitchell's second novel *Number 9 Dream* would also be three-pages long, and in his first novel, *Ghostwritten*, it's possible to find as many as five sections in the space of only two pages. In the short story, David Foster Wallace, whom Zadie Smith has called 'the greatest contemporary innovator in the form'[3] can be found dividing a nine-page story into eight sections.

I'm not recommending without good reason that you model your work on these writers. Beyond the fact that we all live fast and busy lives, and the fact that our culture is highly visual, there's a simple rationale behind this aesthetic of economy and division of the longer into the shorter. Life works that way. We begin work at a certain time, and after an hour or two have a break. An hour or so later, we break for lunch, and so on. Beyond the way we divide the day, the week has its divisions, too; we rest from our labours in the evenings and at weekends. Every few weeks or months, we have short holidays and, for most of us, there is an annual holiday of up to two weeks. The human mind needs regular refreshment. In fact, never mind days and weeks, it's widely accepted that most of us have an attention span of 45 minutes. So, if you ask me, it's advisable to include breathing spaces in your fiction. (For more on this, see Chapter 21.)

Layout Conventions

The way a page in fiction is laid out alters over time. If you went back to the 1980s, you would find subtly different fashions pertaining. However, as things stand, today in 2006, most of what you need to know about layout is listed here. This is how pages in fiction today look. If you are planning to submit your work, it's desirable that it should resemble today's published work.

In section, story and chapter beginnings, the first line of the first paragraph is not indented. Thus, a story or chapter beginning looks like this:

> He answered the phone and tried to switch off the radio at the same time. First he clicked *Pause* on BBC Radio Player, but not being very alert, he also pressed the on-off button on the radio beside his computer. So as he paused the virtual radio he inadvertently switched on the actual radio set.
>   'Sorry,' he said.

And you will denote the end of one section and the beginning of another like this:

> The building shook. She turned to stone where she lay in the bath.
>
> Not having experienced a bereavement, she was a bit shocked when Interflora delivered a bouquet with an 'In Sympathy' card attached.

You can easily find advice on the theory of paragraphing – what a paragraph is and how you can best judge when to start a new one.

All I would say here is that a new paragraph for a new speaker is a good idea. If you imagined the layout used in each spread over a page or more, which of the following would be easier for the reader to follow?

'You don't need to go to Vermont to see some autumn leaves,' Rosie said. 'The leaves are fantastic colours up the road in the Lakes.' 'But there isn't a song called 'Autumn in Keswick,' Sam replied. 'You're too much of an idealist.' 'You're too pragmatic, dear.'

'You don't need to go to Vermont to see some autumn leaves,' Rosie said.
'The leaves are fantastic colours up the road in the Lakes.'
'But there isn't a song called "Autumn in Keswick," ' Sam replied.
'You're too much of an idealist.'
'You're too pragmatic, dear.'

And then there's the whole question of which is easier on the reader's eye...

In addition to starting a new paragraph for each new speaker, I would also suggest you to take a new paragraph when the focus of your fiction shifts from one character to another, as here:

'How would you like to pay?' the waitress asked as she stacked up the pudding bowls.
Beth handed her the credit card she already had out.

Running the second sentence into the previous paragraph wouldn't do much to alert the reader that our focus has shifted from the waitress to Beth.

Beyond aesthetics, as far as the layout of paragraphs goes, all you have to remember is to indent the first line of a new paragraph. Use the tab key on your keyboard to do this.

16 Peer Appraisal

One of the key learning and teaching strategies in Creative Writing is informal peer appraisal. Apart from the many good reasons for engaging in peer appraisal, which will follow in a moment, this is a useful stepping-stone to workshopping, which can be daunting in the early stages of learning your craft. To spell it out, what I mean by peer appraisal is asking a small group of your friends or fellow students to read a draft of your work in progress and give you feedback on it. This feedback is only in the form of comments (which, coming from fellow writers, will be informed comments); peer appraisal does not mean peer assessment.

Peer appraisal allows you to write for an audience wider than the tutor. This is important in building confidence and eliciting feedback for the redrafting process. It is also clear that feedback is a motivating factor, and peer appraisal maximises feedback. Without peer appraisal, you are writing for an audience of one: the tutor. In your Creative Writing degree you may depend on the expert tuition of individual tutors and on their informed assessment and commentary on coursework, but the addition of other, increasingly informed readers (i.e. the other members of your class) has a vital role to play in your development as a mature, autonomous writer.

Not only does peer appraisal build confidence by offering you a more realistic view of your own work, it is also a significant tool in redrafting. As a writer, you depend on being able to estimate an understanding of readers' responses to your work; with peer appraisal, you have the means of making this estimate a little more evidence-based.

I can't recommend too highly the practice of offering first or second draft work to a small group of your peers. You don't have to be a student in further or higher education to acquire the habit. If you belong to a writer's group, for instance, what would be to stop you occasionally breaking into groups of three or four and peer appraising work?

Modus Operandi

Depending on the size of your peer appraisal group (four is ideal), you will need however many copies of your story. The author, obviously, should not be in the same peer appraisal group as his or her work. The group first of all reads the draft, and then discusses it. When they have reached some agreement about the story's strengths, and perhaps about an area in need of development, they should complete the form below.

The object of this exercise is for you to help your peers with their work. Think about how best to achieve that. A bland comment that glosses over significant flaws isn't doing anyone any favours; neither is a destructive comment that discourages the author. Your aim is to encourage an improvement and to increase, not decrease, the author's confidence in his or her writing. If you stick to the requirements of the exercise, you should achieve that.

Remember that you are examining the story on its own merits; you're aiming to make this story as good as it can be. You're not aiming to turn it into a different story, your idea of what it should be.

So, please, select *one* aspect of the story that each of you admired or enjoyed. Then agree between you on just *one* area that needs more work. (It may help to put yourself in the author's shoes.)

When the peer appraisal group has completed the task and filled in the form, they should invite the author over to discuss their responses to his or her work. This is important; it means as appraisers that you have to take responsibility for your comments.

It's a good idea to let the author hang on to the completed peer appraisal form.

The example that follows is a fairly basic form for peer appraisal groups to use.

Peer Appraisal Form

Title ....

Author ....

                                    Comments

Appraiser 1
A strength

Appraiser 2
A strength

Appraiser 3
A strength

Appraiser 4
A strength

(*Each appraiser should sign his or her remarks.*)

Appraisal Group
A suggested improvement you have agreed between you

17 Writer's Workshops

The University of Iowa's Writer's Workshop is the oldest and most prestigious graduate writing programme in the USA. Graduates of the Iowa Writer's Workshop include Flannery O'Connor, Raymond Carver, John Irving and Jane Smiley. Philip Roth taught there in the 1960s, and it was at Iowa that Walter Tevis wrote the story he later expanded into *The Hustler*.

Creative Writing was first introduced into British higher education when the University of East Anglia began its MA in 1971 – with a cohort that included Ian McEwan – but it was as long ago as 1922 that the University of Iowa set the ball rolling by announcing that creative work would be acceptable as theses for advanced degrees. The novelist Madison Smartt Bell, in his teaching handbook *Narrative Design, A Writer's Guide to Structure*, claims 'It was [at Iowa] that the workshop method, now common to about 95 percent of all writing programs across the academic landscape, first evolved. The Iowa workshop, in short, is the Ur-creative writing program.'[1]

I went to Iowa to learn. I surmised that the University of Iowa, with a 50-year head start on universities in the UK, must have learned a thing or two.

A Writer's Workshop

On day two of my visit, I was a guest in Frank Conroy's MFA class. Frank is the Director of Iowa's Writer's Workshop. The kind of class he runs is recognisable as the form of writer's workshop that has been proliferating in Britain since that first postgraduate Creative Writing course at Norwich in the early 1970s. Here's Conroy outlining the conventions of such a writer's workshop:

Every Tuesday at 4.30 in the afternoon I meet with about a dozen students. We have all picked up copies of the material we're going to talk about – texts generated by the two student writers who are 'up' that week – and have read them several times over the weekend, made editorial comments in the margins, and written letters to the authors attempting to describe our reactions to the texts. These letters are quite important – first because they are written before any public discussion and hence are not corrupted by what may be said in class, and second because they tend to be more supportive, more personal, and sometimes more trenchant than what the writer of the letter may say in class. Thus if a story is torn apart during the workshop, the letters, which are read one week later (since I keep them and read them myself during that time), can work to cheer a student up and encourage more work.

We talk for two and a half hours. The author of the text being examined generally remains silent, which some observers find surprising, but which I encourage. If there is a tension between the writer's intentions for the text and what the text, standing alone, appears to actually be doing to the readers, that is a tension the writer should face, and think about. As well, the writer's temptation to defend his or her work can lead to wasted time.[2]

When I sat in on Frank Conroy's MFA workshop, students were asked, one at a time, going clockwise around the room, to comment briefly on the tabled piece. Once this was out of the way – it didn't take long and students offered their observations only with much trepidation – Frank launched into a line-by-line analysis of the story.

First up was a former medic wearing a neck brace, which came to seem like a metaphor for his ordeal. Frank held forth on many aspects of the fiction-writer's craft. He cited Flannery O'Connor, perhaps Iowa's most illustrious graduate, on the necessity of creating a sense of immediacy ('The reader isn't going to believe anything just because you tell them'). He demonstrated the difficulty of achieving 'meaning, sense and clarity.' He discussed choice of verb, choice of action – there was a lengthy debate about the best way to convey a character pinning underfoot a paper napkin that has blown off a table. Much of what was said pertained to the failings of Neck-Brace's story.

'We of course spend 95% of our time finding out what is wrong,' Frank said and then, of a particular aspect of the story: 'This is bad writing.'

Although Frank was a hard taskmaster, and I felt for Neck-Brace, the two-and-a-half-hour session was filled with wisdom about the writer's craft. For example, at one stage Conroy noted one of the fundamental truths about art, one that goes right back to Michelangelo's remark about sculpture already being in the stone before a sculptor lifts a chisel to it: 'The text can be thought of as having a manifest destiny and it's our duty to find out what that destiny is. It's as if the story already exists and it's our duty to uncover it.'

By the end of this workshop, I was in no doubt that anyone passing through the semester that each MFA spends with Frank Conroy would emerge a better writer – so long as they survived. All the writer's wisdom notwithstanding, this class never once ran counter to Madison Smartt Bell's argument (again in *Narrative Design*) that the workshop process amounts to an autopsy: 'The attitude of the group toward the work is surgical. A process of dissection is going on. The text is handled as a machine in need of repair.'[3]

Neck-Brace's firm jaw appeared to recede a little with each flaw analysed, tucking further and further behind his brace. This was more master class than workshop. The criticism was indisputably valid, but students have to be thick-skinned. The fortunate author of the day's second story was praised, amongst other things, for his characterisation – 'Creating a character,' Frank said, 'is like building one layer of filo pastry on the next' – and stumbled from the workshop exuding the kind of glee usually reserved for a successful driving test.

Frank Conroy's philosophy seemed to centre on drumming into his students the strictures of good writing, so that when they were pushed out of the nest they might stand a chance of surviving as writers. If I picked up anything from his impressive, if fearsome, class, it was the value of rigour.

Workshop Limitations

Later in the week one MFA student told me that Conroy believes he isn't doing his job unless the occasional student bursts into tears or faints. This, along with the intense competition there is to gain a place at Iowa, makes for a charged atmosphere.

The short story writer Lan Samantha Chang, a former member of the Workshop, was Visiting Writer at Iowa when I was there. Over a raspberry soda in a downtown coffee shop, she was very positive about the benefits of the Workshop at Iowa, but admitted that at a certain point she had had enough of the workshop experience and just wanted to get on with writing. This was corroborated by another student of the Writer's Workshop I spoke to, Brett Johnston from Corpus Christi, Texas, who said, 'There comes a time when the benefits of the workshop will certainly dissolve.'

Madison Smartt Bell's other misgivings about the value of the writer's workshop rings true to these ears. He suggests that 'Fiction workshops are inherently incapable of recognising *success*.'[4] Having done my fair share of tabling texts in such workshops and, over the past dozen years, leading them pretty much on a weekly basis, I know for sure that tutors and students alike enter the workshop with one question uppermost in their minds: *What's wrong with this piece?* That, and *How can we make it better?* This is the mindset of the workshopper and it often has a reductive effect on the way the work is perceived. I also think that looking at creative work that has been printed straight from the computer has a diminishing effect. Most of us approach a paperback book very differently from a typescript. The glossy presentation of a published work encourages us to regard it more positively than we might regard a stapled sheaf of A4 pages. But my own experience is that, imperfect though it may be, a writer's workshop is a useful means of developing work in progress. As Brett Johnston said during my Iowa visit, 'The job of the workshop is to find the things that five or ten years down the road would embarrass the writer. Hopefully the workshop enables the writer to see that whatever it is is not doing the job he or she wants it to do.'

In order to develop, all creative work needs such responses from readers – in order to reach its 'manifest destiny,' to use Frank Conroy's apposite term. In an article called 'The Rocky Road To Paper Heaven,' Margaret Atwood describes the process of eliciting feedback from friendly readers:

> The work is shown to a few knowledgeable friends, if the writer is lucky enough to have some. Suggestions may be made, which the writer is free to accept or reject.
>   Pitfall 1: If s/he savages the friends for giving the suggestions, they are unlikely to make any more in future.
>   Pitfall 2: The friends may be wrong.
>   Pitfall 3: If all the writer wants from these people is an encouraging 'reaction,' i.e. not real suggestions but a 'Hey, that's great,' it would help matters to say so at the outset. There is nothing illegitimate about such a wish. Everyone needs morale uplift.[5]

If Atwood, one of the most distinguished fiction writers of our era, needs this kind of feedback to produce her finished work, it's a no-brainer that the rest of us do, too.

Benefits Of Workshops

Since workshops will require you to table pieces of creative work reasonably often, perhaps the first and most obvious benefit of being a member of a workshop is that it will provide you with a deadline. To illustrate: if you are in a weekly meeting of 12 students, where two texts are tabled each session, you will have to produce two pieces of work each term. Clearly this means that you will have a readership, which you may never have had before. Not only that, but an increasingly informed readership, who will add to your understanding of what you are doing. Membership of a workshop also puts you in regular contact with other writers, people who share your goals and anxieties, people who are trying to learn the same things you are. Together, you will have the chance to discuss and compare working methods. Being passionate about reading and writing, you will no doubt recommend books to one another, whether fiction or texts on craft.

In Chapter 4, you may have learned one or two things about how to read as a writer. What you do in workshops (as in peer appraisal groups) will help you grow ever more proficient in this discipline. Furthermore, in having your work appreciated and criticised by other writers, you will grow in self-awareness, self-criticism and, let's hope, self-esteem. Which leads me to my next points. Workshops that are worth their salt have two vital components.

First, they build mutual trust amongst their members. By offering your work to others, you are inviting them not to savage you; you are showing that you trust them. This in turn invites a reciprocal response, so that, as the weeks go by, writers who are offering up their own work for critical reaction and responding constructively to the work of others learn increasingly to trust one another.

Second, workshops enhance the confidence of their members. In my experience, many learning writers undervalue their own work. In workshops, they usually come to see that rather than being worse than everyone else's, their writing is as good as most of the work being tabled and may in fact be better than that of some. The corollary of this is that writers who have an over-inflated view of their work will, when they see what everyone else in the group is producing, perhaps arrive at a more realistic view of its merits. In terms of confidence building, though, perhaps the greatest achievement of the workshop is one I've already mentioned: the fact that here you have a group of people who are expecting to read and comment on your work. This, in the experience of every writer I know, is a strange and marvellous thing.

How It Works

Liz Allen says that 'The work you are expected to produce in workshops is first draft raw material for reworking and extending in your own time; a workshop is more about process than product.'[6] The process, I would argue, lies not only in the writing but also in the reading; writers learn as much from reading work by other members of the workshop as by hearing their own work discussed. Thus the workshop procedure begins the week before with every member taking away copies of the work to be discussed and spending some time reading it carefully and annotating it in preparation for the discussion which will take place in the next workshop. In my experience, after that discussion everyone hands over their annotated copy of the tabled work so that the author can see all the detail of the group's feedback. Some Creative Writing tutors – Frank Conroy, for instance, as we saw earlier – ask everyone to write a letter or critique to the author, in which they formally address the strengths and weaknesses of the piece.

In a workshop, you will need a leader or facilitator. In universities, this may well be your tutor, but by Year 3 of the degree, each student should be capable of fulfilling this role. The primary task of the leader is to keep the discussion aloft and moving forwards. Another responsibility is to ensure that each member of the workshop is contributing – and by extension, to prevent any one member of the group from dominating the discussion. The aim is to have a group discussion, not a monologue or dialogue, so if you are facilitating, you will have to do whatever is necessary to achieve this aim. A key part of this will be to ensure that the authors don't pipe up until you want them to. The positive reason for this is to ensure that as good a group discussion as possible takes place – and this discussion is a creative process in its own right; for one thing, in response to what others are saying, spurred by the debate, you will often find yourself having new things to say about the tabled work. The more negative reason for being strict about keeping the author out of the discussion at this stage is that author interjections quickly replace group discussion with a dialogue and destroy any possibility of creative debate. It may help authors keep silent if the facilitator invites them to take notes during the discussion of any points to which they may wish to respond at the end.

As a facilitator, you may want to give the discussion some basic structure. It's helpful to begin with some broad general statements and it eases the author's passage through what some will see as a bit of an ordeal if this general stage of the proceedings can begin with examining the virtues of the tabled work. An added virtue of keeping it general and positive to begin with is that this allows the readers, through making simple statements, to warm up their engines before developing a full-blown discussion.

After these opening, general and more positive statements, it may also be effective for the facilitator to encourage the discussion to go through two separate stages. In *The Fiction Editor, The Novel, and the Novelist*, Thomas McCormack identifies two fundamental short-comings from which a piece of fiction may suffer: 'the dermal flaw' and 'the internal flaw.'[7] The dermal flaw is much easier to deal with and examples of it would include grammar or syntax errors, typos, inelegant phrases, repetitions of vocabulary and redundancies ('six a.m. in the morning...'). The internal flaw has to do with the inner workings of the text and functions at the level of the narrative. Perhaps the tension fails to rise, or questions that the plot raises have not been answered, or at a most basic level, there is not enough at stake. Internal flaws may well most commonly occur at the beginning or end of the narrative. They may concern the quality of the characterisation as much as the efficacy of the narrative. In my experience, it makes most sense for a workshop discussion to begin by looking at the internal and deal with the dermal towards the end of the discussion. Internal flaws are more grievous and take more work to fix, while dermal flaws will be recorded in the annotations that members of the workshop write on copies of the text which can be absorbed by the author later. Whether looking at the dermal or the internal, though, it's good to try and keep a balance by examining the achievements as well as the inadequacies.

When the debate seems to have run its course, the facilitator invites the author to respond to what has been said. Here the author may counter criticisms that have been levelled at the work (or welcome them), clear up any aspects of the text that mystified readers and perhaps discuss the difference between authorial intentions and readers' responses.

I've tried to maintain a balance between the workshop's virtues and vices. Every writer should probably spend a few years as part of a workshop that meets regularly and reasonably formally. However, this does not mean that every writer will spend a lifetime submitting their work in progress to a writer's workshop. In redrafting your work, as Margaret Atwood's experience shows, you will probably always need a small readership on which you may road test your prototypes before putting them into production, but this may mean nothing more formal than sending your fiction out to three or four friends and asking them to read and respond to it.

18 Redrafting 2: Revising

Writing fiction, according to James N. Frey, is a hundred times more difficult than you think it is 'because a writer has a damn hard time evaluating what he has written, and unless he knows the strengths and weaknesses of a manuscript it will not be possible to turn a draft into a finished piece of work.'[1] This is part of the challenge when you come to revise your work. Another difficulty is ensuring that your characters and situations are fully realised. Struggling to imagine himself in the shoes of a young woman who robs a bank, André Dubus had a moment of illumination:

> I could not get inside of her, become her. Then one day or night I decided to try a different approach. I told myself that next day at the desk I would not leave a sentence until I knew precisely what Anna was feeling. I told myself that even if I wrote only fifty words, I would stay with this...
>
> At my desk next morning I held my pen and hunched my shoulders and leaned my head down, physically trying to look more deeply into the page of the notebook. I did this for only a moment before writing, as a batter takes a practice swing while he waits in the on-deck circle. In that moment I began what I call vertical writing, rather than horizontal. I had never before thought in these terms. But for years I had been writing horizontally, trying to move forward (those five pages); now I would try to move down, as deeply as I could.[2]

You might like to bear Dubus' insight in mind as we look at the key areas you will need to tackle when revising your fiction.

Developing Your Characters

As you read your work, you will learn more about your characters, and you should; according to Somerset Maugham, 'You can never know enough about your characters.'[3] What you have down in the existing draft will prompt you to new conclusions about your characters. And as you come to know your characters better, you will sometimes be struck by inconsistencies in your draft. You find that section where Rita tires to unwind with a glass of wine and it occurs to you that unwinding with a peppermint tea would really be more consistent with Rita's personality. You come to know them better the longer they have been living in your mind, but also through the evidence of their characteristics recorded in each successive draft of the fiction. Your characters develop in your mind and in your first draft, but they will also continue to evolve as you contemplate each draft and develop it. They arrive not in one draft, but through many.

Characterisation is widely thought to come before every other element of your craft; it is from your characters that your plot will grow. You have probably read many times the old chestnut that character is plot. Fortunately when it comes to plot, none of us is doomed to settle for our first-draft plot. When we revise, and come to understand better both character and plot – but especially character – we can make our plots stronger and better. 'When you begin to dwell on why he or she acted in this particular way,' the novelist William Kennedy suggests '– that is what moves you forward to the next page.'

A further aspect of the symbiotic relationship between character and plot is the dramatic quality of your characters. If you're aiming to prioritise drama in your fiction, when you come to revise, you may want to check that your characters are somewhat exaggerated for dramatic effect. 'Are your major characters bigger than life?' is Jack Bickham's challenge. 'Are you sure you haven't fallen into the trap of writing about average people in average situations. That can be deadly dull.'[4] I've been criticised for burying both character and plot in domesticity. You may be guilty of the same.

Relationships

You might find your fiction benefits from looking at the dynamics of the relationships in it. Are your characters sufficiently different from one another? Watson's plodding consistency and placid nature act as the perfect foil for Holmes' mercurial genius. Have you failed to use one character as a foil to the other when the opportunity was there? If so, it's not too late. As you redraft and grow in your knowledge of your characters, you can delineate them more boldly, differentiating one from the other ever more clearly, and, ideally, make what distinguishes one character from the other a source of conflict. Joanne is good with money to the point of being tight-fisted, whereas her husband Dan is open-handed, extravagant in every way. The tension between these two personality types will surely generate some useful conflict, which is something that can certainly be developed as you revise. It may even be introduced at the revising stage.

> **Writing Burst**
>
> *My lift is here.*

Dialogue

As you know, dialogue is arguably the best opportunity you have to reveal character. What characters say and the way they say it and indeed what they don't say all show the reader who they are and generate the conflict that makes a story. When you come to revise, there are a few aspects of your dialogue writing that may need checking. Most of us probably include too much dialogue in the first draft and often too much first-draft dialogue is chaff that you will need to remove. Look especially for dialogue with insufficient dramatic tension. The central purpose of dialogue – the central purpose of everything in fiction – is to move the story on. So, for starters, you can lose all the dead things we say, greetings and salutations, those phrases when the dialogue is simply treading water. Keep an eye out, too, for dialogue that is too direct. It's so much more potent and effective when characters say one thing which the reader clearly understands to mean something else. Within that, make sure what your characters say to each other communicates who they are. A handy wheeze when redrafting dialogue is to see if a given speech could have been said by another character. If it could, then it isn't revealing character as much as it might. In revising your dialogue, you will regularly find speeches you've given one character which will be much more appropriate for another character to say. When you spot that, move them and thus sharpen your dialogue. Half of the readers' pleasure in any narrative is in gaining such an understanding of character that they can think, yes, that's exactly what that character *would* say. Finally, remember what it is that you want the reader to take in: that which is said. So make sure as far as it is possible that you remove everything around speech, the clutter that distracts: speech tags and adverbs describing how things are said.

What Belongs

George V. Higgins has this advice: 'It is necessary to remember at all times, especially when most frustrated and cranky, that the writer is always at the mercy of his story.'[5] I've said somewhere else in this book that it often feels as if there already exists, on the far side of consciousness, in another world, a perfect version of the story you are writing. It is in this way that you are at the mercy of your story. You are straining with all your might to try and get down on paper the story you can hear from the other side.

When you're revising your story, one of the important things to consider is what to include in it. To do this, you need a clear understanding of what it's actually about, what it concerns. For instance, Carol Shields' *Larry's Party* is about the emotional life of a contemporary North American man and Vikram Seth's *An Equal Music* is about finding lost love again, and about passion for music. If you know what your story is about, you know what to leave in and what to take out, and what to add. 'The writer,' John Gardner says, 'sharpens and clarifies his ideas, or finds out exactly what it is that he must say, testing his beliefs against reality as the story represents it, by examining every element in the story for its possible implications with regard to his theme.'[6] So if you're Carol Shields revising *Larry's Party* and you find three chapters about ethical investment portfolios in 1960s Latin America, you will twig that you have wandered from the essence of the book and cut the offending chapters. If you happen to be Vikram Seth and find 10,000 words on eighteenth-century French garden design in your draft, you will know what to do.

Openings

Whether they are of scenes, stories or chapters, openings are crucial. Walk into Waterstone's, Angus & Robertson or Barnes & Noble and you will see the fiction section heaving with new releases. In the UK alone, 4000 new books are published *each week*. As far as readers are concerned, the sea is not short of fish, so if you fail to snare readers very early on, they will simply go elsewhere. I know I do.

Spend some time getting your openings right. My tendency is to begin a first draft a paragraph or two before the story kicks in. If you, too, tend to warm up your engines in first drafts, one of the things you will need to check when you come to revise is that the story, or the chapter, or the scene, starts where it should; you may have to remove excess baggage where you have just been easing your way into the story. Check for the appearance of the first hook. If your first draft hasn't generated a reader question in the first or second paragraph, I would think about making sure your second draft does.

Conflict and Drama

One constant consideration when you revise should be examining the quality of the drama. 'Never forget, something must happen!' Barnaby Conrad warns. 'A lot of beginning writers – and too many advanced ones – often forget that there is no drama without conflict.'[7]

Perhaps what your first draft achieves is life, but with the dull parts left in? Perhaps you are, in Scott Fitzgerald's phrase, chewing with no gum? If so, you can in your second draft remove the dull parts, cut the dreariness hanging like a millstone on the drama of your story. You can also find some gum to chew with.

But maybe neither of these is your problem. Maybe you have left the dull parts out and you have achieved the conflict necessary to drama. Is it the right kind of conflict, though? Remember James N. Frey's breakdown of the three kinds of conflict (in Chapter 8). As you revise your story, you will want to make sure that your conflict isn't static or jumping. Steadily rising conflict is what you're aiming to build.

Another thing to consider when looking at your use of conflict is whether the conflict is clear. It's quite easy for you to convey to your readers something different from your own understanding of the conflict. As far as you are able to, it's worth making sure you have communicated with sufficient boldness just what the conflict is and whom it's between. I say *as far as you're able to* because the big problem in writing fiction is putting yourself in the reader's shoes. It's impossible. So you might want to have a friend look at your story and tell you what they think the conflict is.

Action

Through characters and situations, you've managed to build in conflict, but does it result in action? If we think in terms of the simple linear plot, has your character kept pursuing their goal, have they taken action to overcome the obstacles impeding their progress to that goal? In this respect, there are a couple of the ways you can go wrong.

If you have made readers spend any length of time in internal monologue mode, you will have frozen the action. Not only that, but living inside the character's head or heart for any length of time deprives readers of oxygen and eventually makes them lose the will to live, let alone continue reading. You can also impede the action through static description: stopping to describe someone or something. In *Annie Hall*, Woody Allen tells Diane Keaton that a relationship is like a shark, and it dies if it doesn't constantly move forwards. 'I think what we've got on our hands,' he adds, 'is a dead shark.' A story, like a shark, should always be moving forwards. Your description needs to be on the hoof, incorporated into action and dialogue. Describe during action and dialogue – within in the same sentence. When you come to revise, just make sure your shark isn't floating dead in the water.

Chronology

Some of what you do in revising your work is re-ordering. 'I wrote and rewrote sections and moved them around until I had what I wanted' is the way Roddy Doyle describes the process.[8] When I'm revising, I spend a good deal of time moving around bits of text of various sizes. Low-level re-ordering might simply consist of breaking up bits of information that come in too hefty a dose at the start of a story or chapter. In the first draft, I might have included a fair bit of detail about, say, the petrol station where the story was set. Second time through, I would hopefully spot that the level of description involved stops the story advancing. An easy way round this is to break this block of description down into little details and drop them in later in the story, on the hoof, sprinkled, as it were, across the action. Higher level re-ordering might arise because, when I get some distance and perspective on my first-draft novel, I see that the scene where Eddie and Barbara are re-united should come at a completely different point in the novel. Similarly, I might cut a scene at some stage in the writing and leave it aside. Then months later, it could become apparent that this scene, with a nip and a tuck, will fit perfectly a hundred pages away from its original position (see also Chapter 22).

1500-word Story Project: Tuning In

The more you study the craft of fiction, the more you feel burdened when you sit down to write. As you face the blank screen, you may well be wondering how on earth you are going to remember everything you now in theory know. You may be flapping about whether you will be able to balance consistent use of limited third-person viewpoint with steadily rising plot and indirect dialogue – and what was that important tip Helen Newall had for creating convincing characters?

Don't fret about any of what you have been studying. Just trust yourself to remember what you need to remember, even if you can't consciously bring it to mind. Don't forget your unconscious mind is at work all the time and it's in the nature of the unconscious that you aren't aware of what it's up to. You will absorb all you need to absorb from studying the craft of fiction.

For this story, you will need to tune in to the media. Below, I've listed a few formats you can find there and use to inspire a story.

1. The magazine of the London *Sunday Times* has a feature at the back every week called *A Life In The Day*. Here, celebs or members of the public who have distinguished themselves in some way or other describe a typical day, from waking up to going to sleep. Amongst the details of exercise rituals, health supplements, diet and work and play regimes, some of the subject's philosophy of life will emerge. There's a story in this format. Just go online and look at one or two examples of *Life In The Day* in *The Sunday Times'* online archive. Then, once you're familiar with the rough structure, write a pastiche of *A Life In The Day*,

using the most colourful character amongst the teachers you had at school.

2. A couple of similar newspaper formats can also provide starting points for your 1500-word Story Project. The same *Sunday Times* magazine also runs a feature called *Relative Values*, in which two members of a family talk about each other and their relationship. For instance, it might be father and son or two sisters. As before, take a look at a couple of examples of the format before you start. When you've got the rough idea of *Relative Values*, use a variation of it to jot down some notes about the relationship between two of your friends who have an interesting tensions in their relationship. Maybe it's a couple that fight a lot. Maybe it's two competitive friends who are always trying to outdo one another. Use these notes to write your 1500-word story.

3. BBC Radio 4 has a show called *On The Ropes*, in which somebody from public life is grilled about a time when they almost went under. It might be a business person describing how he survived bankruptcy to come back and make a fortune all over again. It might be a famous embezzler who ended up serving a jail term for her crime, a distinguished athlete talking about the loss of a limb or a disgraced politician remembering how he redeemed himself after a spectacular fall from grace. There's a story in any one of these micro-narratives.

4. Maybe your medium of choice is television. If so, how about deriving your story from one episode of a format of your choice? You will find characters and situations in each of the following kinds of shows. Watch one episode of whichever kind appeals and take notes. Then turn your notes into a story.

   ▪ Reality TV (for instance, *Big Brother*)

   ▪ Chat Show (for instance, *The Jonathan Ross Show*)

   ▪ Sitcom (for instance, *Arrested Development*).

Don't forget to write a 250-word self-evaluation and include a bibliography of any texts that have informed the creative work.

IV
How To Manage Fictional Time

19 Some Notes On Handling Time In Fiction

James Friel

Henry James observed that 'the eternal time question is...really a business to terrify all but stout hearts.'[1] Every writer of fiction must confront the question of how to handle time.

In a short story a writer might have to make time pause, accelerate, fall back, leap forward or go in circles. A sentence in a story might distill a decade or even an entire life ('In the end his misfortunes touched her; she grew to love him': Chekhov's 'The Darling'). A story might devote itself to the pivotal events of an hour as in Hemingway's 'Hills Like White Elephants,' or an entire history of the world as in Italo Calvino's 'The Soft Moon.' A story, like Alice Munro's 'Friend of My Youth,' might probe the past and how its secrets surface in the present. A story might plait the past and the present, as in Hemingway's 'The Snows of Kilimanjaro' with its feverous hero recalling his past as he dies in the African heat. A story might concern the passage of time very directly, as in Charles Dickens' *A Christmas Carol* with its visits from the Ghosts of Christmas Past, Present and Future. Tobias Wolf's 'Bullet in the Brain' manages to tell the story of a man's whole life – often by detailing what he failed to do – in the seconds it takes for a bullet to enter his head during a bank robbery.[2] Liam O'Flaherty's 'The Wave' describes the impact of one wave on a cliff face: the work of a moment, but also several millennia.[3]

However else they deal with time, the stories mentioned so far also conform to a conventional structure: they have a beginning, middle and end, and in that order. Each follows the subjective experience of a character as it occurs to that character. However, simply following chronology does not answer or avoid the eternal time question.

For example, where – exactly – should one begin?

Before Or After The Fall?

Take Humpty Dumpty. Round fellow? Sat on a wall, fell off, and was irremediably broken? What if your story was about him? What if you wanted to know why he climbed that wall? What desires provoked him to it? You might wish to probe the mind of such a reckless character. To do so, you might have to go back to the very beginning: his childhood, and the overly ambitious mother who had egged him on? Or you might just step back to the very start of the crucial action – the night before, and the drunken bet that leads to Humpty climbing the wall? Such a beginning is called *ab ovo* – literally 'from the egg.' The writer starts from the beginning, and provides all the *necessary* background events concerning the characters, their circumstances and conflicts.

The familiar nursery rhyme, however, cuts straight to the decisive act: *Humpty Dumpty sat on a wall.* We aren't even told that he climbs the wall – or why. The story begins in the middle of things – or *in media res*. No time is wasted. We jump right in without preamble or explanation. Plot is all. Humpty is now in an action thriller.

One might begin the story at the very end of things – or *in ultima res* – with one of the King's men (or one of his horses) studying Humpty's fragments and wondering how such an event had occurred. Humpty's tale has become a detective story.

A story can begin at any point in time, and, in consequence, its mood and intentions change.

Writing Exercise: Three Beginnings

Look more closely at these three types of beginnings:

Ab ovo
At the age of five, when asked what he wanted to be when he grew up, Isaac said he wanted to be German.

Benedict Kiely, 'The Wild White Bronco'

In media res
The men were speaking in low voices in the kitchen.

V.S. Pritchett, 'Just a Little More'

In ultima res
There was something strange, abnormal, about my bringing up; only now
that my grandmother is dead am I prepared to face it.
                              Mary McCarthy, 'Ask Me Questions'

Now, take a familiar story like *Humpty Dumpty, Hamlet*, or, at random, a
story or event reported in your local newspaper. Ponder how you might
begin to tell the story *ab ovo, in media res* or *in ultima res*. For each one,
write an opening sentence or even a paragraph.
    You don't need to write the whole story. Just think – as storywriters
do – in what ways might you begin to tell this story.

Summary Or Scene

Summary (or telling) *accelerates* a narrative – events are being
compressed. Summary, by its very nature, condenses time. One
can summarise a novel in a sentence or even a title – *War and
Peace?* But with this speed come distance and detachment. It is
much harder to make summary as vivid or immediate to a reader.
Making a scene or dramatising an event (showing) *decelerates* a
narrative. The narrative slows down for dialogue, for the description of a room or a gesture. Detail gives weight, and suggests to the
reader that this moment or this exchange is significant. Too much
scene-making, however, and the pace can be meandering or static.
The story eventually stalls. This is why most fiction shifts between
these two modes.
    In fiction, although we often prize showing over telling, neither
summary nor scene-making is an inherently better narrative method
than the other. Both, ultimately, concern selection: choosing what
to add or omit. What matters, always, is making the writing count.
    This excerpt from Tim O'Brien's 'The Things They Carried' not
only dramatises a crucial event in the story, but also summarises
each of the main characters:

Until he was shot, Ted Lavender carried six or seven ounces of premium dope,
which for him was a necessity. Mitchell Sanders, the RTO, carried condoms.
Norman Bowker carried a diary. Pat Kiley carried comic books. Kiowa, a devout
Baptist, carried an illustrated New Testament that had been presented to him by
his father, who taught Sunday school in Oklahoma City, Oklahoma. When Ted

Lavender was shot, they used his poncho to wrap him up, then to carry him across the paddy, then to lift him into the chopper that took him away.[4]

Except for the last sentence, this is summary. What these characters carry gives clues to their personalities and backgrounds. It is summary, but it is also a very condensed form of showing. For example, is Ted Lavender's dope for consumption or dealing?

But look, too, at those names – *Lavender, Norman Bowker, Kiowa* (a Native American name). O'Brien's choice of names deepens and complicates what we might guess about the characters.

Look at each word O'Brien has chosen. What if O'Brien had written that Bowker had a *journal*, not a *diary*? Bowker's character would subtly change, would it not? O'Brien could have given Kiowa a Bible, but Kiowa has a New Testament – an illustrated one. Every word matters here.

Notice the syntax, too. The shape of each sentence reveals character, too. That fifth sentence? Doesn't it imply that Kiowa is also likely to be rather longwinded and pedantic, repetitious even? And is Mitchell Sanders as curt in all his dealings as the sentence he inhabits?

There is a concentrated thought behind each of O'Brien's choices. These vivid summaries might be O'Brien's answer to the eternal time question.

Writing Exercise: The Things They Carried

Try something similar. Choose either a group of five children going to school, young people out clubbing, a family setting out on a long journey, or commuters in a traffic jam. Suggest their character and history – even their future – by the things they carried, their names, and in the syntax and diction you employ to describe them.

Perhaps, also, as in the excerpt, you could write one more sentence that either moves the story on in time or concludes it.

Flashback/Forwards

The use of flashbacks (or *analepsis*) in fiction is common enough – so many stories begin with a variant of *I remembered* – but flashbacks as a device within a story can seem clumsy if all a character is doing is remembering information that the writer can't fit in any other way. 'Plot,' observed Eudora Welty, 'is not repetition – it is direction.'[5] If you are dealing with flashbacks, ask yourself if you are delaying your story or propelling it forward. Consider whether you need that flashback at all.

The flash-forward (or *prolepsis*), in which the plot or its outcome is given away, is less common but can be effective. In the excerpt from 'The Things They Carried,' the author tells us immediately that Ted Lavender will be shot. An omniscient narrator can see a wider history his characters will never know or even live to see as in William Faulkner's story, 'Barn Burning':[6]

> His father mounted to the seat where the older brother already sat and struck the gaunt mules two savage blows with the peeled willow, but without heat. It was not even sadistic; it was exactly that same quality which in later years would cause his descendants to overrun the engine before putting a motorcar into motion, striking and reigning back in the same movement.

Prolepsis does not destroy suspense; it can create a different and more sophisticated suspense. Rather than wondering how the story will end, the reader is encouraged to wonder how it reaches this point – and why.

Tenses

Tenses indicate time in a sentence. The present tense, for example, suggests that the events in a story are happening simultaneously with our reading it. Modishly, it is thought to be more 'immediate,' but your prose will not be immediate or vivid in any tense if your writing is stiff and uninterested in pace. It is diction and syntax that makes for pace and immediacy, not tense.

Errors in tense make a reader pause or stumble. Sometimes, notes Gerry Visco, the mechanics of the flashback technique can cause you to use cumbersome verb constructions.

If you are writing the story in the past tense, you can begin the flashback in past perfect. You can use 'had' plus the verb a couple of times. Then you can switch to the simple past. I gleaned this nugget from Janet Burroway in her helpful book on writing fiction. As she says, 'the reader will be with you.'[7]

However, tense shifts can be very effective. Timothy J Mason[8] has noted how, in Angela Carter's 'The Company of Wolves,' a young man's actions are reported in the past tense, but his metamorphosis into a wolf and when he kills and eats the grandmother is told largely in the present:

> He strips off his shirt. His skin is the colour and texture of vellum.
> A crisp stripe of hair runs down his belly, his nipples are ripe and dark as poison fruit, but he's so thin you could count the ribs under his skin if only he gave you the time.
> He strips off his trousers and she can see how hairy his legs are. His genitals, huge. Ah! huge.
> The last thing the old lady saw in all this world was a young man, eyes like cinders, naked as a stone, approaching her bed.
> The wolf is carnivore incarnate.[9]

In the penultimate sentence, the tense is changed to the past – the grandmother is dead – and in the last sentence we return to the present tense and the triumphant wolf. Carter does this frequently in her stories. The effect is almost musical. It shapes and modulates her writing voice. The tense changes are deliberate, worked out, chosen. They may have been lucky accidents in the drafting, but they are not errors.

Pace: Get There Smoothly

Chronology matters in fiction because it is about control, a writer shaping the material. Take this piece of prose, for example:

> In a tight-ish tweed coat, un-tanned, ideally bald, and clean shaven, he began rather impressively with that great brown dome of his, tortoiseshell glasses (masking an infantile absence of eyebrows), a thick neck, an apish upper lip, and a strong-man torso, but he ended, somewhat disappointingly, in frail-looking, almost feminine feet and a pair of spindly legs.

It is cumbersome but syntactically correct. It has some pleasing phrases, but it reads lumpily. It fails to impact. There is a reason. It does not occur chronologically. The reader's eye must first take in a coat and then a bald head. A domed skull is described next and then we slip down to his glasses. We then zip down to his neck and back up again for his lips only to plummet past his torso to his feet and finish with a flick back to the legs. Dizzying, yes?

If this were written chronologically, if we followed as the eye would take in this sight or as a camera might – that is, as it occurs in time – then we have this magisterial panning shot:

> Ideally bald, sun-tanned, and clean shaven, he began rather impressively with that great brown dome of his, tortoiseshell glasses (masking an infantile absence of eyebrows), an apish upper lip, thick neck, and strong-man torso in a tightish tweed coat, but he ended, somewhat disappointingly, in a pair of spindly legs and frail-looking, almost feminine feet.[10]

A great deal of writing commits the sins of the former passage. There is so much to do in writing that one gets flustered. In redrafting and shaping sentences, one can make one lose sight of common sense. Events occur in time. A description of a place or person is an event. Follow time.

This also applies to action. Graham Greene wrote that he learned never to interrupt an action; a man walks through a door with a gun and fires it. This is not a moment to describe the clouds.

Endings

Some stories reach a full stop, say, with marriages or murders. Such endings are called *closed*. Others are called *open*. The story need not have reached its end in time, but arrives at a point where what follows can be intuited – for example, the ending of James Joyce's 'The Dead' – or where it would spoil the effect to spell it out.

In Chekhov's 'Sleepy,' the climactic act is delivered as a devastating summary.

> Laughing and winking and shaking her fingers at the green patch, Varka steals up to the cradle and bends over the baby. When she has strangled him, she quickly lies down on the floor, laughs with delight that she can sleep, and in a minute is sleeping as sound as the dead.[11]

An even more brutal summary brings Raymond Carver's 'Popular Mechanics' to a dead halt:

> She would have it, this baby. She grabbed for the baby's other arm. She caught the baby around the wrist and leaned back.
> But he would not let go. He felt the baby slipping out of his hands and he pulled back very hard.
> In this manner, the issue was decided.[12]

In Elizabeth Bowen's 'The Demon Lover,' a woman returns to a neglected and boarded-up house. The story builds up an eerie and threatening atmosphere. The house is chillingly evoked. We wait for the demon lover to appear before her, but, at the very close of the story, she leaves the house and climbs into a waiting taxi. There is almost relief, and then the driver turns and she recognises her dead lover:

> They remained for an eternity eye to eye...Mrs Drover's mouth hung open for some seconds before she could issue her first scream. After that she continued to scream freely and to beat with her gloved hands on the glass all around as the taxi, accelerating without mercy, made off with her into the hinterland of deserted streets.[13]

These stories work by creating scenes, but their real coup is to cut away to summary or a muffled silence – those *gloved hands*.

Writing Exercise: Suspense

In 'Sleepy,' Chekhov conveys the poor maid's miserable life in such detail that we understand why she kills the child: it is one more dull and deadening task in a life filled with too many such tasks. The story appears to pay the child's death no more mind than she does and so we notice it all the more. In 'The Demon Lover' the house looks at Mrs Drover with 'a damaged glare.' Inside, the wallpaper looks 'bruised.' A piano has left 'claw marks' on a carpet. These details threaten. Something terrible *will* happen. It does – a woman is dragged off to a hell all the worse for it not being presented to us.

Take a simple or mundane event:

   a trip round a supermarket

   the cleaning of a kitchen

   taking a bath

   making a bed.

Imagine at the end of each of these events something terrible occurs:

an accident happens

a lie is told

a murder is committed

the world ends.

Try very hard not to announce this terrible conclusion. Show how it grows out of the event you describes or cuts across it in a way only you as writer could anticipate.

The eternal time question is one you must confront each time you tackle a story. We have only touched upon it here. I have had only 3000 words and, for a writer, time is also space – and word counts. I have not answered the question fully. I never will. Nor will you. That's one more reason why the question of time might terrify, but, if writing held no terrors, we would be uninterested in pursuing it. Love the questions. In the writing of fiction, a question takes you further than any answer.

20 Foreshadowing

According to James N. Frey, 'Foreshadowing is the art of raising story questions.'[1] Every time you raise a question in the reader's mind, you are foreshadowing and – not just because it is crucial to raise questions in the reader's mind – this is a key storytelling technique.

In a way, foreshadowing is connected to cause and effect: because this happens, that should follow. If Raymond Chandler's Philip Marlowe is shown taking a gun with him at the start of one of his adventures, we expect a follow-through. The expected effect of this private eye setting out with a gun is that he will use it later. But he better use it. In *Words Fail Me*, Patricia T. O'Connor sees foreshadowing as a promise the author makes to the reader, and warns of the dangers in unfulfilled promises:

> A careless hint or a subject that's raised and then dropped is a gun left in plain view but never fired. It's a promise to the audience – 'Trust me to deliver the goods' – that's never kept.[2]

Another way of looking at it is Frank Conroy's. In a class of his at the Iowa Writer's Workshop, I once heard him liken broken promises such as this to equipping the reader for a stiff uphill walk. If you give the reader things they will need later in the journey (a compass, a pen-knife, water, a packed lunch), fine. But if you make them carry a lot of things up the hill they find out later they didn't need (a laptop, thermal clothes, a walkie-talkie with heavy battery pack, etc.), not so good. In other words, don't piss your reader off by burdening him with superfluous things to carry.

Foreshadowing may also act like an omen – or at least what will come to seem like an omen later on. A minor action at the start of a story may suggest a major action at the end. For example, Pip's dramatic encounter with the convict Magwitch at the start of *Great Expectations* foreshadows the novel's climax. In the minor action, our first impression of the child Pip as kind-hearted and brave is formed when Magwitch, a frightening escaped convict, orders him to bring him food. In the major action, the climax of the novel, the adult Pip almost loses his life while attempting, once again, to help Magwitch escape. Dickens underlines the relation between these two scenes by setting both of them on murky marshland. But there's another level to foreshadowing in this example. Yes, the minor action foreshadows the major one, but the way Pip is characterised in it is confirmed in the major action. We were initially led to believe that he was brave and noble, which the major action confirms for us; he's so much so he almost gets himself killed. 'What a character does under a little stress,' says James N. Frey, 'is very telling about what he might do under a lot of stress.'[3]

The screenplay guru Robert McKee has a lovely definition of foreshadowing; he says it is 'the arrangement of early events to prepare for later events.'[4] I'm a great admirer of Pixar screenplays, which are nearly always instructive about narrative craft. Their most recent hit, *The Incredibles*, is awash with exemplary storytelling. At the start of the film, we see the superhero Mr Incredible in action, rescuing those in peril, and being tagged by Buddy Pine, a kid who idolises him and wants to become his sidekick. But Mr Incredible sees Buddy as a liability and rejects the offer more than once. These early events prepare us for later events, when the adult, embittered Buddy becomes Mr Incredible's greatest ever super-foe, Syndrome.

> **Writing Burst**
>
> *I wish you had told me this before.*

Plants

'Some promises,' Patricia T. O'Connor advises, 'are subtle; the reader recognizes them only in retrospect. They may be as unobtrusive as a recurring image.'[5] These subtle promises may be seen as plants, little seeds the author sows and which the reader unconsciously stores away for future use.

My favourite example of this comes in Rose Tremain's novel *The Way I Found Her*. Here the teenage narrator, Lewis, offers regular updates on the progress his father, Hugh, is making with constructing a garden hut. It is to be a homecoming present for Lewis's mother when she returns to London, with Lewis, after a summer working in Paris; it will be a place for her to work in peace. Each of the several times the garden hut is mentioned it seems that, largely because building it appears futile – Lewis is aware of his mother's growing estrangement from his father – it has been included in the narrative for comic purposes. But then Tremain pulls off a wonderful sleight of hand: the novel ends after Lewis's terrible rites of passage, when he comes home bereaved and scarred and electing to move into the garden hut himself. What was the sleight of hand? We thought the garden hut was comic relief, so we didn't notice at the time that Tremain was furiously planting. So, when she reaches the pay-off of this series of subtle promises, it seems like a kind of magic. Of course he will move into the garden hut. Since it symbolises the way his epic journey has wrenched him from the world of childhood, what could be more appropriate than moving from his family home into a shed in the garden?

Two things to learn from Rose Tremain here. One, you need to plant adequately for the information being planted to register, as Barnaby Conrad recommends here:

> If the fact that a character is left-handed is vital to the plot, show the reader in Chapter One or possibly Chapter Five or Six, but well before Chapter Thirteen when that fact becomes important.[6]

Two, you want the reader to register the plant without noticing they are registering it and an efficient way of doing that is to disguise it by making it seem like something else (as Tremain does here; it seems to be comic relief) or distract the reader by having something dramatic happening beside the plant. (In *The Usual Suspects*, when we first see the notice board in the police interview room, our attention is on Kevin Spacey's character, Verbal, being interviewed by a police officer about a waterfront explosion. This distracts us from any significance the notice board might have.)

Foreshadowing isn't always about wrong-footing the reader the way Tremain did with the garden hut. Sometimes it's a matter of satisfying an expectation the story has created. When Buzz Lightyear arrives at Andy's house at the start of *Toy Story*, his defining characteristic is that he thinks he can fly. When he demonstrates, he only, as Woody the Cowboy says, manages to 'fall with style,' which fools the other toys but not the viewer. At the end of the story, though, he and Woody are shot hundreds of feet into the air on a rocket and then, having survived everything that has been thrown at them in the previous half-hour, seem to be doomed to tumble to the ground. Just the perfect moment for Buzz to pop out his wings and glide them safely home. The gun in the first act (Buzz thinking he can fly) goes off in the third act (he flies, and saves the day). 'With each line of dialogue or image or action,' Robert McKee says, 'you guide the audience to anticipate certain possibilities, so that when events arrive, they somehow satisfy the expectation you've created.'[7]

Writing Exercise: Foreshadowing

Like a lot of writers I know, I only ever have a vague idea of where I am going with a story, so thinking about plants and pay-offs in advance isn't really an option. What I have found, though, is that when I discover a pay-off in a first or second draft, it's quite simple and fun to go back and insert the plants for it afterwards. In its most basic form, this may be a case of realising at the end of a short story that your protagonist needs, for dramatic purposes, to be asthmatic. So you go back and show him being asthmatic a couple of times earlier in the story.

This is an exercise to use with an existing draft of a story. Read it carefully and see if you can find a pay-off looking for a plant, see if you can find something it will be helpful to go back and foreshadow. Say the story ends with your protagonist heroically rescuing his fellow passengers after an air-crash; you could foreshadow that by going back and inserting an opening scene where he takes a risk to help somebody in some minor difficulty – the minor action that will prepare your readers for the major action.

21 Transitions

One aspect of the pressure to be dramatic is the need for movement. I've said already that a story has more in common with a movie than a photograph; it ought to involve movement almost all the time. In attempting to keep your story moving, you will need a variety of means for a variety of purposes to move your reader around.

Perhaps the most obvious movement — and it is prompted by wanting to leave the dull parts out — is moving through time. Watch how Amy Tan in this passage from *The Joy Luck Club* achieves the most elementary moving through time:

> When Harold returns from the store, he starts the charcoal. I unload the groceries, marinate the steaks, cook the rice, and set the table. My mother sits on a stool at the granite counter, drinking a mug of coffee I've poured for her. Every few minutes she wipes the bottom of the mug with a tissue she keeps stuffed in her sweater sleeve.
>
> During dinner, Harold keeps the conversation going. He talks about the plans for the house: the skylights, expanding the deck, planting flower beds of tulips and crocuses, clearing the poison oak, adding another wing, building a Japanese-style bathroom. And then he clears the table and starts stacking the plates in the dishwasher...[A dialogue passage follows and then this:]
>
> After dinner, I put clean towels on the bed in the guest room. My mother is sitting on the bed.[1]

The opening line is the beginning of a new section within the chapter and follows an extra space on the page, so the reader has been moved from an earlier scene, on a previous day, to Harold returning from the store. Tan shunts us through time again at the beginning of the second paragraph. We had been at some earlier time in the day and now we are in the evening: 'During dinner, Harold etc.' The following sentence, beginning 'He talks about the plans for the house...' includes a summary of the conversation while the family are eating, so that moves us along again. In the last sentence of the second paragraph ('And then he clears...'), Tan uses ellipsis again, that is, she cuts out another piece of time. In the first sentence of the final paragraph, we have moved from the conversations while clearing up after dinner to a later point in the evening and then, shoving us swiftly on, to another point a little after that ('My mother is sitting on the bed.').

This means that in only the 150 words I have quoted here, Amy Tan has moved the reader through time or space five times (if we count the plans for the house summary as one movement). This has several beneficial effects for readers. Number one, it's a moving picture, skipping through time and space and omitting less interesting business. Movement is desirable. Clearly it creates pace, since motion and pace are interrelated. By leaving out the inconsequential, it also gives air to the scene and helps it get off the ground. (If you have young children whose comprehensive summary of their escapades, or of a film's storyline, leaves nothing out, you will know how desperately long a complete account of any series of actions can feel.) And the fact that you register at some level that the author has been editing the fictional reality into a palatable narrative, removing the irrelevant to help you focus on the pertinent, must reassure you that you are in competent hands, that this story is being crafted for your reading pleasure.

All of these movements are transitions, which Jack M. Bickham defines as 'passages that get a character from one place to another, or from one time to another.'[2] These particular transitions were between one paragraph and another, between one sentence and another or within a sentence. However, transitions may also be between one scene and another, as we see in the following brief extract from Andrea Levy's *Small Island*. The first paragraph ends a short scene in which Hortense, the narrator, has arranged a marriage of convenience with Gilbert.

Gilbert nodded like a half-wit as the minister went on. He threw his head back, looking to the church roof, when asked the question, 'How long have you and your wife-to-be known each other?' Tapping the side of his face with his fingers, mumbling, 'Now let me see ...' he lingered so long with this deliberation that the minister resumed his sermon without receiving an answer. As the minister talked of the joy of seeing two young people embarking on a cherished life together after a period of unprecedented upheaval, Gilbert, satisfied with his trickery, looked furtively to me and winked.

'Married!' Mrs Anderson yelled. 'But how long have you two known each other?'
'Oh, now, let me see ... Five days,' Gilbert said.[3]

Why use this sort of transition, which requires a break between two scenes? It gives the reader a break, offers some breathing space, and in that space she can rest from reading, and perhaps allow her unconscious to process the information that has gone before the break. The alternative is a monolithic text without breaks of any kind. It's preferable to cut your fiction up into sections which have some relation to the attention span of the human mind. Although my wife accuses me of having the attention span of a goldfish, I can, if pushed, concentrate pretty well for up to 45 minutes without stopping for breath. The same is probably true of you. And your readers – so make some allowances.

> **Writing Burst**
>
> *She's been told.*

As you know, one of the great priorities in writing fiction is engaging the reader. Assuming you have succeeded in that, another pressure on you is to retain that engagement. You don't want to lose or confuse your reader. In the passage from *Small Island*, Andrea Levy illustrates one of the characteristics of transitions. They are bridges, with feet on both sides of the divide. Signalling the bridge, the connection between the end of one scene and the beginning of the succeeding one, can be a smart idea because it lets the reader know that these scenes are closely related. This way you can fight against losing or confusing your reader.

In the example given, the earlier scene has concerned the subject of marriage and to build a bridge, to demonstrate that the next scene is related, Levy places a marker ('Married?') right at the start of the second scene. As a result, the relationship between the two scenes is established and the reader has a handy little bridge on which to cross from one scene to the next. Better than that, emotion has been built into that bridge: somebody (Mrs Anderson) is outraged that Hortense and Gilbert are getting married in such haste. Outrage is a strong emotion and there is a direct correlation between strong emotion and drama. *Drama*, let's not forget, is the name of the game.

In both of the examples given so far, a transition, whether or not it involves a section break, has been used to show that the narrative has moved through time or space, or has omitted some irrelevant action. A further example of a transition is similar to the one from *Small Island* in that it involves a section break, an extra space on the page to denote some kind of change. This time, though, the change is not from one place to the other, or from one time to another; it is from one viewpoint to another – in Pat Barker's *Regeneration*.

In the taxi, going to Craiglockhart, Sassoon began to feel frightened. He looked out of the window at the crowded pavements of Princes Street, thinking he was seeing them for the first and last time. He couldn't imagine what awaited him at Craiglockhart, but he didn't for a moment suppose the inmates were let out.

He glanced up and found the taxi-driver watching him in the mirror. All the local people must know the name of the hospital and what it was for. Sassoon's hand went up to his chest and began pulling at a loose thread where his MC ribbon had been.

For conspicuous gallantry during a raid on the enemy's trenches. He remained 1½ hours under rifle and bomb fire collecting and bringing in our wounded. Owing to his courage and determination, all the killed and wounded were brought in.

Reading the citation, it seemed to Rivers more extraordinary than ever that Sassoon should have thrown the medal away. Even the most extreme pacifist could hardly be ashamed of a medal awarded for *saving* life.[4]

The earlier section, obviously, is in the viewpoint of the poet Siegfried Sassoon. The second is that of Rivers, the doctor who will treat him. Pat Barker and Andrea Levy use the same technique to help the reader make the transition from one scene to the next. In the *Small Island* extract, the subject of marriage is used as a marker on either side of the divide. Here in *Regeneration*, subject matter is again used as a bridge. This time the subject is Sassoon's rejection of his Military Cross. There's a subtle difference between the Levy and the Barker, though. The subject matter – marriage – was the same in both *Small Island* scenes. In *Regeneration*, the first scene isn't about Sassoon dispensing with his medal; it's about his anxiety as he approaches Craiglockhart, the psychiatric hospital in which he will be treated. The medal may well have been introduced for the specific purpose of helping the reader make the transition from one scene (and viewpoint) to the other. 'Sassoon's hand went up to his chest and began pulling at a loose thread where his MC ribbon had been' is where the feet of the bridge rest on one side of the divide. 'Reading the citation, it seemed to Rivers more extraordinary than ever that Sassoon should have thrown the medal away' is where the feet rest on the other. In other words, the whole subject of Sassoon and the Military Cross he threw away seems to have been introduced here as a means of hanging onto the reader during the transition from Sassoon in the taxi to Rivers in the hospital.

In a nutshell, the function of transitions is like that of anything which connects two separate things – a hinge holding door and frame together, a stitch holding the arm of your shirt to the body, or a lead connecting owner to dog. Transitions connect two patches of fiction together. You need transitions because in fiction you have to omit and leave spaces. You don't always have to insert those markers to help the reader along, though. Readers are as smart as you and maybe smarter. They've read post-modern novels with fragmented chronologies and can leap from here to there without you holding their hand. But some of the time, though, as we've just seen from these highly sophisticated novelists, using markers to help the reader is desirable. Even when it's not, you may want to plant markers on either side of a transition just to be elegant, to show that the author has devoted some thought to the construction of the fiction, as Margaret Atwood does here, in her story 'The Sin Eater':

'The old fart,' I said. I was furious with him. It was an act of desertion. What made him think he had the right to go climbing up to the top of a sixty-foot tree, risking all our lives? Did his flowerbeds mean more to him than we did?

'What are we going to do?' said Karen.

What am I going to do? Is one question. It can always be replaced by What am I going to wear? For some people it's the same thing.[5]

Writing Exercise: Transitions

Using an existing draft of a piece of fiction, see if you can't make it more cohesive and engaging by introducing transitions between sentences and paragraphs. Then introduce more breathing space for the reader by introducing transitions between scenes which move from one place to another, from one time to another or from one viewpoint to another.

22 Crossing Timelines And Breaking Rules

Heather Leach

How fast or slow does time go? Most people will answer 'It depends' because we are all very well aware that time seems to go too fast when we are doing things we enjoy and extremely slowly when we're bored. The writer can simply *describe* this experience:

> The long afternoons I spent in the Maths class nearly drove me mad with boredom

or

> I was so much in love with Jenny that the hours I spent with her went by in a flash and were over far too soon.

But it is much more challenging and interesting for the writer to try to *show* the subjective experience of time in a story.

In David Foster Wallace's 'Forever Overhead,' the protagonist is a boy on his thirteenth birthday. The story is told in the second person, an unusual point of view that enables the writer to add another time-shift: that of the boy narrator himself and of the omniscient narrator/writer remembering. The boy is rapidly turning from child to adolescent and is both thrilled and alarmed by his new sexual awareness and his changing body. On this special day he decides to make his first dive into the swimming pool from the top board. As he climbs the ladder, things get scary and time begins to shift:

> There's wind. It's windier the higher you get. The wind is thin; through the shadow it's cold on your wet skin. On the ladder in the shadow your skin looks very white. The wind makes a thin whistle in your ears. Four more rungs to the top of the

tower. The rungs hurt your feet. They are thin and let you know just how much you weigh. You have real weight on the ladder. The ground wants you back.

Now you can see just over the top of the ladder. You can see the board. The woman is there. There are two ridges of red, hurt – looking callous on the backs of her ankles. She stands at the start of the board, your eyes on her ankles. Now you're up above the tower's shadow. The solid man under you is looking through the rungs into the contained space the woman will look through…

Time slows. It thickens around you as your heart gets more and more beats out of each second. [...] No time is passing outside you at all. It is amazing. If you wanted you could really stay here forever, vibrating inside so fast you float motionless in time, like a bee over something sweet.[1]

As the line of swimmers move forward and up the ladder, rung by rung with a machine – like regularity, the boy's perceptions of time are transformed by fear and adrenaline. He shifts out of 'normal' time into something close to timelessness. The story is told using short sentences, with many repetitions. Notice how often the words 'thin,' 'wind' and 'rungs' are used in the first small paragraph alone. And also, even though this is prose, there are a number of rhymes and half-rhymes – thin / skin / wind; ladder / shadow – which work to reinforce the anxiety the boy feels about his own weakness and vulnerability, and also to add a lyrical, mythical quality. The boy notes the smallest detail: *the red hurt-looking callus on the backs of her ankles.* These precise observations, along with the patterned, rhythmic texture of the language, slow down the action into a series of small, almost meditative moments.

I guess that this story is based on experience. I think it would be difficult for any writer to write in this way without having some subjective knowledge of how it feels. For the first part of the next exercise, dig down into your own experience to find the precise quality of your own time-shifting memory, its taste and texture, its colours and patterns. Then in the second part of the exercise you will have the materials to begin to re-frame these qualities into a fictional story.

Writing Exercise: Slowing Down Time

1. Bring to mind an event in your life when your normal experience of time was altered and your perceptions changed. Try to re-enter the experience, to re-imagine how it felt, using all your senses.

2. Imagine two people: any age or gender. One person is in life-threatening danger; the other is trying to rescue them. The endangered person could be someone who has fallen over a cliff, balanced precariously on the ledge of a building, with their foot trapped in a railway line, etc. Write a page of the story plunging straight into the action, no preliminaries. Try to create a powerful sense of immediacy. Experiment with some of David Foster Wallace's methods: staccato sentences, repetition, tiny details. Time is tick-tocking somewhere in the background, but in this place, for the two of you, time has almost stopped.

Travelling In Time

Time travelling has long been a popular fictional theme. H.G. Wells' *The Time Machine*[2] is a classic example and one of the first to reach a mass audience. Published in 1895, it pre-dated Einstein's theories by 10 years and has inspired two film versions. An earlier story, *Rip Van Winkle*, by Washington Irving[3] depicts a man sleeping his way into the future, waking to find the world transformed. Today's most well-known time fictions are probably television series: *Star Trek* and *Dr Who*, for example, both of which translate actual science (black holes, time warp, wormholes) into fantastic fact, jumping freely back and forth in time as if the Universe was a dog and they were its fleas.

Martin Amis' *Time's Arrow* uses a reversed chronology to disrupt the way we normally perceive events. The main theme of the book is the Holocaust. At that point, in real historical time, *Time's Arrow* implies, human history and progress were reversed. The novel also draws on semi-scientific speculation that if the Universe's Big Bang were to reach its limit and then begin to implode, time, including human time, would start to go backwards. Amis also explores the idea of reversal in many contexts, using it to create surprising and very odd effects. A doctor speaks of what happens in a hospital:

Some guy comes in with a bandage around his head. We don't mess about. We'll soon have that off. He's got a hole in his head. So what do we do? We stick a nail in it. Get the nail – a good rusty one – from the trash or wherever. And lead him out to the Waiting Room where he's allowed to linger and holler for a while before we ferry him back to the night.[4]

This passage summarises (in reverse) the way a person is treated in hospital and is odd, shocking and funny. The key to this, I think, is that Amis takes us through each step of the expected time structure – person coming into the hospital from outside, yelling in the waiting room, rusty nail taken out of his head and thrown in the trash, hole in his head bandaged – and then carefully reverses them. Of course, it doesn't work perfectly but there is a strange logic to this reverse world, as if we are looking through the writing to another dimension, through a quantum looking-glass.

Stuart: A Life Backwards by Alexander Masters[5] is the story of an actual person described on the book cover as 'a chaotic, knife-wielding beggar.' Masters collaborates with Stuart to recount his crazy, violent life-story, which has involved many spells in prison, drug-addiction, alcoholism and life on the street. The added twist is that this story, as the title says, is told backwards. It begins at the end, as Stuart and Alexander meet,[6] and works its way through to the beginning of Stuart's life.

The key point is that in both of these texts this reversal of time is not simply a piece of clever but empty experimentation, but a method of exploring meaning and character in greater depth. The main theme of *Time's Arrow's* is the Holocaust, when human progress seemed to go into reverse. Masters' book uses reversal to trace some of the possible causes of Stuart's chaotic and unhappy life. It leads the reader back from half-deranged and threatening man step by worsening step to small and vulnerable child. These texts also work by being grounded in the real world, by focusing carefully on the 'normal' order of events. Try it for yourself but don't force every detail into reversal and don't comment on the strangeness. Let the writing speak for itself.

Time Loops And Jump Cuts

One of the most well-known time-loop stories is the film *Groundhog Day*, directed by Harold Ramis, in which the central character, a bored and cynical television reporter, is forced to repeat the same day over and over until he learns the value and meaning of his life. Margaret Atwood's also uses this relentless repetition in her short story 'Happy Endings.'[7] A number of alternative boy-meets-girl romantic scenarios are set out in a series of blocks. Each block is labelled A, B, C and so on., beginning with the happy-ever-after version:

A. John and Mary fall in love and get married. They both have worthwhile and remunerative jobs which they find stimulating and challenging. They buy a charming house. Real estate values go up. Eventually when they can afford live-in help, they have two children, to whom they are devoted. The children turn out well. John and Mary have a stimulating and challenging sex-life and worthwhile friends. They go on fun vacations together. They retire. They both have hobbies which they find stimulating and challenging. Eventually they die. This is the end of the story.

Atwood is, of course, over-egging the perfection, her tongue firmly in cheek in order to offer a critique of this idealised vision in which everything turns out perfectly. The use of the formulaic names and short formal sentences, the repetition of the words 'stimulating' and 'challenging,' is spooky, making John and Mary come over as robotic, unreal. In the other versions, things don't always turn out so well:

B. Mary falls in love with John but John doesn't fall in love with Mary. He merely uses her body for selfish pleasure and ego gratification of a tepid kind. He comes to her apartment twice a week and she cooks him dinner, you'll notice that he doesn't even consider her worth the price of a dinner out and after he's eaten the dinner he fucks her and after that he falls asleep, while she does the dishes so he won't think she's untidy, having all those dirty dishes lying around and puts on fresh lipstick so she'll look good when he wakes up, but when he wakes up he doesn't even notice, he puts on his socks and his shorts and his pants and his shirt and tie and his shoes, the reverse order from the one in which he took them off. He doesn't take off Mary's clothes, she takes them off herself, she acts as if she's dying for it every time, not because she likes sex exactly, she doesn't, but she wants John to think she does because if they do it often enough surely he'll get used to her, he'll come to depend on her and they will get married but John goes out of the door with hardly so much as a goodnight and three days later he turns up at six o'clock and they do the whole thing over again.

Note how this block begins with a similar formal and cool tone as version A, but within a sentence or two the story slips into something more painfully human, more real and the language becomes richer, the sentences running on without full stops, like a voice speaking. In Block C the power struggle is reversed:

> John, who is an older man, falls in love with Mary, and Mary, who is only twenty-two, feels sorry for him because he's worried about his hair falling out. She sleeps with him though she's not in love with him. She met him at work. She's in love with someone called James, who is twenty-two also and not quite ready to settle down.

Atwood's method gives us a series of mini-sagas, each one entertaining in its own right but the repeating form also echoes and resonates with deeper patterns and meanings: the universality of love and sex; expectations and experience; the patterns we find ourselves stuck in; and the truth that we all must eventually learn: that all stories, even love stories, will come to an end.

Writing Exercise: Writing In Pieces

Create two characters in a relationship (not a romantic one). For example, Human–Pet; Teacher–Pupil; Parent–Child.

Tell the story of this relationship in ten sections – number the sections one to ten. Think of possible permutations from the familiar to the bizarre and unexpected. Start formally but then let the stories take off, allowing characters and events to develop. Use the final section to draw a conclusion – to make some kind of fictional statement about the nature of such relationships. However this statement should be implicit, not explicit: *shown, not told.*

Remember that, although there is repetition, there still needs to be narrative development – something must always change in a story. But the change can be in the reader's mind.

There are many other ways of playing with time and form which I don't have space to explore here. The important thing is that you are aware that not all writing follows, or needs to follow, the classical linear narrative. There are as many ways of telling stories, of writing the world, as there are writers. If you are someone who finds the traditional forms difficult and restrictive, this is an opportunity for you to try out some of the alternatives for yourself. Learn the rules first. Then learn to break them.

V
How To Write With Style

23 Meaning, Sense And Clarity

As you will remember, during my visit to Iowa in 2001, I was a guest in Frank Conroy's workshop. During the workshop I witnessed, while Conroy was offering a critical reading of a piece of student work, he was at pains to convey to his students the difficulty of achieving 'meaning, sense and clarity.' In the following, from his essay 'The Writer's Workshop,'[1] Frank Conroy expands on his beliefs about accurate expression.

Writing Burst
Meet the gang.

In my opinion the struggle to maintain meaning, sense and clarity is the primary activity of any writer. It turns out to be quite hard to do, demanding constant concentration at high levels, constant self-editing, and a continuous pre-conscious awareness of the ghostly presence of mind on the other side of the zone [the reader] . . .

1. Meaning. At the literal level, the writer's words must mean what they say . . . *He sat down with a sigh* means that the sitting and the sighing are happening at the same time, which precludes a construction such as *'I'm too tired to think,' he said as he sat down with a sigh.* The reader will undoubtedly get the drift and will separate the sighing from the saying, but the writing is sloppy from the point of view of meaning. It doesn't, at the literal level, mean what it says. Errors of meaning are quite common in lax prose, and there are more ways of making them than I can list here.

2. Sense. The text must make sense, lest the reader be excluded. *The boy ate the watermelon* makes sense. *The watermelon ate the boy* does not, unless the author has created a special world in which it does. Unmotivated behaviour in characters doesn't make sense to the reader, who is also confused by randomness, arbitrariness, or aimlessness in the text. The writer must recognise the continuous unrelenting pressure from the reader for the text to make sense. It can be a strange kind of sense, to be sure, but the reader must be able to understand the text to enter it.

3. Clarity. Strunk and White[2] tell us not to use ten words where five will do. This is because the most compact language statement is almost always clearer than an expansive one. The goal is not brevity for its own sake, but clarity. The reader expects the writer to have removed all excess language, to have distilled things to their essences, whether the style is simile or complex…As well, clarity has aesthetic value by itself.

In using language, accuracy and direct communication are essential. It's also an important consideration to keep language in its place. Language is, if you like, a medium, while your fiction is the message it delivers. Remember that your use of language is just a tool.

Years ago I went on a lighting course at the Royal Exchange Theatre in Manchester. The most helpful advice during that week was made by Vince Herbert, then in charge of lighting at the Royal Exchange. 'Lighting is there to allow the show to be seen and to create effects,' he said. 'If the audience notice your lighting, you've failed.' Joyce Carol Oates says virtually the same thing about the way we as writers use language:

> I think that's one of the problems with the really elegant writers; you stop reading and start admiring the words. So you lose the narrative flow. I don't want that to happen.[3]

I'm as fond of beautifully crafted prose styles as the next person, but I think the point being made here is worthy of your attention. All of us want to use words beautifully, but the beauty of the style should never distract from the function of language in fiction, which is not primarily to be attractive.

Writing Exercise: Meaning, Sense and Clarity

If you're at university or college, it shouldn't be too hard to find a play to see, or a gig. Whatever kind of performing rings your bell, go and see a live show of some kind.

Your brief is to write a record of what you saw and experienced, but not to express the kind of opinions that a reviewer might. Instead, stay at the level of what happened, both onstage and in the audience. You have 500 words in which to produce a record of your chosen event, one which complies with Frank Conroy's observations about meaning, sense and clarity.

Do it properly: word-processed, double-spaced and include drafts.

24 Description
Ursula Hurley

Good fiction conjures an alternative world, gives you a window into someone else's life, takes you somewhere other. Above all, it's convincing. Effective description is fundamental to this process. The aim is to entrance your reader by the cunningly set stage to the extent that they don't notice the ropes and pulleys supporting it all. The art is in judging what is salient and what is boring, when to zoom in and when to draw back, when to show and when to leave intriguing gaps, when to elongate and when to contract. Effective description, just like a palatable brew, takes skill and judgement: too much cloys, too little is bland; get it right and the good times roll.

Less Is More

Narrative drive is paramount, a lesson I learned the hard way after wasting a lot of time and effort on pages and pages of beautiful (to me) but pointless (to everyone else) description. As Stephen King says,

> In many cases when a reader puts a story aside because it 'got boring,' the boredom arose because the writer grew enchanted with his powers of description and lost sight of his priority, which is to keep the ball rolling.[1]

Just because you can doesn't mean that you should. When it comes to setting the scene, the bare minimum can be more than enough. Alessandro Baricco's *Ocean Sea* begins thus:

> Sand as far as the eye can see, between the last hills and the sea – *the sea* – in the cold air of an afternoon almost past, and blessed by the wind that always blows from the north.
> The beach. And the sea.[2]

Baricco gives us little to work with, and yet what he does give us has a powerful effect. The concept of the sea finds fertile ground in the imagination, rich in metaphor and association. Are the fading afternoon and north wind symbolic? Do they signal decline, winter or menace? The very sparseness of the description loads it with significance; every word is weighed and pondered. I would bet my laptop that you have already conjured a beach for yourself; a hybrid of childhood memories, imagined paradises, lonely walks. You might even hear the sigh of the waves, taste the salt on your lips, feel the spray on your face. Giving the reader's imagination room to work is often the most powerful thing that a writer can do.

Writing Exercise: Using Description For Specific Effects

Readers have a horizon of expectation. If Baricco's opening lines went on to describe a corpse bobbing gently in the waves, we would be justified in suspecting that we were probably embarking upon a murder-mystery. Alternatively, if two young women in sequins and sunglasses came laughing along the surf, we would brace ourselves for some Chick Lit. Innovative fiction may toy with that horizon, leading the reader to expect one thing and then surprising them with something else.

Practise manipulating the reader's horizon of expectation by completing Baricco's opening paragraph in two or more contrasting styles. Here are some suggestions: Horror, Crime, Chick Lit, Romance, Historical.

Think about the kind of description you will need to deploy in order to achieve the desired effect. Which details will you need to highlight? What does the reader need to see or understand? With Chick Lit, it might be the brand of sunglasses; with historical it might be the style of dress or the ship on the horizon.

Then ask someone to read your paragraphs. Ask them to explain the effect that your description has on them. What does it look like in their imagination? What have they understood or anticipated from your writing? How do their impressions differ from your intentions? What would you change in the light of their comments?

Multi-Tasking

Description is the consummate multi-tasker. Amongst other things, it can:

- Create atmosphere
- Explain something the reader needs to know
- Help the drama
- Show character
- Contribute to the plot
- Work on symbolic, allegoric and prosaic levels.

One of the most atmospheric novels that I have read is Rupert Thompson's *Air & Fire*. What might be a predictable tale of an unfulfilled wife seeking refuge in the arms of another man becomes intensely absorbing because of the barren Mexican landscape in which the drama is played out. The searing heat and unforgiving light create a hyper-reality where the emotional tension is as unbearable as the climate. Here's a particularly rich passage, which occurs just before the plot's climax:

There were lava fields now, shades of coral and maroon. Like raised roads, they curved towards him. This was where the elephant trees put down their roots. Perverse trees, to choose such desolation. Nothing else grew here. From a distance the lava looked smooth, but up close you saw that it was flakes of rock stacked tightly, pages in a book. And each flake sharp as glass; they could slice through boot leather, horses' hoofs. He let his eye climb towards the mother of the fields. Its slopes striped with lava stains. The shocked blue air above the crater's edge. The last time it erupted had been a century and a half ago. But the air did not forget.[3]

The heroine, half-dead from heat exhaustion, is lolling on the back of the 'other' man's mule. Lives are hanging by a thread. Why stop to tell us about the shades of lava and the species of tree? Thompson is using the helpful trick of elongating the moment. Stretching things out with salient description can get your reader panting with anticipation – as long as you pull the narrative taut without letting it snap. Notice how Thompson zooms in, from fields of lava to the individual flakes of rock. He points out how sharp they are, especially to hooves. Rather than telling us how dangerous the situation is, Thompson shows us by focusing his microscope on the local geology.

Drip-Feeding

If Thompson had tried to give us a geology lesson in the first chapter, we would have thought 'Yeah, and?' It's *where* he introduces the
fact that transforms it from boring background padding into a
vitally important plot device. The key here is to sugar the pill – the
reader digests description much more easily when it comes in little
snippets that punch well above their weight in terms of significance.
Why, for example, does Thompson describe the volcano as the
'mother' of the fields? It could be self-indulgent cleverness were it
not for the fact that the heroine's childlessness is a theme which
runs throughout the book (her barren state matching the barren
landscape). Using the word 'mother' reminds the reader of circumstances and motivations that may otherwise have been forgotten at
this moment of intense drama.

   Description offers an opportunity to echo and amplify themes,
adding resonance and richness. This technique comes in really
useful for all sorts of fiction, but its use is especially visible with
historical novelists: it's a way of telling readers what they need to
know without sending them to sleep. Manda Scott's *Boudica* opens
with a detailed account of the heroine (Breaca) casting metal,
narrated from her father's point of view. Each stage of the process is
used to introduce important information about character, context
and previous events:

> The mould cooled slowly. The time from pouring the metal to cracking it open
> had always been the hardest part for her. Of his three children, Breaca was the
> worst for acting on impulse. Twice as a child she had reached forward too soon
> and had had to be taken afterwards to the elder grandmother to have the
> scorched flesh bound with dock leaves and fennel root to keep it from
> festering.[4]

Within the overarching narrative drive, which invites the reader to
speculate as to what it is Breaca might be making as well as introducing the metaphorical theme of the heroine herself being forged,
this waiting for the metal to cool creates a space in which we can
learn something of Breaca's character, her family, the social structure of her tribe and the primitive herbal remedies at their disposal.
At no time do we feel we are being lectured on archaeology. Indeed,
despite all the clever things going on behind the scenes, Scott's
description is simply a pleasure to read:

The fire, unfed, grew cooler, throwing redder light and softer shadows into the corners of the forge, drawing out the autumn tones of her hair and her eyebrows, making of the rest a silhouette.[5]

It's atmospheric, convincing, a fireside seat. And above all else that's what description can do: enrapture your reader until they drink down your words like the finest champagne.

Writing Exercise: Description Without The Exposition

Using the techniques and strategies that we have covered in this section, write about an everyday process, such as making a cup of tea, cleaning your teeth or switching on your computer. You could use description to reveal character, develop a story or add atmosphere. Above all, make it a gripping read.

25 Sentences

Concision is a matter of removing the superfluous and the redundant, two slightly different things. You might say the superfluous is what you can manage without. The redundant, I suppose, is that phrase or word which amounts to stupid repetition of one kind or another: 'Sunrise at this time of the year comes at 6.30 a.m.' (It's never going to be p.m., is it?) Or 'This CD was electronically recorded.' (How else?)

I can see all kinds of reasons to keep your prose not only concise but also economical. For instance, adjectives, used sparingly, are effective. In her story 'The Allies,' Katherine Dunn has this sentence: 'Her eyes went soft, turning to the grey sky outside the window.' Two adjectives, both of which tell you something significant the reader can easily absorb. How about this, though:

> You understand it at once when I say, 'The man sat on the grass'; you understand it because it is clear and makes no demands on the attention.
>
> On the other hand, it is not easily understood, and it is difficult for the mind, if I write, 'A tall, narrow-chested, middle-sized man, with a red beard, sat on the green grass, already trampled by pedestrians, sat silently, shyly, and timidly looked about him.'
>
> That is not immediately grasped by the mind, whereas good writing should be grasped at once – in a second.
>
> Anton Chekhov, in a letter of 1899

The second, long-winded version has too much detail for the reader to take in. You need to leave space for readers to work. For one thing, readers need that space so that they can engage with your text and they engage by being allowed work to do, work such as supplementing your outline of something with more detail from their own minds. An additional reason to keep it brief is that since the last century – the century of the image, of photography, billboard advertising, cinema and television – people have become visually oriented. Also impatient of lengthy descriptions of what they will already be familiar with from the TV. Less is almost always more.

Following on from Chekhov's aesthetic of simplicity and economy, two twentieth-century writers have particularly influenced fiction writers to be succinct. The first was Ernest Hemingway, a great theorist of style. One of Hemingway's ideas about fiction is that it is strengthened by omission. He speaks of leaving out the fact that his protagonist commits suicide at the end of one story:

> This was omitted on my new theory that you could omit anything if you knew that you omitted it and the omitted part would strengthen the story and make people feel something more than they understood.[1]

Hemingway elaborates by using the allegory of an iceberg:

> There is seven-eighths of it under-water for every part that shows. Anything you know you can eliminate and it only strengthens your iceberg. It is the part that doesn't show. If a writer omits something because he does not know it then there is a hole in the story.[2]

Omission is perhaps a first cousin of concision, and Hemingway majored in keeping it succinct. He seems to have taken to heart the advice for writing put forward by Ezra Pound in a letter of 1913:

- direct treatment of the 'thing,' without evasion or cliché
- the use of absolutely no word that does not contribute to the general design and
- fidelity to the rhythms of natural speech.[3]

Every fiction writer you've read from the second half of the twentieth century who writes tight, mean and lean, from Raymond Chandler all the way through to Pat Barker, owes a debt to Hemingway. He is possibly the most influential prose fiction writer of the twentieth century (which is not to say that he is the best).

> **Writing Burst**
>
> *Connection.*

In style, Hemingway's heir was Raymond Carver. Carver's work has been perceived as minimalism, though he himself preferred to see it as 'precisionism.' Jay McInerney finds in Carver's work 'the naïve clarity ... of Hemingway's early stories.'[4] Carver may not have done anything much that Hemingway hadn't half a century earlier. Carver giving a rationale for his precisionism should sound familiar:

> What creates tension in a piece of fiction is partly the way the concrete words are linked together to make up the visible action of the story. But it's also the things that are left out, that are implied, the landscape just under the smooth (but sometimes broken and unsettled) surface of things.[5]

Economising

If you want to avoid the clutter that Chekhov was talking about in his letter, you might think about writing with verbs and nouns. This means as far as possible avoiding adjectives and, especially, adverbs. It has to do with hitting the nail on the head first time, so that the reader accesses the information immediately. Compare:

- Buffy walked angrily out of the room.
- Buffy stormed out of the room.

Which is more direct? An adverb ('angrily') and the verb it qualifies can usually be replaced with a single verb that means the same thing. This is concision. This is choosing to leave out words you can manage without. But Hemingway was talking about something else: the omission of information. What his theorising of omission says to me is that we will often have far more material for a piece of fiction than we actually use. Yes, you should know the world you have imagined inside out, but you don't have to exhibit that knowledge in the final cut. Above and beyond Chekhov's concision and Hemingway's omission, what Carver brings to the table is precision ('the language must be accurate and precisely given'). Let's look at some examples of each of these cousins of economy in fiction writing.

Concision

Chekhov's story 'The Kiss' includes the following: 'The horse turned, danced, and retired sideways; the messenger raised his hat once more, and in an instant disappeared with his strange horse behind the church.'[6] How clean is that? You can picture the scene he describes as easily as reading it, but this is only one sentence with only one adjective (and no adverbs).

Omission

In Ernest Hemingway's story 'Hills Like White Elephants,' a couple sit at a bar in Spain waiting for a train. Reading between the lines of their conversation – information is conveyed indirectly (see 'Dialogue') – it is clear that they are going to a city where she will have an abortion. As we approach the end of this very short story, we know the train is close. Here are the last two lines of the story:

> 'Do you feel better?' he asked.
> 'I feel fine,' she said, 'There's nothing wrong with me. I feel fine.'[7]

Do the man and woman get on the train? Does the woman have an abortion? If so, do they remain together afterwards? It's possible that Hemingway had some or all of the answers to these questions, but it's certain that the story is made stronger because he has decided to omit all of this apparently vital information. As with words, with information, less can be more.

Precision

In promoting precision, Raymond Carver said that 'the words can be so precise they may even sound flat; but they can still carry; if used right, they can hit all the notes.' This excerpt, from Carver's story 'One More Thing' may include flat words, but they carry, and, I would say, hit all the notes:

> [Maxine] unbuttoned her coat and put her purse down on the counter. She looked at L.D. and said, 'L.D., I've had it. So has Rae. So has everyone who knows you. I've been thinking it over. I want you out of here. Tonight. This minute. Now. Get the hell out of here right now.'
> L.D. had no intention of going anywhere. He looked from Maxine to the jar of pickles that had been on the table since lunch. He picked up the jar and pitched it through the kitchen window.[8]

Writing Exercise: Concision, Omission, Precision

Write a scene 500 words long and composed of concisely, precisely expressed prose in which you omit what you might yesterday have considered key information. In the manner of Hemingway in 'Hills Like White Elephants,' try to avoid your characters communicating directly or expressing emotion.

A sentence to start you off:

Mamie arrived back earlier than Lewis expected.

Here's Henry James, one of the great novelists, and here also is a pretty good illustration of why I favour the concise and precise:

> The money was far too much even for a fee in a fairy-tale, and in the absence of Mrs Beale who, though the hour was now late, had not yet returned to the Regent's Park, Susan Ash, in the hall, as loud as Maisie was low and as bold as she was bland, produced, on the exhibition offered under the dim vigil of the lamp that made the place a contrast to the child's recent scene of light, the half-crown that an unsophisticated cabman could pronounce to be the least he would take.[9]

I mean, for crying out loud, man, get a grip!

What this sprawling, Elvis-on-super-sized-cheeseburgers sentence means, I think, is: *Maisie had in her hand far too much money to pay the cabby, but Susan Ash produced a half-crown and paid him.* Does Henry James's passage communicate this directly and effectively? No. Is this scenic route sentence in some way stylish? Not to me.

Long Sentences

Long sentences make long paragraphs and long paragraphs make dense pages and, in our visual era, none of us is very good at reading monolithic chunks of black ink. We prefer some white space on our pages. However, not all longer sentences are bad. Longer sentences offer more opportunities to vary the rhythm and to build musicality. There's something beautiful about a sentence that extends for line after line without losing your attention, like Richard Fords' sentences here:

Karl Bemish, a saved man now in his white, monogrammed tunic, paper cap and
shiny dome, was of course promptly established as owner-operator, yukking it up
with his old customers, making crude half-assed jokes about the 'bun man' and generally feeling like he'd gotten his life back on track since the much-too-early death
of his precious wife. And for me, for whom it was all pretty simple and amusing,
our transaction was more or less what I'd been searching for when I came back
from France but didn't find: a chance to help another, do a good deed well and
diversify in a way that would pay dividends (as it's begun to) without driving myself
crazy.[10]

Ford sets one phrase on top of another, like someone building a
house of cards; with each new card that the author sets successfully
in place, the reader is more enthralled.

Lush

Hemingway and Carver are famous for cutting their prose to the
bone, so it isn't just writing longer sentences that's a viable alternative to the models of economy in the last chapter – it's also the texture of the writing.

The fringed lampshade glowed with a warm light that exposed the lovers on the
bed. Her mother was transformed into a round, rosy, moaning, opulent siren, an
undulating sea anemone, all tentacles and suckers, all mouth and hands and legs
and orifices, rolling and turning and cleaving to the large body of Bernal, who by
contrast seemed rigid and clumsy, moving spasmodically like a piece of wood
tossed by inexplicable high winds.[11]

This passage from Isabelle Allende's story 'The Wicked Girl' shares
the house of cards layering of phrase upon phrase, but in addition
the prose is also more sensual, more lush and lavish. It is ornate if
not baroque. After Carver's American cold cuts and salad, Allende's
prose is Chilean *empanadas*; the meat and vegetables have been
stewed in an exotic blend of spices and herbs. If you're having difficulty coming to terms with the contrasting models in this chapter, it
might help to think of my friend who, when he's on his bike, thinks
motorists are a pain in the ass, but when he's in his car, thinks
cyclists are. You get my drift. Flowery and elaborate has its uses just
as much as lean and wiry.

Lyrical

One of Hemingway's major concerns was to eschew emotionalism and sentimentality in his work. In 'Hills Like White Elephants,' cited recently, powerful emotions are at work between the man and the woman, but none of these emotions is directly alluded to or expressed. Lyrical writing is just the opposite. Rather than being ducked, character's emotions are poured out in an effusive manner, as Ishmael Chambers' are here, in David Guterson's *Snow Falling On Cedars*:

> Sometimes at night he would squeeze his eyes shut and imagine how it might be to marry her. It did not seem so farfetched to him that they might move to some other place in the world where this would be possible. He liked to think about being with Hatsue in some place like Switzerland or Italy or France. He gave his whole soul to love; he allowed himself to believe that his feelings for Hatsue had been somehow preordained. He had been meant to meet her on the beach as a child and then to pass his life with her.[12]

It seems a reasonable proposition to suggest that effusive characters with deep emotions, such as we see in this Guterson passage, will engage readers' emotions, up to a point. The American film director Frank Capra, whose emotive, populist work includes *It's A Wonderful Life*, once said in an interview on French television, 'I made mistakes in drama. I thought drama was when actors cried. But drama is when the audience cries.'[13]

I think I'm probably guilty of making that mistake and perhaps you are, too. I try to put my characters in dramatic situations and these involve them in powerful emotions. The aspiration implicit in this is that the reader will have a strong emotional response. What Capra is suggesting is that the latter is not an inevitable result of the former. If you remember, 'Hills Like White Elephants' concludes like this:

> 'Do you feel better?' he asked.
> 'I feel fine,' she said, 'There's noting wrong with me. I feel fine.'

All of the dialogue prior to this point suggests – in an impressively indirect way – that tension between this couple is riding high and that she, in particular, is feeling very far from 'fine.' The question is, which is likely to give the reader the emotional experience – being effusive like Guterson or restrained like Hemingway? You'll have to decide for yourself. But maybe this is a good point to look at a model that bridges these two extremes – an extract from Cormac McCarthy's *All The Pretty Horses*. The protagonist, John Grady, is sitting in a lake.

The water was black and warm and he turned in the lake and spread his arms in the water and the water was so dark and so silky and he watched across the still black surface to where she stood on the shore with the horse and he watched where she stepped from her pooled clothing so pale, so pale, like a chrysalis merging, and walked into the water.

She paused midway to look back. Standing there trembling in the water and not from the cold for there was none. Do not speak to her. Do not call. When she reached him he held out his hand and she took it. She was so pale in the lake she seemed to be burning. Like foxfire in a darkened wood. That burned cold. Like the moon that burned cold. Her black hair floating on the water about her, falling and floating on the water. She put her other arm about his shoulder and looked toward the moon in the west do not speak to her do not call and then she turned her face to him.[14]

Deep feelings are involved here, but they remain implicit rather than explicit. There is no pouring out of emotion, but neither is there the repressed restraint of the Hemingway. Is it a case of the character or the reader having an emotional experience? Again, you decide.

Musical

Another interpretation of lyrical writing is that it suggests music in its rhythms. Creating musical prose is about descriptive writing, but there are other ingredients beyond descriptive prose. This kind of lyrical writing has to do with sculpting and shaping your words and clauses, so that they are more beautiful than their function demands. It's also about having a love for words, for their sounds as much as their meaning. We are approaching the realm of poetry here, and it's no coincidence that Helen Dunmore, the author of this next passage, is as much acclaimed for her poetry as for her fiction.

We were by the orchard. On the left was the close lacework of the trees, their branches striped black and white like the skunks' tails in Rob's *Picture Almanack of the World.* Just here was the place where the wall had collapsed into a pile of soft yellow stone years back. This was the oldest part of the orchard, where a thicket of burly apple trees grew close together, unpruned, bearing fruit on their highest branches. We used to scramble through the gap in the wall to fill a sack with the big, winey apples, easily bruised. They never kept. They were always furred white before we could eat them all.[15]

This paragraph features sibilance throughout, alliteration ('On the left was the close lacework of the trees'), assonance ('striped black and white like') and consonance ('furred white before'). In addition, hard and soft sounds have been artfully knitted together ('where a thicket of burly apple trees grew close together'). All of these devices work together to create music.

You're a writer; you love words. You could do this. But bear in mind the wise words of Elmore Leonard: 'If it sounds like writing, I rewrite it.'[16]

Writing Exercise: Long, Lush, Lyrical, Musical

In the previous exercise, you wrote a concisely, precisely expressed prose scene, starting with this sentence:

Mamie arrived back earlier than Lewis expected.

See if you can learn from the authors you have just been reading, and re-write that exercise so that it becomes almost the opposite of itself.

2000-word Story Project: Dental Surgery

Your next Story Project is set in a dental surgery. Your protagonist is the vivacious, slightly zany receptionist. She has fallen for the new dentist at the practice, whose surgery is the one closest to reception, and your story is about what she does to try and win him over.

You are allowed to use the waiting room, the reception desk and the small storage area just behind it. Your characters might include receptionists, dental nurses, dental hygienists, dentists and patients. People might come in to collect or deliver dentures. Repairmen might call.

Write a 2000-word short story, either as comedy or drama, particularly incorporating what you have learned recently about managing time and about style. There's also an opportunity here for you to research data relating to dental surgeries.

Write a 250-word self-evaluation and include a bibliography of any texts that have informed the creative work.

VI
How To Broaden
Your Canvas

26 Demons And Angels: Using A Persona

Jenny Newman

'Man is least himself when he talks in his own person,' says Gilbert in Oscar Wilde's *The Critic As Artist*. 'Give him a mask and he will tell you the truth.'[1]

But which truth will he tell?

We all have many people under our skins, waiting to be tapped. The most striking way of expressing yourself as a writer is to choose a 'persona' (the Latin word for 'mask'). A persona narrates a novel or short story, is the main and not a minor character, and always uses the first person ('I'). This device empowers you as writer to choose a voice which is probably not the same as the one you use every day. For example, the American writer Mark Twain was forty eight when he created his teenage narrator in *The Adventures of Huckleberry Finn*. Note how at the start of his novel he detaches himself from his hero: 'You don't know about me, without having read a book by the name of *The Adventures of Tom Sawyer*, but that ain't no matter. That book was made by Mr Mark Twain, and he told the truth, mainly.'[2]

As we can see from Huck's direct address, persona writing resembles a dramatic monologue on television or stage. You could say the form has its roots in classical Greek drama, and that it blossomed in Shakespeare's soliloquies. It also fuelled the rise of the novel – think of Daniel Defoe's feigned memoir, *Moll Flanders*, or Laurence Sterne's witty, digressive *The Life and Opinions of Tristram Shandy, Gentleman*. Yet persona writing's link with living voices makes the modern versions I shall discuss below seem freshly minted and original.

Preparing To Write

People's voices grow strong when they are gripped by a strong emotion. This is true of writing voices, too. Josip Novakovich quotes Evelyn Waugh, author of *Brideshead Revisited*: 'An artist [...] has to stand out against the tenor of the age and not go flopping along; he must offer some little opposition. Even the great Victorian artists were all anti-Victorian, despite the pressure to conform.'[3] So learn to be combative, at least in your fiction, to stand out from the crowd and, as the poet Emily Dickinson said, 'Tell all the Truth but tell it slant.'[4]

Any distinctive voice is born out of the speaker's confidence that they know how to engross or entertain. For this you need to find out what sort of person you are and how to chart your periods of change, regression, development, whim, good and bad moods, shifting opinions, and wildest flights of fancy.

Writing Exercise: What You Love, What You Hate

Make a list of 10 things you love. They will change each time you do the exercise. That is part of the point. While you write, remember that:

■ Precision lends authority. Rather than writing 'music,' write 'Bootlegged recordings of Joy Division from the early eighties.' Rather than 'beaches' write 'a beach on Hilbre island on a warm September day, with seals bobbing offshore.'

■ Sense memories enliven prose. Instead of listing simply 'Persian carpets,' describe how they feel under your bare feet; or imagine the texture of moss or dewy grass or sun-warmed stone.

■ Follow poet Gerard Manley Hopkins by treasuring 'All things counter, original, spare, strange.'[5] He mentions, for example, finches' (not birds') wings and 'rose moles' on trout (not fish).

■ Now make a list of ten things you hate – but not straight after watching the news. Avoid abstractions (prejudice; cruelty) and think instead of people who have frightened or disgusted *you*. Or how you feel when ill (for inspiration read the extract from Irvine Welsh's *Trainspotting*, below). Or how you dislike double glazing, or finding a hair in your *fusilli*.

Choosing A Voice

Novakovich says that the puzzling thing called 'voice' that you as a writer are often urged to cultivate is simply 'a metaphor for a writer's vigour.'[6] Just because you choose to don a disguise does not mean that your words will sound phoney or archaic. Instead, like an actor, you learn to log on to another part of your psyche, describing a scene, for instance, or spinning a yarn, or sharing your views and feelings, all in the voice of your speaker. Your reader is buttonholed. She has to 'listen.'

As the extracts below will remind you, the most distinctive speech is often heard on society's margins, spoken by those who are not allowed or who would not want to communicate through official bulletins, newspaper leaders or the legal system. This does not mean that to adopt a persona you need to have taken heroin, or run away from home, or belonged to an underground gang. Nor does it mean that you have to use dialect or inner city slang. You may, however, wish to listen to people whose views differ from yours or whom you would not usually mix with, or to what the Irish short story writer Frank O'Connor called 'submerged population groups.'[7] Likewise, children and teenagers have their own cultures, so you can always mine your childhood for suitably wayward voices, like Twain, who spent his boyhood on the banks of the Mississippi. Many jobs have their own lexicon and patterns of speech (Twain, for instance, grew up to work as a river boat pilot). Watch and listen to butchers, auctioneers, estate agents, hairdressers, mechanics – the list is endless. Or you could draw on household members, as does the Irish novelist and short-story writer Bernard Mac Laverty, who grew up among strong and talkative women. But persona writing is more than mimicry: whatever your idiom, you need to link it with an aspect of your personality; not the self you present to the world but no less authentic for that.

Writing Exercise: Use A Spy Notebook

Take your writer's notebook to a place where you do not normally go but to which you feel drawn: a horse fair, for example, or a wrestling match or a fashionable night club. Transcribe all the conversations that you can, as exactly as you can, using phonetic spelling wherever possible.

Style

A persona voice can be demotic, regional, flowery, racy, ungrammatical, profane or even high-flown – as long as it is consistent. Your goal is to carry your reader along so convincingly that she 'suspends disbelief'; that is, she never pauses to question the gap between you and your central character. For this, your style needs to look effortless. But this seeming ease will be the result of skill, calculation and redrafting – and of reading other writers and studying their techniques.

You could start with a triumph of style, *Huckleberry Finn*, mentioned above and shaped by the Black and white voices of Twain's boyhood. In the following extract, Huck is in the dining room of the kindly widow who has taken him into her home, where she lives with her disagreeable sister, Miss Watson:

> One morning I happened to turn over the salt-cellar at breakfast. I reached for some of it as quick as I could, to throw over my left shoulder and keep off bad luck, but Miss Watson was in ahead of me, and crossed me off. She says, 'Take your hands away, Huckleberry – what a mess you are always making!' The widow put in a good word for me, but that warn't going to keep off the bad luck, I knowed that well enough. I started out, after breakfast, feeling worried and shaky, and wondering where it was going to fall on me, and what it was going to be. There is ways to keep off some kinds of bad luck, but this wasn't one of them kind; so I never tried to do anything, but just poked along low-spirited and on the watch-out.[8]

Do not be misled by the casual tone: this is a deft portrayal of an ideological clash. The tone is lightly ironical (Huck's belief is irrational) but not at Huck's expense (his apprehension will prove well-founded). Note Twain's sparing use of adjectives, and the informal effectiveness of his concluding verb, 'poked along.' Also note his delicate touch in creating a colloquial voice. The first two sentences are more or less standard English, and so is Miss Watson's rebuke. Non-standard verb forms such as 'warn't' (used only once for 'wasn't') are sparingly used, and never subtract from the meaning's clarity. Most important is the episode's tight construction. Although this passage does not further the plot, Huck's adolescent mix of naivety and knowingness raises reader anxiety. These few lines also convey the vulnerability of a generally optimistic hero, and the poignancy of his constraint.

Conventional novels and short stories comment not only on the self but on society, directly or obliquely. They also include diverse voices: even a short story can represent several. Persona writing is closer to soliloquy and can sometimes seem self-absorbed. This is part of the purpose of, say, Kazuo Ishiguro's *The Remains of the Day*, with its narrow, deluded narrator. But, unless your touch is sure, such writing can seem narrow or misanthropic. If you want to avoid claustrophobia, include a large and talkative cast, like Twain in *Huckleberry Finn*, whose dialogue not only reveals character but shows the illogic of slavery. Or, like Irvine Welsh in *Trainspotting*, you can switch between several narrators. All 'speak' in a profanely demotic language, cocking a snook at London literary style. But Welsh's paragraphs are so skilfully constructed that his meaning is always clear. Thanks also to his attention to narrative and pacing, non-Scottish readers all over the world have enjoyed the dialect words and grown used to phonetic spellings such as 'pit,' 'ah,' and 'tae.' Here Renton, one of the narrators, is trying to come off heroin.

> The great decline is setting in. It starts as it generally does, with a slight nausea in the pit ay ma stomach and an irrational panic attack. As soon as ah become aware ay the sickness gripping me, it effortlessly moves from the uncomfortable tae the unbearable. A toothache starts tae spread fae ma teeth intae ma jaws and ma eye sockets, and aw through ma bones in a miserable, implacable, debilitating throb. The auld sweats arrive oan cue, and lets no forget the shivers, covering ma back like a thin layer of frost oan a car roof.[9]

Note how Welsh eases us in, like Twain in the preceding extract, with two or three lines of fairly standard English, including the opening, easy generalisation. He also, like Twain, sustains pace by compressing the passage of time: despite the painful slowness of the process, one symptom seems to quickly succeed another. Though not as obviously funny as the passage from *Huckleberry Finn*, Welsh includes a glint of humour ('from the uncomfortable to the unbearable'). Despite his often uninhibited descriptions and rebellious views, Welsh has established a register which can include the Latinate ('miserable,' 'implacable' and 'debilitating') and the Middle English, onomatopoeic 'throb.' 'Lets no forget the shivers' is an easy appeal to his audience, and the passage concludes with a poetic urban simile. Above all, Renton sounds rawly singular, like all other effective personae.

Writing Exercise: An Experiment With Style

Reread your transcript from the spy notebook exercise above, then write it out again. This time, experiment with spelling. How does it look, for example, if you miss the last letter off present participles (*missin'* or even *missin*); or use *me* instead of *my*, or a grammatically incorrect verb form (such as *ain't* or *innit*)? Or spell some words phonetically? Or incorporate dialect words (like *nesh*); or slang (like *chav*)? Or words from an invented argot, as in Anthony Burgess's *Clockwork Orange*? Do short sentences suit your purpose? Or ones without a main verb? Does it weaken or strengthen your style if you use the above sparingly or even inconsistently?

Frank O'Connor speaks of the narrowness and 'hysterical clarity'[10] of a child's view of the world. If you want to hone your narrative skills, you might experiment by adopting a child's voice: a popular choice among postmodern writers because of the child's fragmented view of the world: its half-comprehending vision can be easily pushed to an extreme of subjectivity. But if, as with any persona, you miscalculate the tone, it can grow over-insistent, so why not experiment in a short story with a voice you might not want to sustain throughout a novel? Here is the opening of Donna Tartt's 'The Ambush,'[11] which deals with a child's trauma over his father's violent death, the narrator's estrangement from her family, and adult inability to cope with prejudice and grief. The story is narrated by eight-year-old Evie:

> Before I met Tim – who, in spite of everything I'm about to tell you, would be my best friend for the next four or five years – my mother warned me on the way over to his grandmother's house that I had to be nice to him. 'I mean it, Evie. And don't mention his father.'
> 'Why?' I said. I was expecting to hear: *Because his parents are divorced*. (This was why I had to be nice to John Kendrick, who I couldn't stand.)
> 'Because,' my mother said, 'Tim's father was killed in Vietnam.'
> 'Did he get shot?'
> 'I don't know,' said my mother. 'And don't you ask him.'

Evie is in the process of learning – and failing to learn – adult codes. Note that, as with Huck, her use of the second person ('you') signals an ingenuous directness, and emphasises her storytelling role. As she is looking back over at least four or five years, it seems unlikely she would remember the dialogue. No matter. The opening plants a powerful hook. Will she upset Tim by asking about his father? If so, how will he respond? (The story turns this question on its head.) Note the slight but predictable flaw in the grammar ('*whom* I couldn't stand' would make Evie sound pretentious) and also the mention, albeit bracketed, of the barely relevant John Kendrick – Evie is naively confident of our interest. In the narrative that follows, Tartt excludes crucial information, asking her reader to stay alert to clues. It is we and not the child-narrator who anticipate the crisis.

Tom, the narrator of Daren King's *Tom Boler*, is a year older than Evie but far less knowing, and victim of an even less stable society. In this experimental novel, King daringly abandons standard diction to approximate a child's thought processes in what one (highly favourable) reviewer described as 'small-lunged' sentences:

> When you broked somethin. What happens is. You get told off. So. Do runnin off. Then. Carnt get told off.
>   I have broked it that train set train. Fatwa Jihad not telling me off but. Not looking at me looking cross lookin at train mendin it shaking his head sayin. That boy that boy. Me runnin out of front bedroom runnin down stairs runnin out goin out side in garden.[12]

Breaking the train was Tom's (inadvertent? unconscious?) response to his neighbour Fatwa Jihad's sexual abuse: an incident which the reader is left to decode and which Tom never mentions again. This is a plausible strategy. The small, unprotected Tom knows no adult in whom he can confide, and probably cannot conceptualise what has happened.

'The Ambush' looks at the trauma of Vietnam through a suburban lens. *Trainspotting* deals with life on the Edinburgh schemes. Anthony Burgess's *A Clockwork Orange* pits anti-social behaviour against civil liberties. *Tom Boler* locks us into a nine-year-old's world where an episodic structure and King's choice of the present tense reveal what it is to be Tom, tiny, neglected yet game. All – and many more wonderful books and short stories – bring out other writers' angels and demons. Read them, and summon up your own.

27 Looking For The Drama
Ursula Hurley

There used to be an insurance advert about 'not making a drama out of a crisis.' As far as fiction writers are concerned, the opposite is the goal: drama and lots of it at every opportunity. Of course, a crisis is the obvious place to find drama, but there are ways of presenting it that can effect a transformation from mildly interesting to absolutely nail-biting. An excellent example is Ian McEwan's *Enduring Love*. The first chapter sucks you in and chews you up, creating a hurricane of narrative drive that keeps you turning the pages right through the book.

Setting The Stage

McEwan is so successful at creating drama because he knows how to hook the reader and keep them dangling. Point of view is useful here: in *Enduring Love* the narrator is recounting a personal experience, trying to make sense of what happens as he tells us. This gives plenty of scope for non-linear narrative, for justification and digression. In other words, he takes his time cutting to the chase. McEwan keeps the reader from frustration by dropping a trail of tantalising hints. Thus on page 1, we are told: 'this was the moment, this was the pinprick on the time map' so we know that everything which follows is hugely significant. Then we switch to a buzzard's eye view — showing us the situation that we need to understand, but not yet revealing what happened. On page 2, we get the old 'knowing what I know now' chestnut, before the admission that 'I'm holding back, delaying the information.' And the reader yells back: 'You can say that again, but I'm so desperate to find out what happens that I can't put this down! Now will you get on with it?'

Halfway down page 3, the catastrophe is revealed. The language is matter of fact; it doesn't need to be hysterical because the stage has been set; we're already on the edge of our seats:

> At the base of the balloon was a basket in which there was a boy, and by the basket, clinging to a rope, was a man in need of help.[1]

McEwan could have told us this in the first sentence of the book. He doesn't because he knows, as most successful writers do, that readers like to be titillated. The repeated deferral and ultimate fulfilment of curiosity is one of the great pleasures of reading. Therefore, this juicy fact is not given away cheaply but bought by the reader at the price of their utter involvement. If the balloon had just bobbed away into the sky, most readers would shrug and maybe think about buying a more interesting book. The clear sense of impending doom and the knowledge that we have an out-of-control hot air balloon, a helpless child on board and a man clinging by his fingertips to the rope make for compulsive page-turning. Knowing what's at stake inflames our curiosity even further. *People could die.* And if they do, we want to see how.

Having dangled this morsel, McEwan then has the nerve to give us four and a half pages on how the narrator spent his morning (information that will be important to the rest of the book) before returning on page 8 to the situation with the balloon. Then we change focus and we are back in real time, the drama playing out before us in all its horrible fascination. The boy seems to be rescued once, twice; the rescue fails; time passes in heartbeats; the balloon breaks free and, second by second, the man slides down the rope and falls to his death. McEwan has toyed with us outrageously and we can't wait to start Chapter 2.

So, the lessons here are,

- use point of view to withhold information, but:
- leave a trail of tasty morsels
- hint at something momentous
- make clear what is at stake
- add twists, turns, near-triumphs and near-disasters
- change pace and focus

- don't sell your plot cheaply
- get maximum mileage from your material.

Writing Exercise: Making A Drama Out Of A Crisis

Using some or all of the techniques listed above, turn the following account of a shipwreck into a dramatic reconstruction. Aim for 500–1000 words, longer if you want.

At 15.45 on 21st June, the *MV Tern* sank in calm seas off the Cornish coast. All four crew-members, believed to be local fishermen, were rescued by the lifeboat service. However, the ship's cat is still unaccounted for. Coastguards are currently investigating the cause of the accident. A spokeswoman said: 'These were experienced sailors in calm seas. It is very unusual for a boat to sink in such circumstances.' She refused to comment on allegations that the boat had been sabotaged by environmental campaigners.

Mining For Hidden Drama

McEwan is describing a grand drama; he wouldn't be doing his job if he didn't make some capital out of that. However, not all plots will have a grand event. Certainly, you don't usually have one every few pages – the aim is compelling narrative, not melodrama. Colm Toibin's *The Master* is a great example of how to create drama from what isn't seen and what isn't said. Subtle suggestions and conspicuous silences intrigue the reader like a carrot and a stick. The following episode takes place when James, accompanied by a younger male acquaintance, visits the grave of his friend Constance (whose suicide may have been related to her unrequited love for James):

> He immediately checked that there was nobody in view before allowing the embrace to continue, feeling the other man's warm, tough body briefly holding him, wanting desperately to allow himself to be held much longer, but knowing that this embrace was all the comfort he would receive.[2]

Of course we could also read this encounter as a human being trying to console another, but Toibin's overtly sensual descriptions of James' various male friendships and his furtive unfulfilled longing make us wonder; we create our own dramatic speculations, twisting them this way and that as we consider how these permutations may affect our interpretation of the rest of the book. From my experience in writers' workshops, readers' imaginations can be far more devious than your own: all you have to do is create a whiff of ambiguity and off they go.

You would be right to argue that Henry James isn't exactly an ordinary subject, being a star of the literary firmament and therefore possessing a great deal of dramatic potential. What about everyday life? Is there a drama of the mundane? Carol Shields is often regarded as one of the best chroniclers of the daily grind:

> Larry could be someone else, but he's not. He's Larry Weller, an ordinary man who's been touched by ordinary good and bad luck.[3]

Shields' work may seem prosaic, just the simple recounting of the detail of somebody's life. But if you think of *Ulysses* – James Joyce's gargantuan attempt to record the thoughts and events of a day in one man's life – it becomes clear that Shields has been extremely selective in the apparent flotsam that she does include. It's all doing a job. Thus, in Chapter 13 a middle-aged Larry lies alone in the marital bed, his stream of consciousness babbling gently about nicknames and other trifles. Then, in parentheses, we are thrown the following afterthought:

> (If you're living a life without sex, you start talking to yourself.)[4]

The enormity of his loneliness and the fragility of his psychological state are delineated so lightly that it takes a moment to sink in. This guy may be a flawed, ordinary screw-up, but we feel for him. Perhaps it's his very ordinariness which makes us relate to him, want him to be okay, want to read on so we can watch over him. And then:

> The morning light is explicit and cruel, its first slapping steps on the floor grotesque. There lies his suitcase, open. There is the bed with its bare mattress ticking and rimmed stains, blood, semen, sweat, his and Beth's, but now the bedsprings are preparing for a transfer of power.[5]

The image of the bare mattress is pathetic, grubby, elemental. Far more effectively than a lengthy exposition on the history of Larry's personal life, it encapsulates a past of lost intimacy and a future of bleak uncertainty. The bodily fluids lend the visceral starkness of a Greek tragedy, while also prompting us to think of mattresses we have known, to consider the state of our own relationships and to ponder what it feels like to be in Larry's situation. Succinctly, eloquently, this old stained mattress pulls us into Larry's world, makes him real, makes us care about what happens. The mattress has become a powerful representation of what's at stake. As the blurb on the back cover says:

> The mundane is made magnificent by a perception which finds the drama in life's detail – poignant, peculiar or simply absurd.[6]

Writing Exercise: Using Detail To Create Drama

Write a dramatic episode which hinges on one or more of the following objects. Add more detail if you need to.

■ A battered old arm chair, once chintz but now mostly grey, with worn patches on the arms and head rest.

■ A bunch of freshly picked, sweetly scented daffodils, still wet with morning rain.

■ A leather-bound family Bible, ancient flowers pressed between its pages.

■ A brand new notebook, with blue velvet covers and thick creamy-white pages.

■ An apple tree, gnarled and bent, the names of generations of sweethearts carved into its trunk.

3000-word Story Project: Literary Revision

You may have come across the term 'literary revision.' Put simply, it's where a work of fiction by one author is used by another writer as the starting point for a new, related work of fiction. For example, Jean Rhys' *Wide Sargasso Sea* is born out of Charlotte Brontë's *Jane Eyre*. In it, the central character is Antoinette, Rochester's first wife – the celebrated madwoman in the attic. More recently, Valerie Martin's *Mary Reilly* is a revision of Robert Louis Stevenson's *The Strange Case of Dr Jekyll and Mr Hyde*; Mary Reilly, the point-of-view character, is one of the maids in the house of Dr Jekyll. J.M. Coetzee's *Foe* has a similar relationship to Daniel Defoe's *Robinson Crusoe* and *Ahab's Wife* by Sena Jeter Naslund has been inspired by one of the characters in Herman Melville's *Moby Dick*.

This exercise will require you to do a bit of extra reading, but it's reading which I hope will appeal to you. Choose one of the following short stories cited earlier in this book, chase it up in its original location and read it carefully.

- Richard Burns, 'Perfect Strangers' in Duncan Minshull (ed.), *Telling Stories* (Coronet, 1982).

- Amy Hempel, 'In the Cemetery Where Al Jolson is Buried' in Tobias Wolff (ed.), *The Picador Book of American Stories* (Picador, 1993).

- William Trevor, 'The Ballroom of Romance,' *The Collected Stories* (Penguin, 2003).

- Flannery O'Connor, 'Everything That Rises Must Converge,' *The Complete Stories of Flannery O'Connor* (Faber, 2000).

- Denis Johnson, 'Emergency' in Denis Johnson (ed.), *Jesus' Son* (Faber, 2004).

- Anton Chekhov, 'The Kiss' in Richard Ford (ed.), *The Essential Tales of Chekhov* (Granta, 1999).

- Ernest Hemingway, 'Hills Like White Elephants' in James Fenton (ed.), *Collected Stories of Ernest Hemingway* (Everyman, 1995).

Once you've read the story of your choice, write one of your own from the point of view of one of the non-viewpoint characters in it. To make it easier for you, stick with the same storyline; all you have to do is see it from another character's point of view and find out how the whole will change as a result. Afterwards, don't forget to write a self-evaluation, with an annotated bibliography.

28 The Longer Story

There are a great many rewards for the writer in choosing the short story form. It is a practical option, which may be fitted into the schedule of those of us (most of us) who have to earn a living. There's also the advantage offered by the limitations of length. You aren't committing years of your life to a short story, which, with the novel, you often are. The variety of writing short stories may appeal to you, too, as it did to Henry James: 'I want to leave a multitude of pictures of my time, projecting my small circular frame upon as many different spots as possible.'[1] It's certainly the case that most writers find it difficult to begin their fiction writing lives with a novel, and working with a shorter form is a helpful way of learning your craft. This is not to say that the only purpose or virtue of writing short stories is as a staging post on your journey to becoming a novelist. Far from it. If anything, the short story is a more difficult form than the novel, as William Faulkner, for example, thought. But it is the case that learning fiction writers, certainly in university programmes, begin by practising the short story.

Whatever your reasons for choosing to write short stories, you will inevitably want to tackle writing to different lengths. The Story Projects in this book begin at 1000 words and work up from there. If you spend a prolonged period writing 2000-word short stories, you will sooner or later want to stretch your legs by moving on to three or five thousand words. Perhaps you've reached the stage where you want to try something not harder, not better, but different from the short story.

In this chapter, we're going to be looking at writing longer stories and, in the following chapter, at something called the short story cycle.

How Long?

Edgar Allan Poe and others have bandied about the idea that a short story is something that may be read in one sitting. Of course, some of us read faster and can sit longer than others. Around 2000 words, the approximate length of the BBC Radio 4 short story isn't a long sit for anyone. But Alice Munro's story 'Carried Away' weighs in at 15,000 words and the eleven works collected by Richard Ford in *The Granta Book of the American Long Story* (1999) are as long as that and more. As you can see, what we may broadly call the short story is subject to a good deal of variation.

In her book on the form, Valerie Shaw gives up trying to define the short story: 'It seems reasonable to say that a firm definition of the short story is impossible.' Perhaps Ailsa Cox offers a good reason for this, when she suggests that 'The short story is a protean form, encompassing infinite variations and, just like the novel, shading into other genres.'[2] It probably doesn't matter what anyone calls the fiction you produce; your concern is how it may best be achieved.

How will you need to alter your approach if you move from writing 2000-word to 10,000-word stories? To find out, we're going to do a close study of a longer story by Alice Munro, whom I've just mentioned. Munro, if you haven't come across her work, is widely regarded as one of today's finest short story practitioners, and tends to write longer stories. 'The Jack Randa Hotel'

> **Writing Burst**
>
> *I was trying to estimate how tall he was.*

runs to about 9000 words. Before reading on, it will make my comments on this story a lot less abstract if you can find 'The Jack Randa Hotel' and read it. (It's in Munro's 1995 collection, *Open Secrets*.)

Breaking Stories Into Sections

In the same way that it is common to break a novel down into chapters (and, often these days, chapters will, like short stories, be divided into shorter sections), it is common to break a story down into sections, which may or may not be scenes. The guiding aesthetic behind this impetus, like so much in the craft of fiction writing, is to keep the reader engaged. We have limited concentration spans, and breaking up longer passages of fiction into shorter, more easily digested sections is desirable if you want to retain the reader's interest. So perhaps the first lesson to be learned from 'The Jack Randa Hotel' is that its 9000 words have been broken down into seven sections. Towards the end of the story, these sections, the longest of which is probably about 3000 words, become very short: the fifth and sixth sections are each roughly 200 words long. At this length, the idea can hardly be to allow the reader a breathing space. It's much more likely that such brief sections have been used at the end of the story to increase the pace.

A further reason for organising your fiction into sections is that it facilitates changes of setting and moving through time. The opening section of 'The Jack Randa Hotel' shows us the protagonist, Gail, landing in Honolulu on a plane to Australia in pursuit of Will, the man who has left her. In the second section, Munro takes us back through Gail's recent history, so the section break has been used as a means of disrupting the story's chronology, and this second section has taken us from Gail and Will's earliest days as a couple right through to a washroom at Brisbane airport when Gail arrives in Australia. Organising your work in sections allows you to change setting (from Honolulu to Canada to Australia in these two sections) and manipulate time (from 'now' to 'then' and back, passing through some key points in between).

Different Discourses

Using sections also allows you to create patches of fictional fabric of different nature and for different purposes. In this story, the longest section includes the correspondence Gail has with Will, through the *alter ego* of Catherine Thornaby, purporting to be a recently deceased relative of his, a disguise she adopts to gain the upper hand in their relationship. In 'Jack Randa,' the nature of the sections is mostly conventional dramatic fiction, with dialogue and narrative passage. However, for much of the longest section of 'Jack Randa' Munro uses the epistolary, where the story is advanced through letters exchanged by Gail and Will, thus:

Dear Ms Thornaby,

You do not know me. But I hope that once I have explained myself, we may meet and talk. I believe that I may be a Canadian cousin of yours...

Dear Mr Thornaby,

The name we share may be a more common one than you suppose, though I am as present its only representative in the Brisbane phone book. You may not know that the name comes from Thom Abbey, the ruins of which are still to be seen in Northumberland...[3]

Moving from one kind of writing to another offers a desirable variety of discourse, while the epistolary as a technique gives you the chance to get right inside the consciousness of your characters. It is the equivalent in fiction of Shakespeare's soliloquies. Characters may, as they pour out their thoughts and feelings on paper, open their hearts and address the readership directly. This adds another string to your bow. As you will see in looking at 'Jack Randa,' the use of the epistolary has pretty much the same effect as multiple viewpoint: in allowing Will to open himself up in his letters, Munro almost gives him the status of second viewpoint character. (And while I mention it, using multiple viewpoint may well be a motivating factor in choosing to write longer fiction.)

Sub-Plots

A further advantage of the longer story is that it permits you the space to develop sub-plots. In 'Jack Randa,' which is primarily about Gail's adventure in going to Australia to try and rescue her relationship with Will, there is time and space for Munro to develop three sub-plots, one in each country and one that bestrides both. In Canada, there is Gail's relationship with Cleata, Will's mother, while in both Canada and Australia, there is the story of Will and Sandy, the young Australian woman he has left for whom he abandons Gail. In Australia, there's a narrative Gail observes, which concerns an old man and his younger companion, a potentially gay couple, who act as an allegory for the relationship between Gail and Will as well as that between Will and Sandy. However, arguably the greatest advantage of writing the longer story is its potential for increased complexity and psychological depth.

Extended Not Distilled

The short story has often been said to depend on distillation. It has been compared to the photograph and there's a sense in which short stories are snapshots. Poe wrote of 'a certain unique or single effect to be wrought.'[4] The brevity of the form, the focus on distilling the essence of character or situation is borne out by Chekhov when he wrote that 'In short stories it is better to say not enough than to say too much.' I think, however, that when you write longer stories, when you get up to five, ten or fifteen thousand words, you begin to benefit from some of the attributes of the novella, that halfway point between story and novel.

John Gardner's definition of the novella, 'a single stream of action focused on one character and moving through a series of increasingly intense climaxes,'[5] seems more apposite when looking at 'Jack Randa' than Chekhov's 'not enough' being preferable to too much. Gardner compares the novella to a tone poem in music, whereas a novel, in his view, has more in common with a Beethoven symphony. 'The chief beauty of a novella,' he argues, 'is its almost oriental purity, its elegant tracing of an emotional line... [It] moves through a series of small epiphanies or secondary climaxes to a much more firm conclusion.'[6] 'The Jack Randa Hotel' seems to me to be much closer to Gardner's description of the novella than to many accepted notions of the short story.

If you wish to write stories of 5,000 words and upwards, I think the extra length enables you to go beyond the snapshot, the distillation, and produce a more extended effect, something a little closer to the prolonged exploration of character and more developed narrative of the novel. It gives you a little more space to stretch your legs, to flex your muscles, and in this space you may move your characters through a narrative where you steadily build the tension towards the kind of climax and resolution more usually found in the novel. 'Many of the differences between writing short stories and writing a novel,' Ailsa Cox suggests, 'are related to questions of structure and pace.'[7]

Greater Psychological Depth

In the following passage from 'Jack Randa,' it's possible to see how writing a longer story may permit greater psychological depth than a story of 3000 words or less.

She liked to watch him at rehearsals, or just talking to his students. How skilled and intrepid he seemed as a director, how potent a personality as he walked the high-school halls or the streets of Walley. And then the slightly quaint, admiring feelings he had for her, his courtesy as a lover, the foreign pleasantness of his house and his life with Cleata – all this made Gail feel like somebody getting a unique welcome in a place where perhaps she did not truly have a right to be. That did not matter then – she had the upper hand.

So when did she stop having it? When he got used to sleeping with her, when they moved in together, when they did so much work on the cottage by the river and it turned out that she was better at that kind of work than he was?

Was she a person who believed that somebody had to have the upper hand?

There came a time when just the tone of his voice, saying 'Your shoelace is undone' as she went ahead of him on a walk – just that – could fill her with despair, warning her that they had crossed over into a bleak country impossible to challenge. She would stumble eventually, break out in a rage – they would have days and nights of fierce hopelessness. Then the breakthrough, the sweet reunion, the jokes, and bewildered relief. So it went on in their life – she couldn't really understand it or tell if it was like anybody else's. But the peaceful periods seemed to be getting longer, the dangers retreating, and she had no inkling that he was waiting to meet somebody like this new person, Sandy, who would seem to him as alien and delightful as Gail herself had once been.[8]

Of course, this extract is in itself an example of skilful distillation: in the space of only 300 words, Munro shows us what Gail first found attractive about Will before tracing the decline in their relationship and bringing us to the point where he was ready to pursue another woman, Sandy. However, distilled as it may be, I hope it will give you a glimpse of the in-depth understanding of character which the extended length of this story affords. To present characters in this kind of depth, I suspect it is necessary to live with them for some time, and the ability to do this is probably connected to the story's length. Clearly writing a story of 10,000 words takes longer than writing one of 2000 words, but it's worth noting that the length of time spent producing it may require you to live with your characters for longer and come to understand them more fully. As a result, your story will not only be longer, but with a bit of luck, deeper.

From Alice Munro's story, it's possible to learn a few valuable lessons about writing the longer story.

1. You may break your longer fiction down into digestible sections, which will allow you to:

   ▪ manipulate time

   ▪ change setting

   ▪ alter the nature of different sections (epistolary; dramatic fiction).

2. You may, as Munro almost does here, make use of more than one viewpoint character.

3. In addition to the main plot of your story, you will have space to include sub-plots.

4. You may use short sections when you want to step up the pace.

5. Perhaps the most important lesson to take away from a study of this, or any other Alice Munro story, is that when you come to write longer fiction, making your text as various as possible – using a greater variety of narrative techniques – is a good idea. You can learn a lot about using the epistolary from Munro's story, but another related technique is to use extracts from the journal of one of your characters. You'll find a good example of the use of this technique in Sarah Waters' *Affinity*, which you will remember we looked at in Chapter 10. This dual viewpoint novel is half told through the use of the spiritualist Selina Dawes' journal. If you read it and compare it with the conventional narrative of Margaret Prior, the other viewpoint character, you will see that the effects of these two approaches are quite different.

6. Writing a longer story may well require you to live with your characters for longer, which ought to result in a greater psychological and emotional depth. After reading 'Jack Randa,' think how you may emulate the sense it gives of a character and situation fully explored, comprehensively understood.

Story Project: The Longer Story

Using as many of the techniques listed at the end of the last chapter as you feel comfortable with, write a story of 4000–6000 words.

Many writers speak of being inspired by just one image. John Fowles, for example, credits the inspiration for *The French Lieutenant's Woman* to seeing a woman at the harbour in Lyme Regis. Go to Google, select 'Image Search,' type in 'Harbour' and see what the search engine brings up for you. Select an image from the first page of listings and use it as the starting point for your story.

This time, given the length, go for a 500-word self-evaluation as well as including a bibliography of any texts that have informed the creative work.

29 The Short Story Cycle

In 'Only Connect,' a short essay on form in the online magazine *salon.com*, Robert Morgan, the author of *Gap Creek*, suggests that the short story cycle has 'the advantages of the integration and interconnection of a novel and the intensity and compression of a short story.'[1] 'Short story cycles' may be the most common term for collections of linked short stories, but they have also been dubbed 'novels-in-stories,' 'composite novels' and, simply, 'linked story collections.'

Publishers' marketing departments often pass off short story collections as novels. You will probably have read one such 'novel' – Seamus Deane's *Reading in the Dark*, for instance, or Alice Munro's *The Beggar Maid*, perhaps, but possibly the best-known examples are Carol Shields' *Larry's Party* and Amy Tan's *The Joy Luck Club*. It is a mark of publishers' success in passing short story cycles off as novels that Julian Barnes' *A History of the World in 10 1/2 Chapters* (1989), Carol Shields' *The Stone Diaries* (1993), Ali Smith's *Hotel World* (2002) and David Mitchell's *Cloud Atlas* (2004) have all been short-listed for the Mann Booker Prize, an award for novels.

Generally speaking, short story cycles do not have a single, unifying plot or a single point of view – though, of course, the latter is true of many novels – but are linked by other attributes. In James Joyce's *Dubliners* and Robert Olen Butler's *A Good Scent from a Strange Mountain*, the element that links the stories is place. In Denis Johnson *Jesus' Son*, Melissa Banks' *The Girls' Guide To Hunting and Fishing*, Sheena Joughin's *Things To Do Indoors*, Pam Houston's *Cowboys Are My Weakness* and, let's face it, a volume of Sherlock Holmes stories, it is the focus throughout on a central character that unifies the collection, while in William Faulkner's *Go Down, Moses*, Sherwood Anderson's *Winesburg, Ohio*, Tim O'Brien *The Things They Carried* and anything by

Amy Tan or Louise Erdrich, what connects the stories is their focus on a set of characters, often a family. However, as the critic Susan Garland Mann argues, 'there is only one essential characteristic of the short story cycle: the stories are both self-sufficient and interrelated.'[2]

In David Mitchell's first book, *Ghostwritten*, which the title page bills as 'A Novel In Nine Parts' (although, impishly, Mitchell includes 10 chapters), what the publishers are marketing as a novel is really, if you'll excuse the pun, a slightly different spin on the short story cycle. The first nine chapters are to all intents and purposes short stories – well, actually, long stories; many of them are over 20,000 words. What connects the chapters is movement across the globe (England, China, Japan, Russia, Mongolia) and the way protagonists in some stories crop up as minor characters in others. You'll get the idea just by looking at the connections in the three opening chapters. At one point in the first, 'Okinawa,' the point-of-view character, Quasar, makes a phone call to the Secret Service of 'the Fellowship,' the terrorist cult to which he belongs. When the call is answered, there is only silence on the other end of the line. Later, in another story, we are present when Satoru, the young protagonist of the second chapter, 'Tokyo,' receives this phone call. It is a wrong number and Satoru is so bemused by what Quasar says that he can think of no reply. 'Tokyo' ends with the implication that Satoru will follow his Chinese girlfriend Tomoyo back to Hong Kong. Chapter 3, 'Hong Kong,' concerns Neil Brose, an English corporate lawyer and to begin with the only link with what has gone before is the setting.

> **Writing Burst**
>
> *Out of sight.*

But then some way into the story, Brose sees Satoru and Tomoyo together in a coffee bar and, without knowing them or meeting them, envies their love affair. As the novel progresses, the links that connect characters and stories become no less coincidental but gradually these chance encounters have more consequence. Marco, the point-of-view character of the seventh story, 'London,' wakes up in bed in London with Katy, Neil Brose's wife, which connects backwards, but more significantly, he connects forwards by saving the life of Dr Mo Muntervay, the protagonist of the following story, 'Clear Island.' And so on.

Connections are made across time and space in the world of *Ghostwritten*, making it read less like a short story collection and more like the unified construct of a novel. In addition, the book is nudged further away from short story collection and closer to the form of the novel by including a final chapter which returns us to Quasar, taking his story up where we left it at the end of the first chapter. This completing the circle technique, ending where we had started, suggests the cohesion and completion of the novel without actually providing it, an old and useful trick. Apart from the fact that in this final chapter he refers, however obliquely, to all the other narratives, that's how Mitchell disguises his collection of linked short stories as a novel.

When it comes to endings, another way of doing it is a technique used by Amy Tan in *The Joy Luck Club*. The novel has been about the relationship between Chinese mothers and their Chinese-American daughters and specifically about the difficulty the daughters have had in coming to terms with the two halves of their identity. The final story is narrated by one of the daughters, Jing-Mei, and in it she goes to China to meet her half-sisters, the daughters her mother was forced to leave behind when she had to flee to America. When the half-sisters finally meet, Jing-Mei feels she is becoming fully Chinese for the first time; she finally comes to terms with being both American and Chinese. This bringing together of the two worlds, the two identities of the novel, achieves a similar effect to the one I have just described at the end of *Ghostwritten*. It suggests a cohesion and a completion that perhaps isn't in reality present.

The connections between characters and locations that you may devise will link your short story collection and give it some of the fulfilment that a novel may offer the reader, but to pull that off, it seems to me that there will have to be some sort of drawing together of the threads of the different narratives at the end of your short story cycle. I've looked at two models here. Another is the one Carol Shields uses in *Larry's Party*, where the final chapter suggests this concluding feel not only by being about the eponymous party, but also by drawing together at it most of the major characters from Larry's life, from the rest of the book, in other words. There are no doubt many, many ways of suggesting resolution and conclusion to a short story cycle and you will no doubt find yours in the writing.

Writing a novel is a hard slog and most of us seem to find the knack of making a long-haul narrative cohere difficult; so, if you feel you have written as many short stories as you want to for the moment and want to try something longer, longer even than a story like Alice Munro's 'Jack Randa Hotel' – a short story cycle, your next Story Project, might be a reasonable and feasible place to start.

Story Project:
The Short Story Cycle

Take one of the stories you have produced earlier, but choose one no shorter than the 1500-word story. This is the foundation stone of your short story cycle.

First of all, look at this story very carefully and select a secondary character from it, no matter how minor. The character you use may be no more than an extra (to pinch one of the terms Helen Newall uses in her chapter, 'Characters'). Now write a story of approximately the same length as your foundation story, with this minor character as the protagonist.

For your third story, a little more flexibility is possible. You could repeat what you have just done and turn a minor character into the point-of-view character for your next piece – except don't forget that this time you have two stories from which to select a minor character. Alternatively, write a story that has the same *setting* as either of the first two.

See how you feel when you have three stories with the connections between them that you have chosen. If the idea of spending more time with specific elements of these three stories appeals, you're well on your way to having a short story cycle under your belt.

If you're ready for a fourth story, the starting point this time is to think of how the characters in your first three stories are connected. Are they members of the same family? Friends? Do they all work together? For your fourth story, bring all your point-of-view characters so far together in a particular setting: a Christmas meal, a trip to the cinema or in their workplace.

If you get as far as four stories, I recommend that you spend some time studying the work of any of the authors I've mentioned whose novels are to a greater or lesser extent short story cycles: Amy

Tan, Carol Shields, David Mitchell. Apart from anything else, if you want to try and publish a short story cycle, you will need to learn from the ways in which these authors conclude their cycles.

As with your longer story project, your self-evaluation here should be 500 words, with a bibliography included of any texts that have informed the creative work.

30 Structure – What Is It Good For?

Gareth Creer

Few people would set out on a trek across the Sahara without a map or a compass. Only a fool would build an office block without plans. And nobody would build anything without foundations, a means of supporting the building's outer shell. I would not attempt to write a novel without knowing where it was going, without something to support and guide the characters.

The first time you hear a favourite song, you think, 'I've heard that before.' It seems to have always been around. A favourite painting first drew you in because there is something in it whispering for you to come closer: a tale being told, a moment captured. Beneath the surface are gridlines and bridges but all that is there by the time it is hung or played for us are the curves and tones that make us swoon. The structure is buried, deep.

And so it is with the canon of novels that I carried around to guide me. My favourite novelists – Greene and McEwan; Moore and Dickens; Moravia and Ellroy – all had a way of beckoning you along on the coat tails of their characters, but the methods they employed were tracks well covered. How did they do it? What I needed was a method for deconstruction. I was on the lookout for a template of some sort and it came to me quite by accident – on a scriptwriting module.

Nothing New Here

You have probably realised, or heard it said, that there is nothing new under the sun in terms of what we all write about. Some people say that there have only ever been seven different stories told. George Polti[1] compiled what he claimed to be an exhaustive list of

36 dramatic situations which encompass all stories told throughout the entire course of recorded literature. And, so it goes, these have all been in place for 3000 years: revenge or self-sacrifice or remorse or a coming of age...

What we write about has been handed down from generation to generation of storytellers since myth began, but what we are looking at here is how the dramatic structure within myths affects HOW we write, not simply WHAT we write.

In *The Hero With A Thousand Faces*, Joseph Campbell[2] posited that modern storytellers could not help but arrange the unfolding of their dramas into a template established by thousands of years of oral and written tradition. We are so accustomed to hearing stories perform in a certain way, that we quite naturally tell stories in that way. More importantly, our readers have been conditioned to expect certain narrative behaviour at certain points in a story's unravellment. We are dealing with a human's inclination to mimic.

Chris Vogler, a reader of Hollywood scripts, took Campbell's ideas and delved into cinema's canon to see if a common structure to myths and Hollywood films could be established. We're not here to argue the toss as to whether Vogler's premise is proven; let's just assume he is right. All we need is a formula that might help some of us some of the time. Remember, this particular journey started with us trying to make life easier for us on that 80,000-word marathon from the title page to *ends*.

It might seem that this is about to become a dumbed-down guide to writing by numbers, but in my experience having a self-conscious and firm take on the structure beneath your story can actually help the writer to take risks. With the readers' expectations sated on one level, the writer is free to take risks with point of view and voice, style and characterisation. Furthermore, the confidence that can flow from having a rigid structure is likely to bring the best out in the writer, released from inhibitions that may stem from not knowing whether the story is 'working.'

A Circus Tent That Won't Fall Down

Somebody once described novels to me as great swathes of material that the writer has to lift but which want to fall down. What we need are pillars to ensure that the main characters' travails are supported and given the shape that both writer and reader need. Readers want highs and lows in a story; light and shade, and they also want to be pulled along – each high getting higher than the one before. Stakes rise and rise and rise until the writer and reader and the story can barely take it any more. Then, and only then, there is a gradual coming down until the reader is released, like a fish after a great fight being put gently back into the water, not entirely unharmed but free nonetheless to get on with its life, changed.

The Way It Is (And Can't Remain)

Vogler describes 12 stages that are apparent in mythic story structure and he splits these into three groups: the ordinary world, the special world, and the (enriched) return to the ordinary world. There is nothing too different here from Aristotle's observations on dramatic structure of beginning, middle and end. In the first stage, we have a character (perhaps more than one, but let us assume one) with whom the reader can engage and in whose plight the reader can invest. The character is introduced in their ordinary world. The ordinary world may be colourful and chaotic, but there is a sense that things must change. There is an instability which pervades the status quo and matters are brought towards the surface with a call to adventure. The call to adventure is typically followed by a refusal of the call and what follows is dramatic tension: quite simply the reader wanting the character to do something they don't do, but fearing for their well-being whatever they do.

With the call to adventure refused, the protagonist meets a mentor. This can be another character or part of their own value system. In a blockbusting thriller it might be an exogenous force such as a political treaty. In a romance it might be the recollection of some lost, unrequited love. It might even be an old tramp with a lifetime of ignored wisdom. Whatever it is, the protagonist wills herself to cross the threshold, to accept the call to adventure. The ordinary world is left behind and the special world, probably foreshadowed throughout these opening chapters, is embraced.

In summary, the protagonist has identified a lack in her life and is now hell-bent (or something milder) on overcoming that lack.

In terms of getting to the end, we are on our way. Let's say the beginning should be 20,000 words. All you need is five chapters of 4000 words, that's 12 pages each on the ordinary world, the call, the refusal, the mentor and the crossing of the threshold. Suddenly the end isn't so far away. Somebody is putting the lights on.

Change And Challenge: Rising To The Occasion

If we think in terms of the main character's journey (and this may be an individual or an ensemble), the middle of the story is where they face challenges, discover their failings, and find ways to overcome. In this new world, they have to pass tests along a road of trials. They will form allies who may be archetypes or who might even represent elements of the hero's own character. Enemies will be encountered and here it may be necessary to co-opt traits from others. Most interestingly, in terms of dramatic tension and reader curiosity, some characters will present themselves as allies, but may not be what they appear and vice versa. These characters are shapeshifters, and the travails of the hero in the middle of the book take the reader towards the hero's inmost cave, the second threshold which makes them face up to their innermost fears. Think of it as a throne room where another status quo has to be disturbed.

Only when placed under the severest pressure will the hero be able to show the reader what they are really made of. And unless the writer presents the obstacles, neither the hero nor the writer will truly discover the hero's character. What a rigid structure allows is a dynamic model for character development.

Keep Upping The Stakes

The hero's quest may be a physical challenge, a psychological battle or an emotional journey. They may be striving to learn to say 'I'm sorry' or to save the world. What is being established here are the stakes. Your challenge, whilst using a blueprint such as this, is to make the story and situations as vivid and original as you can, and to also use this dramatic structure as flexibly as you see fit. The structure is here to help, not hinder. The key, not the lock.

It is important in the middle of the story that the stakes rise, and rise, and rise, and after the Inmost Cave comes the Supreme Ordeal. This is the crisis (not the climax) and here we may wish to remember that heroes have to die, that they may be reborn. It may be that the Supreme Ordeal witnesses the death of the ego. As they say, tasting death allows you to sit in God's seat for a while. Time for apotheosis, if that's what you want.

The Supreme Ordeal is followed by the Reward. Gaining the Reward is a life-changing affair, not always immediately for the better and at this point in the story, the hero may have heightened powers or perceptions. This is the time they will see through deceptions, seeing shapeshifters for what they are. There may be profound self-realisation or even a moment of epiphany.

In terms of a three act play, we have now experienced the final 'turn.' We are on The Road Back.

Full Circle

If the beginning is The Decision To Act and the middle The Action, then the end is The Consequences Of The Action. On the road back, the hero will return, in some sense, to the ordinary world, enriched from the journey and seeing it in a new light.

Initially, there may be a refusal to return. Refusals are always good for tension. There may a setback and this is where subplots are played out. The hero may be set a new goal and a rededication to the adventure will often be required before Resurrection can take place. This is a final purge before re-entering the Ordinary World. A final test will prove that the hero has retained the wisdom gained from the Supreme Ordeal. This may be a time for laughter or tears, but it's serious stuff and the reader needs proof that the hero has truly changed and this might require the sacrifice of something precious from the world they left.

Finally, we need unravellment, denouement, and there may be a circularity here in which the old has new meaning. This is the hero's Return With The Elixir and they may even be re-presented with a task previously failed before fully assuming a new life, made better for the lessons learned, the road travelled.

Writing Exercise: Suck It And See

This exercise will take an hour if you do it properly. Make six copies of this table:

1. Ordinary World

2. Call To Adventure

3. Refusal Of The Call

4. Meeting The Mentor

5. Crossing The First Threshold

6. Tests, Allies, Enemies

7. Approach To The Inmost Cave

8. Supreme Ordeal

9. Reward

10. The Road Back

11. Resurrection

12. Return With The Elixir

NB: The 12 stages do not command equal 'page time,' nor must they religiously follow the above sequence.

Now, think long and hard about your three favourite films. Think about the sequence of events. For each film, in turn, above, enter the recalled action against the numbered headings. Does the film fit the model?

Now, think long and hard about your favourite three books. Do the same.

Finally, make a cup of tea, potter about round the house or garden, all the time thinking about your story and your main character(s). What is the journey? Are the stakes high enough? Will the reader care? Now, thinking in terms of the challenges your character might face, see if their journey can be broken down and described in summary form in the table you have copied, but don't break them trying to cram them into the box.

All this only works if you've got everything else – energy, voice, an interesting character about whom the reader cares deeply, a vividly evoked sense of place, searingly effective dialogue... You need to care and can't just put your hero through these hoops, they've got to burn to do it for themselves. What I hope you will find is that once you have everything that a good story requires, The Pillars Of Hercules will help you get to the end, and a firm structure will liberate you as a writer to take risks with the individual elements of storywriting. As a case in point, here's a brief case study of how the Pillars helped me through my most challenging novel.

The Pillars In Action

In *Big Sky*,[3] I was attempting to tell a traditional crime story in a literary style from the highly stylised point of view of Jimmy Mack, a mute ne'er-do-well with 'the voice of an angel.' I was taking risks with the hybrid of style and genre, and on top of this I wanted to tell Jimmy's 'real time' story going forward (one last big scam goes wrong) interwoven with the exposition of how he came to lose his voice (an infancy of abuse in a lesbian homestead and an adolescence in children's homes).

It occurred to me that what I could do was follow the Hero's Journey in both directions. As Jimmy Mack moves forward, across thresholds and into new worlds, meeting allies, enemies, mentors and shapeshifters, the stakes rise and Jimmy's character is tested to the full. Interwoven with this (and I'm as wary as the rest of you about over-egging flashbacks) is another linear narrative explaining Jimmy's evolution from abandoned child to king of his own small castle – but in reverse. The novel therefore crescendos with Jimmy returning to the scene of his infancy and abandonment by his mother – on the day he lost his voice. This scene is also the crucible in which he is entasked to overcome his principal antagonist in 'real time.' In other words, this one scene is the older Jimmy Mack's *Road Back*, and the establishment of young Jimmy Mack's *Ordinary World*, from which he is called to adventure – birth and resurrection if you like.

The novel begins and ends at an abandoned shack on a desolate stretch of cliff on the coast of East Yorkshire. Jimmy has returned to the place he lost his voice. It is a journey of self-discovery in which he exorcises the ghosts of his relationship with his mother. Lying in wait is the drug baron who can cut Jimmy free from his old world and allow him to find a new life. But will she?

It is also a voyage of discovery for the reader who has been told, by Jimmy, how he grew up to be the person he is today. It is not clear whether Jimmy is withholding the back-story or struggling to break through the barriers his mind has constructed to cover the pain he has suffered. Either way, such an extended back-story – told through interior monologue, third-party dialogues and flashbacked action sequences – is a dangerous game to play. The reader may switch off.

Jimmy lost his voice whilst being brought up by his lesbian mothers. He was abandoned by his biological mother and had to make himself unhurtable, ridiculed as he was in children's homes. His heart breaks when he plays a part in the death of the girl he loves, and he then dedicates his life to saving the soul of Angela, the junkie twin sister of his dead and unrequited love.

In telling this back tale, I plotted Jimmy a path through Vogler's 12 phases and told it backwards. For example, the book begins with Jimmy having to steal the overdosing Angela away from it all. He has resolved to dedicate his life to saving her soul. This is the end of his emotional journey and we work back to find out why he should want to do this. At the same time, in order to save her, he needs to settle her debts and get her out of their ordinary world. This precipitates the one last scam (which, of course, goes wrong). The scene is the end of one story, the beginning of another.

Conversely, at the end of the book, we discover how Jimmy's journey began and in the same scene, Jimmy has to pull out of the scam-gone-wrong and overcome the drug baron who is holding him to ransom. Similarly, the two emotional climaxes are revealed to the reader: going forward, can Jimmy make himself love the woman who loves him; and going backwards, under what circumstances can a mother abandon a son?

It is not for me to say if the dovetailing of the narratives work, but at least the mythic structure helped me get there and achieve the other, riskier objectives I had set myself in terms of voice and style.

Reflection Project 3: Where You Are Up To Now

At this stage in the proceedings – the end of the book – it may be beneficial to look back, to study the journey you have been on as you have been using *HTWF*. To help you prepare for a longer and deeper piece of reflective writing, I first of all offer a few comments from my students. A few months ago, I asked my first-years to complete a questionnaire on the use of reflective writing in their Creative Writing studies. Here are a few examples of what they had to say about the practice of reflection. To make sense of their responses, I've also included the relevant questions from my questionnaire.

How have you learned to reflect?
Partly through Self-Evaluations, though these tend to be short-term and specifically focussed. For a longer view I look back over my work at regular intervals – assignments, course notes, journal, etc. I have kept a journal of my latest creative piece. I'm surprised how useful it's been. I don't like reflecting even now, but I know I must do it.

How has having to produce reflective writing affected your development as a writer?
It's helped – I am more of an activist than a reflector so being forced to consider what has worked for me and what has been a waste of my time has been valuable. I then use that knowledge to help me in my next piece of work.

Would your growth as a writer this year have been different without the use of reflective writing?
I think I wouldn't have learned as much so quickly. At this stage, because I've really thought about what works, I feel I can produce a piece of work without having to edit as drastically. Without reflective writing, I would've been spending a great deal more time trying out different ways. Knowing what works and what doesn't, I settle down to the task more quickly.

From where has your awareness of what you have learned this year come?
From being made to think about my writing rather than just being given time to write (as in previous classes).

This Reflection Project may be simply summarised: I would like you to reflect on what you have learned from *HTWF* about writing fiction and about yourself as a writer. It can be succinctly expressed, but I suggest to you that it will take a fair amount of time and effort to produce this reflection. Before you do, let's just recap on some of the avenues possible to you when you reflect more broadly in this way.

How To Reflect

- Be self-critical and self-aware.

- Examine the creative processes involved in writing and express your understanding of them.

- Write about the growth in your understanding of how you function as a writer.

- Write about yourself as a fiction writer:

  What kind of writer are you?
  What kind would you like to be?
  What is your philosophy of writing; your writer's aesthetic?

- Write about what you have come to understand about the craft of fiction.

- Write about how you came by that understanding.

- Discuss the elements of craft you've studied: dialogue, narrative, structure, pace.

- How have you applied them in your work, and what you have learned as a result?

- Write about some of the problems you've come up against in your creative work and how you've dealt with them.

- Write a short commentary on any work by contemporary practitioners that may have influenced you: in what ways can their influences be traced?

- Discuss your approaches to re-drafting – what I have referred to in this book as editing and revising.

- How did you decide what was good and what needed to change?

- If anyone has read your work in progress, write about the ways that the response has influenced your redrafting.

How Not To Reflect

- Making value judgements about your work.

- Explaining your work.

- Analysing your work for meaning – interpreting it (Leave that to your readers).

- Retelling the story (It's pointless and won't make very interesting reading).

You've had a few reminders there how to go about writing a reflection, but let's not forget that you have written a self-evaluation of each of the Story Projects you have produced and you have already written two Reflection Projects; you are probably more adept at writing reflectively than you think you are.

In between 2000 and 3000 words, reflect on what you have learned from *HTWF* about writing fiction and about yourself as a writer. As usual, include a bibliography.

Afterword: How To Go The Distance

Assuming you have established a writing discipline and have begun to produce work you want to share with the world, the next step is to remember to submit it. If you're going to devote your life to writing, you will need to set aside time – quite a bit of it – to make sure that what you write reaches an audience. And if you're uncertain how to go about it, you can learn everything you need to know in the pages of *The Writer's & Artist's Yearbook* and *The Writer's Handbook*, both of which are revised annually.

If you are writing short stories, keep sending them off to magazines and broadcasters. And when they come back, send them off again. Rejection does not mean that the story is no good. It just means that you landed on the wrong desk on the wrong day. Remember the much-quoted advice that nobody knows anything. Fourteen publishers turned down J.K. Rowling before Bloomsbury stuck their neck out on the first Harry Potter book. Twenty-two publishers turned down James Joyce before he was taken up; with J.P. Donleavy it was 33.

Rejection

Nobody likes being rejected, but every writer has to put up with it, often for years. Richard Ford, by most reckonings a major figure in American literature, writes affectingly of how it feels to deal with blanket rejection.

> I could not get my stories published. I sent them to many – very many – of the magazines that were on everyone's checklist...I kept a log, a little notebook in which I had lined off little boxes, inside which I wrote where this story was sent when, and when it came back, where it went next...[which] would give me something to do while I awaited my own good news, offer solace when there wasn't good news. And there wasn't.[1]

In a catalogue of his struggles as a young writer, Ford details the desperation and downright embarrassment of the stubborn submitter, all of which are far too uncomfortably familiar to me and, I suspect, every other writer on the planet: the check, for instance, to see if the returned story was still in good enough condition ('undented by paper clips') to send out again. Ford concludes his reflection on getting started as a writer with some encouragement, gleaned from his hard experience:

> Writing is dark and lonely work, and no one has to do it, and no one will even care if it doesn't get done at all, so that choosing to do it and trying to do it well is enough of an existential errand, enough of a first step, and for whatever my money and counsel's worth, enough of a last step too[2]

You will be rejected, perhaps for years. You will be discouraged. You will feel disillusioned. You will feel bitter towards publishing's gatekeepers who seem to have singled you out for special contempt. You may make a fool of yourself, as Ford did (and as I have, too) by telling some cruel and uncaring editor where he can stick his magazine. But keep submitting. The alternative is giving up, and it's unlikely, having got this far, that being a person who *used* to write fiction is going to make for a happy old age. 'Nobody asked any of us to become a writer,' George V. Higgins warns. 'No one will care if you don't become one. No one but you, that is.'[3]

Representation

If you have written a novel, get an agent. With my first book, I tried two or three agents before just getting on and pitching it to publishers myself. Once I had found a publisher, one of the agents who turned me down got in touch again to ask if she could represent me. Being young and proud, I thanked her and declined. On mature reflection, the correct answer would have been to say, 'Yes, please.' Agents are business people who understand how the publishing trade works. If they are any good, they will know every trick in the book. Also, because their payment is inextricably linked to yours, one of their primary motivations is to make sure you get paid as much as possible. This is a good thing. So, get an agent.

It's at least as hard as finding a publisher, and you will already have come cross Catch 22: can't get a publishing deal without an agent, but it's not easy to get an agent without a publishing deal. When I did eventually get an agent, I had been turned down by far more other agents than I have ever been by publishers. I'm not going to tell you how – I only have a little space left in this book – but, again, you can learn how to go about finding an agent in *The Writers & Artists Yearbook* and *The Writer's Handbook*, both of which should be in your local library.

Self-Publishing

But it's a buyer's market out there. What if nobody is willing to publish your novel?

One option is to do it yourself. Because of the difficulty of getting picked up by conglomerates like Random House, Transworld and Penguin Puttnam, self-publishing has become increasingly respectable over the past two or three years. Stephen Clarke self-published *A Year In The Merde*, managed to get it serialised on BBC Radio 4 and, on the back of that, it was picked up by Bantam, who have turned it into a hefty bestseller. Then there's G.P. Taylor, a curate from Whitby, Yorkshire, who wrote a children's novel called *Shadowmancer*, a Christian parable with some similarities to C.S. Lewis' *Narnia Chronicles*, for which, fiction editors at major publishing houses told him, there was no market. Taylor promptly sold his motorbike, raised £3500 and self-published his first book. It sold well in his locality on word of mouth alone, which, with some good reviews, led to Faber and Faber taking the book up. The Faber edition quickly went top 10 in the bestseller lists. This in turn led to an American three-book contract worth £300,000, soon followed by a seven-figure film rights deal.

I had been having nearly three years of doors closing in my face as I tried to place my novel *Holy Joe*, which is a kind of Lad Lit story set in the world of evangelical Christianity. I found an excellent agent with it, Judith Murdoch, who amongst her other accomplishments handles the Chick Lit big hitter Lisa Jewell and helped Kate Atkinson to break through with her Whitbread-winning novel *Behind the Scenes at the Museum*. Judith works with all the major publishers and they all said the same thing: they liked the writing but didn't think there was a market for a book with religion at its centre 'in the present climate.' My view was that the book inevitably reflected much of my own experience and that hundreds of thousands of other people in the UK were having very similar experiences, so why would there not be a market for it?

That was when I read a little news story in *The Guardian's Review* section about Deborah Lawrenson, an author who had published three novels with Heinemann and had her fourth, *The Art of Falling*, rejected. Believing it to be her best work to date, she was unwilling to shelve the manuscript and so approached Troubador Publishing who offered to partner-publish her book and get it distributed for her. In this arrangement, as the term 'partner-publishing' suggests, publisher and author share the cost of getting the book printed and the author pays the publisher for marketing and securing distribution. Troubador held up their end of the deal so well that after strong sales through the Ottakar's bookstore chain and on Amazon, as well as favourable national media coverage, Lawrenson's agent made a very profitable sale of paperback rights for *The Art of Falling* to Arrow – who had been the paperback publisher of Lawrenson's previous three books. Remember what I said about nobody knowing anything?

Armed with the feel-good qualities of the Deborah Lawrenson story, I contacted Troubador, who said they would be interested in *Holy Joe* if they could see a market for it. I sent it to them – the whole 73,000 words by e-mail, which was a new experience in submitting work – and Jeremy Thompson offered me a contract within weeks.

At the time of writing, after yet another draft and much proofing of text and cover, *Holy Joe* has been out for five months and is into its second print run. While it's receiving very good word-of-mouth, it's too early to say whether the novel will duplicate the success of G.P. Taylor, Stephen Clarke and Deborah Lawrenson. As each of them has done, I'm faced with promoting the book as effectively as I can without the clout of Random's or Transworld's publicity office, which brings me neatly on to the next topic in this chapter.

Promoting Your Work

'These days even the most ardent apostles for art roll up their sleeves, hold their noses against the meretriciousness of the market-place and practice a little economic determinism.'[4] In other words, even the big guns get out and try to stump up an audience for their work. Michael Norman, the author of the article this comes from, cites Cormac McCarthy, Don DeLillo and William Gaddis as examples of literary heavyweights who descend from the mountain to shift a few more units. In the UK, bestselling authors of literary fiction, the McEwans and Tremains of this world – whose novels may sell six figures in paperback – are regularly to be found giving readings at bookshops and festivals. Is this because they're lonely? Is it because they're charitable and want to give their readers the chance to meet them? Possibly not.

Twenty-six new novels are published every day in the UK (but only 30 novelists in Britain every year can live off the income from their books),[5] so when yours comes out, you are going to have to make a song and dance about it – in a dignified way, of course – if you don't want it to sink without trace. But surely such tawdry commerce is for the publishers' sales, marketing and publicity staff? Surely your job is to sit in the lonely eaves of your rooftop and slave at the keyboard to produce *literature*? As I've indicated, I haven't much experience to go by, but what I have I'll share with you.

I've had a book out with a major publisher and the sales push they organised for that amounted in its entirety to a four-day trot around London, Birmingham, Wolverhampton and Liverpool, being interviewed for newspapers and putting in appearances on local radio. We started on a Monday and finished on a Thursday. By Friday the friendly publisher's publicist had moved on to her next title and my book was left to make its own way in the world. I've also had a book published by a tiny independent, whose promotional efforts compared quite favourably with the major, given the massive difference in clout between the two. With the independent, there was a little drinks party in Camden to launch several of its new titles and then one day of being trotted round some not particularly huge parts of London's media (Galaxy FM and the *Catholic Herald* were amongst them). With the tiny independent, that was my lot. I've been known to quip that it sometimes feels less like a book launch and more like having your heartbreaking work of staggering genius set on the doorstep with the empty milk bottles.

The conclusion I'm taking you to by the scenic route is that you will have to get to work promoting your books off your own back. You cannot afford to leave it to somebody else. The situation is succinctly summarised by Harcourt Brace's director of publicity in that same Michael Norman article: 'Writers are no longer content to sit by while publishers market their books.'

Let's say you are published by a small, independent publisher, who will go to some lengths to market your book, but not nearly as far as you would like. Not nearly as far as you need them to. What are you going to do to build on their efforts? A good idea is to try to raise the profile of your novel locally. Having a bookstore launch won't hurt. Last I heard, the two big UK chains, Waterstone's and Ottakar's (who at the time of writing might be about to become one), are willing to co-operate with you in setting up a book launch. Waterstone's in Manchester may agree to a launch in their store if you can guarantee a turnout of 50 punters. With that independently published book I mentioned, the Deansgate branch agreed to a launch if the publisher met the fairly modest cost of wine and a few savoury snacks, which they kindly did. I know Ottakar's are open to similar arrangements. The key thing is ensuring you can get a decent turnout of your friends and acquaintances. These events last between one and two hours, and if Waterstone's can shift 30 or 40 copies in that length of time, they won't be too unhappy.

As well as inviting every reading friend you have to the local launch, you would like some of the wider public come along too. To this end, you want to mount a local publicity campaign. Here in Manchester, there are two large-scale weekly free-sheets and a local evening newspaper, in all of which I could reasonably hope to get a story. Then there's the local BBC radio station, two or three commercial stations and a community radio set-up or two. Your town or city will have equivalents, and if you want people to attend your launch or buy your book at any other point during its early days in the marketplace, you will produce a press release yourself, mail it out, and then ring round to see if any of your targets are willing to follow through with a story. Local news, unless you live in Jerusalem or Baghdad, isn't filled with the world's most exciting stories, so finding an angle with which you can interest your local media should not be beyond most of us. For instance, *Holy Joe* is set in Chorlton, the Manchester urban village where I live, so that was one selling point I used to get local media coverage.

What about outside of your hometown? Well, your novel might have an angle that would interest special interest periodicals. To stick with the example of *Holy Joe*, because it is set in a contemporary church, I picked up a fair amount of coverage in the national Christian press. Such specialist coverage isn't going to bring your book to the attention of the wider public, but it is a kind of direct marketing that might well result in increased sales. Maybe your book is issue-based. If it's about a teenage mother, you might do well to approach some carefully selected woman's magazines, or, say, the *Parents* page in *The Guardian*.

You've done local and special interest. How about national media coverage? Maybe you think you're too small-fry for a daily newspaper, but I bet if you went out and bought any three of them today, you would find coverage of stories no more newsworthy than the launch of your new book. Obviously the place to start is with the books pages. You want to be reviewed. When book-loving *Observer* readers see Robert McCrum enthuse about a new novel, they will often have the urge to go out and buy a copy. And besides, if you don't get it reviewed, how are you going to be able to find any quotes for the cover of the paperback edition? Obviously it's fearsomely difficult to get reviews in the national press, but somebody has to get reviewed and it might as well be you. You've nothing to lose by sending your book in and then phoning afterwards to see if you can persuade somebody to write a review. That's how all those other books pick up coverage: somebody asks the books editor for a review and that somebody doesn't have to be Vintage's chief publicist. It could be you, the author. Another way in is knowing somebody who can lobby on your behalf. If you think about it, you may know somebody with contacts on a national newspaper. Let's face it, many of the novels you see reviewed in Sunday papers are written by Sunday paper journalists and how do you think they get their books reviewed?

I have spent more than half of my life writing and trying to get published. I wouldn't say I had been at all successful in the latter, but what keeps me going with the former is the realisation I had quite early on in the game: the best part of being a writer is what happens as you are writing. Here's novelist Kurt Vonnegut on how writers may overcome the difficulties involved in our vocation:

> It's like having a pharmaceutical school with no pharmacies for the graduates to work in afterwards. There are no careers in writing when you come out of this programme. Van Gogh is a totem for writers: sold one painting in his lifetime, to his brother. You should write for its own sake. What you write is a print-off of whom you are, where you are, when you are. You can say, *This came out of me. I am adding this to the universe.*[6]

If that resonates, you too may decide to keep writing, however little you are published.

Notes

1 How A Writer Works

1 Guy Claxton, *Hare Brain, Tortoise Mind: Why Intelligence Increases When You Think Less* (London: 4th Estate, 1998), p. 3.
2 Dorothea Brande, *Becoming A Writer* (New York: Harcourt Brace & Company, 1934), p. 149.
3 Madison Smartt Bell, *Narrative Design: A Writer's Guide To Structure* (New York: Norton, 1997), p. 14.
4 Brande, pp. 159–60.
5 Brande, p. 164.
6 Natalie Goldburg, *Wild Mind* (London: Rider, 1991), pp. 32–3.
7 Smartt Bell, p. 15.
8 Brande, pp. 45–46.
9 Bell, p. 15.
10 Goldburg, pp. 1–4.

2 Making Notes

1 John Fowles, 'On Work Habits' in George Plimpton (ed.), *The Writer's Chapbook* (New York: Penguin Books, 1992), p. 55.
2 Natalie Goldburg, *Wild Mind: Living The Writer's Life* (London: Rider, 1991), p. 204.
3 Joseph Heller, 'On Work Habits' in George Plimpton (ed.), *The Writer's Chapbook* (New York: Penguin Books, 1992), p. 57.
4 Joan Didion, 'On Keeping A Notebook,' *Slouching Towards Bethlehem* (London: Flamingo, 2001).
5 Jack Kerouac, 'Believe & Technique in Modern Prose,' cited in Oakley Hall (ed.), *The Art and Craft of Novel Writing* (Cincinnati: Story Press, 1989), p. 161.
6 Natalie Goldburg, *Wild Mind* (London: Rider, 1991).
7 George V. Higgins, *On Writing* (London: Bloomsbury, 1991).
8 Carol Shields, *Larry's Party* (London: Fourth Estate, 1998), pp. 53–4.

3 Keeping Journals

1 Patricia T. O'Connor, *Words Fail Me: What Everyone Who Writes Should Know About Writing* (New York: Harcourt Brace and Company, 199), p. 19.

2   Jennifer Moon, *Learning Journals: A Handbook for Academics, Students and Professional Development* (London: Kogan Page, 1999).
3   Daniel Price, *How To Make A Journal of Your Life* (Berkeley: Ten Speed Press, 1999), p. 7.
4   Ibid., p. 9.
5   Bernard Mac Laverty, interviewed by Sharon Monteith and Jenny Newman in Monteith, Newman, Wheeler (eds), *Contemporary British and Irish Fiction: An Introduction Through Interviews* (London: Arnold, 2004), p. 111.
6   Dorothea Brande, *Becoming A Writer* (Basingstoke: Pan Macmillan, 1983), p. 73.
7   O'Connor, pp. 18–19.

4 How To Read As A Writer

1   Joyce Carol Oates, *Telling Stories* (New York: W.W. Norton & Co., 1997), p. xv.
2   'Why Bother?' from Jonathan Franzen, *How To Be Alone* (London: 4th Estate, 2002), p. 74.
3   John Gardner, *The Art of Fiction: Notes on Craft for Young Writers* (New York: Vintage, 1991), p. 10.
4   Stephen King, *On Writing*. New English Library (London: Hodder and Stoughton, 2000).
5   John Updike, *More Matter: Essays and Criticism* (New York: Fawcett Books, 2000), p. 418.
6   Gardner, p. 10.
7   From an interview in Bonnie Lyons and Bill Oliver (eds), *Passion and Craft: Conversations with Notable Writers* (Chicago: University of Illinois Press, 1998), pp. 76–7.
8   Heather Leach, 'Reading As A Writer,' in Graham *et al.* (eds), *The Road to Somewhere: A Creative Writing Companion* (Basingstoke: Palgrave, 2005), p. 74.
9   Tom Bailey, *A Short Story Writer's Companion* (New York: Oxford University Press, 2001), p. 109.
10 Ernest Hemingway, quoted in George Plimpton (ed.), *The Writer's Chapbook* (New York: Penguin Books, 1992), p. 12.

Reflection Project 1: The Writer Reading

1   Francis Spufford, *The Child That Books Built* (London: Faber and Faber, 2002), p. 18.
2   From the introduction to Clare Boylan (ed.), *The Agony and the Ego: The Art and Strategy of Fiction Writing Explored* (London: Penguin Books, 1993), p. xii.

5 A Brief Tour Around The Short Story

1 From the introduction to Joyce Carol Oates (ed.), *The Oxford Book of The American Short Story* (Oxford: OUP, 1992).
2 Valerie Shaw, *The Short Story: A Critical Introduction* (London: Longman, 1983), p. 3.
3 From the introduction to Jay McInerney (ed.), *The Penguin Book of New American Voices* (London: Penguin Books, 1995).

6 The Distance Between: Author, Narrator, Reader And Point Of View

1 Janet Burroway, *Writing Fiction: A Guide to Narrative Craft*, Sixth Edition (New York: Longman, 2003), p. 254.
2 George Eliot, *Silas Marner* (Harmondsworth: Penguin Books, 1967), p. 51.
3 Burroway, p. 289.
4 Richard Burns, 'Perfect Strangers' in Duncan Minshull (ed.), *Telling Stories* (London: Sceptre, 1993), p. 30.
5 Amy Hempel, 'In the Cemetery Where Al Jolson is Buried' in Tobias Wolff (ed.), *The Picador Book of Contemporary American Short Stories* (London: Picador, 1994), p. 321.
6 Orson Scott Card, *Characters and Viewpoint* (London: Robinson Publishing, 1990), p. 144.
7 John Gardner, *The Art Of Fiction: Notes on Craft for Young Writers* (New York: Vintage Books, 1991), p. 56.
8 Jenny Newman, 'Short Story Writing' in Newman *et al.*, *The Writer's Workbook*, Second Edition (London: Arnold, 2004), p. 57.
9 William Trevor, 'The Ballroom of Romance,' *The Stories of William Trevor* (Harmondsworth: Penguin Books, 1983), p. 185.
10 Gardner, p. 111.
11 Mark Haddon, *The Curious Incident of the Dog in the Night* (London: Vintage, 2004), p. 83.
12 Haddon, p. 193.
13 Gardner, p. 158.
14 Flannery O'Connor, 'Everything That Rises Must Converge' in the collection of the same name (Harmondsworth: Penguin Books, 1975), p. 13.
15 Joyce Carol Oates, 'Is Laughter Contagious?' in Robert Stone (ed.), *The Best American Short Stories* (Boston: Houghton Mifflin Company, 1992), pp. 218–9.
16 Alice Hoffman, *Here on Earth* (London: Vintage, 1998 details), p. 256.

7 Characters

1 John Gardner, *The Art of Fiction* (London: Vintage, 1991), p. 43.
2 Larry W. Phillips (ed.), *Ernest Hemingway on Writing* (New York: Simon and Schuster, 1984), p. 71.

3 L.P. Hartley, *The Go Between* (London: Penguin, 2004).
4 Gardner, p. 45.

8 Living Elsewhere: Plot

1 Quoted in George Plimpton (ed.), *The Writer's Chapbook* (New York: Penguin, 1992), p. 191.
2 Raymond Carver, 'On Writing' in Anne Charters (ed.), *The Story and its Writer* (New York: St. Martin's Press, 1995), p. 1529.
3 Ashley Stokes, 'Plotting A Novel' in Julia Bell and Paul Magrs (eds), *The Creative Writing Coursebook* (Basingstoke: Macmillan, 2001), p. 207.
4 Online interview with Anne Tyler in Readers' Club. http://www.readersclub.org/meetAuthor.asp?author=7, accessed 25 July 2005.
5 Michèle Roberts, interviewed by Jenny Newman in Monteith, Newman, Wheeler (eds), *Contemporary British and Irish Fiction: An Introduction Through Interviews* (London: Arnold, 2004), p. 128.
6 Ansen Dibell, *Plot* (London: Robinson Publishing, 1990), pp. 5–6.
7 Anne Lamott, *Bird By Bird – Some Instructions on Writing and Life* (New York: Anchor Books, 1995), p. 55.
8 Michael Baldwin, *The Way to Write Short Stories* (London: Elm Tree Books, 1996).
9 Dibell, p. 74.

9 Scenes

1 William Goldman, *Which Lie Did I Tell?* (London: Bloomsbury, 2000), p. 198.
2 James N. Frey, *How to Write a Damned Good Novel* (Basingstoke: Macmillan Publishers Limited, 1988), p. 127.
3 Gardner, p. 111.
4 Gardner, pp. 110–1.
5 Ansen Dibell, p. 8.
6 Barnaby Conrad, *The Complete Guide to Writing Fiction* (Cincinnati: Writer's Digest Books, 1990), p. 118.
7 Dibell, p. 8.
8 Ibid.
9 Denis Johnson, 'Emergency' in Robert Stone (ed.), *Best American Short Stories 1992* (New York: Houghton-Mifflin, 1992), pp. 111–2.
10 William Goldman, p. 104.

10 Dialogue

1 Sarah Waters, *Affinity* (London: Virago, 2000), pp. 44–5.
2 John Singleton, 'Dialogue in Prose Fiction' in Graham *et al.*, *The Road to Somewhere: A Creative Writing Companion* (Basingstoke: Palgrave, 2004), p. 158.

11 Setting

1 David Park, *Swallowing The Sun* (London: Bloomsbury Publishing, 2004), pp. 22–4.
2 Park, pp. 230–3.

12 Epiphany

1 Valerie Shaw, *The Short Story: A Critical Introduction* (London: Longman, 1983).
2 Daniel J. Schwarz (ed.), *The Dead: Case Studies in Contemporary Criticism* (New York: Bedford Division of St. Martin's Press, 1994), p. 66.
3 James Joyce, 'The Dead,' *Dubliners* (Harmondsworth: Penguin Books, 1971), pp. 206–7.
4 Ibid., pp. 218–9.
5 Tom Bailey, *A Short Story Writer's Companion* (New York: Oxford University Press, 2001), p. 75.

13 Reflection: How To Think About Your Writing

1 Thom Jones, 'I Am A . . . Genius!' in Will Blythe (ed.), *Why I Write: Thoughts on the Craft of Fiction* (London: Little Brown, 1998), p. 32.

14 Redrafting 1: Editing

1 Tom Wolfe in George Plimpton (ed.), *The Writer's Chapbook* (New York: Penguin Books, 1989), p. 137
2 From a letter by Gustave Flaubert, quoted in Barnaby Conrad, *The Complete Guide To Writing Fiction* (Cincinnati: Writer's Digest Books, 1990), p. 204.
3 James Laughlin quoted in Plimpton, as before, p. 60.
4 Rita Mae Brown, *Starting From Scratch: A Different Kind of Writers' Manual* (New York: Bantam, 1989), p. 69.

15 Page Design

1 John Haffenden (ed.), 'Fay Weldon,' *Novelists in Interview* (London: Methuen, 1985), pp. 305–20.
2 Michael Chabon, *The Amazing Adventures of Kavalier & Clay* (New York: Picador USA, 2001), p. 415.
3 Zadie Smith in the introduction to her micro short story collection *Martha and Hanwell* (London: Penguin Books, 2005), p. vii.

17 Writer's Workshops

1 Madison Smartt Bell from his chapter 'Unconscious Mind' in *Narrative Design: A Writer's Guide to Structure* (New York: W.W. Norton & Co., 1997), p. 4.
2 Frank Conroy, 'The Writer's Workshop' in Tom Bailey (ed.), *On Writing Short Stories* (New York: Oxford University Press, 2000), p. 81.
3 Madison Smartt Bell, p. 9.
4 Madison Smartt Bell, pp. 6–9.
5 Margaret Atwood, 'The Rocky Road To Paper Heaven,' on the Margaret Atwood Information Site, http://www.web.net/owtoad/road.html, accessed 27 February, 2006.
6 Liz Allen, 'The Workshop Way' in Singleton and Luckhurst (eds), *The Creative Writing Handbook* (Basingstoke: Palgrave, 1996), p. 18.
7 Thomas McCormack, *The Fiction Editor, The Novel, and the Novelist* (New York: St. Martin's Press, 1988), pp. 16–17.

18 Redrafting 2: Revising

1 James N. Frey, *How to Write a Damned Good Novel* (Basingstoke: Papermac, 1987), p. 151.
2 Andre Dubus 'The Habit of Writing' in Tom Bailey (ed.), *A Short Story Writer's Companion* (New York: Oxford University Press, 2001), pp. 138–9.
3 Quoted in George Plimpton (ed.), *The Writer's Chapbook* (New York: Penguin Books, 1992), p. 195.
4 Jack M. Bickham, *Writing the Short Story: A Hands-On Guide for Creating Captivating Short Fiction* (Cincinnati: Writer's Digest Books, 1994), p. 177.
5 George V. Higgins, *On Writing* (London: Bloomsbury, 1991), p. 85.
6 John Gardner, *The Art of Fiction: Notes on Craft for Young Writers* (New York: Vintage, 1991), p. 70.
7 Barnaby Conrad, *The Complete Guide to Writing Fiction* (Cincinnati: Writer's Digest Books, 1990), p. 207.
8 Roddy Doyle, interviewed by Pat Wheeler and Jenny Newman in Monteith, Newman, Wheeler (eds), *Contemporary British and Irish Fiction: An Introduction Through Interviews* (London: Arnold, 2004), p. 64.

19 Some Notes On Handling Time In Fiction

1 Henry James, 'Preface to Roderick Hudson' at http://www.henryjames.org.uk/prefaces/text01.htm
2 Tobias Wolff, *Collected Stories* (London: Bloomsbury, 1997).
3 Tim Akers and Jerry Moore (eds) *Short Stories for Students: Vol. 5* (Detroit: Gale, 1999).
4 Tim O'Brien, *The Things They Carried* (London: Flamingo, 1991).

5 Eudora Welty, *The Eye of the Story* (New York: Random House, 1978).
6 William Faulkner, *Selected Short Stories* (New York: Modern Library, 1993).
7 http://www.writersstore.com/article.php?articles_id=7
8 http://www.timothyjpmason.com
9 Angela Carter, *Burning Your Boats* (London: Penguin, 1997).
10 Vladimir Nabokov, *Pnin* (New York: Vintage, 1989).
11 Anton Chekhov (trans. by Robert Payne), *Forty Stories* (New York: Vintage, 1991).
12 Raymond Carver, *What We Talk About When We Talk About Love* (New York: Vintage, 1989).
13 Elizabeth Bowen, *Collected Stories* (London: Cape, 1980).

20 Foreshadowing

1 James N. Frey, *How to Write a Damn Good Novel* (Basingstoke: Papermac, 1987), p. 116.
2 Patricia T. O'Connor, *Words Fail Me: What Everyone Who Writes Should Know About Writing* (New York: Harcourt Brace & Company, 1999), p. 165.
3 Frey, p. 119.
4 Robert McKee, *Story* (London: Methuen, 1998), p. 200.
5 Patricia T. O'Connor, p. 169.
6 Barnaby Conrad, *The Complete Guide to Writing Fiction* (Cincinnati: Writer's Digest Books, 1990), p. 186.
7 Robert McKee, p. 200.

21 Transitions

1 Amy Tan, *The Joy Luck Club* (London: Minerva, 1990), pp. 162–3.
2 Jack M. Bickham, *Writing the Short Story: A Hands-On Guide for Creating Captivating Short Fiction* (Cincinnati: Writer's Digest Books, 1994), p. 39.
3 Andrea Levy, *Small Island* (London: Review, 2005), pp. 97–8.
4 Pat Barker, *Regeneration* (London: Penguin Books, 1992), pp. 7–8.
5 Margaret Atwood, 'The Sin Eater,' *Bluebeard's Egg* (London: Vintage, 1980), pp. 216–17.

22 Crossing Timelines And Breaking Rules

1 David Foster Wallace, 'Forever Overhead,' *Brief Interviews with Hideous Men* (London: Abacus, 2001), pp. 10–12.
2 You can read a free online version at http://www.online-literature.com/wellshg/timemachine/ but be warned that the story takes until the third chapter to get into the time travel journey.

3 Washington Irving, *Rip Van Winkle* (London: Puffin Books, 1996).
4 Martin Amis, *Time's Arrow* (London: Vintage,1991), p. 76.
5 Alexander Masters, *Stuart: A Life Backwards* (London: Fourth Estate, 2005).
6 Although this isn't the true end, which is given to us in the introduction, but to say anymore would be to give it away.
7 Atwood M, 'Happy Endings' in Hermione Lee (ed.), *The Secret Self* (London: J.M. Dent, 1985), pp. 370–1.

23 Meaning, Sense And Clarity

1 Frank Conroy (ed.), 'The Writer's Workshop' in Tom Bailey *On Writing Short Stories* (New York: Oxford University Press, 2000).
2 William I. Strunk and E.B. White (eds), *The Elements of Style* (New York: Allyn and Bacon, 1999) and online at: http://www.bartleby.com/141/
3 Joyce Carol Oates, quoted by William F. Buckley in his essay, 'Style and Language' in Barnaby Conrad (ed.), *The Complete Guide to Writing Fiction* (Cincinnati: Writer's Digest Books, 1990), p. 94.

24 Description

1 Stephen King, *On Writing* (London: New English Library, 2000), p. 207.
2 Alessandro Baricco, *Ocean Sea* (London: Hamish Hamilton, 1999), p. 3.
3 Rupert Thompson, *Air & Fire* (London: Penguin Books, 1993), pp. 273–4.
4 Manda Scott, *Boudica: Dreaming the Eagle* (London: Bantam, 2003), p. 36.
5 Ibid., p. 37.

25 Sentences

1 Hemingway, *A Movable Feast*, p. 75.
2 Quoted by Anne Charters, *The Story and Its Writer* (New York: St. Martin's Press, 1995), p. 614.
3 Ibid.
4 In his introduction to Jay McInerney (ed.), *The Penguin Book of New American Voices* (London: Penguin, 1995).
5 From Raymond Carver, 'On Writing' in Anne Charters (ed.), *The Story and Its Writer* (New York: St. Martin's Press, 1997), p. 1524–7.
6 Anton Chekhov, 'The Kiss' in Richard Ford (ed.), *The Essential Tales of Chekhov* (New York: HarperCollins, 1998), p. 51.
7 Ernest Hemingway, 'Hills Like White Eyes' in *The Essential Hemingway* (Harmondsworth: Penguin books, 1964), p. 378.

8 Raymond Carver, *Where I'm Calling From: New and Selected Stories* (New York: Vintage, 1989), p. 148.
9 Henry James, *What Maisie Knew* (London: Everyman, 1997), p. 135.
10 Richard Ford, *Independence Day* (London: The Harvill Press, 1995), pp. 134–5.
11 Isabelle Allende, 'The Wicked Girl' in Janet Berliner and Joyce Carol Oates (eds), *Snapshots: 20th Century Mother–Daughter Fiction* (London: Vintage Books, 2001).
12 David Guterson, *Snow Falling On Cedars* (London: Bloomsbury, 1995), p. 150.
13 Quoted in J.M. and M.J. Cohen (eds), *The Penguin Dictionary of Twentieth Century Quotations* (London: Penguin Books, 1995), p. 67.
14 Cormac McCarthy, *All The Pretty Horses* (London: Picador, 1993), p. 141.
15 Helen Dunmore, *A Spell Of Winter* (London: Viking, 1995), p. 95.
16 J.M. and M.J. Cohen, p. 230.

26 Demons And Angels: Using A Persona

1 Oscar Wilde, *The Critic as Artist: With Some Remarks on the Importance of Doing Nothing and Discussing Everything* (Los Angeles: Sun & Moon Books, 1997), p. 41.
2 Mark Twain, *The Adventures of Huckleberry Finn* (London: Penguin Classics edn., 1884), p. 1.
3 Josip Novakovich, p. 202.
4 Thomas H. Johnson (ed.), *The Complete Poems of Emily Dickinson* (London: Faber and Faber, 1975), p. 506.
5 Gerard Manley Hopkins, 'Pied Beauty,' *Poetry and Prose* (London: Everyman, 1998), p. 48.
6 Novakovich, p. 201.
7 *The Lonely Voice* (London: Macmillan, 1993), p. 72.
8 Mark Twain, p. 10.
9 Irvine Welsh, *Trainspotting* (London: Minerva edn., 1994), pp. 15–16.
10 *The Lonely Voice* (London: Macmillan, 1993), p. 57.
11 *The Guardian Weekend*, 25.06.05, pp. 17–21.
12 Daren King, *Tom Boler* (London: Jonathan Cape, 2005), p. 45.

27 Looking For The Drama

1 Ian McEwan, *Enduring Love* (London: Vintage, 1998), pp. 1–3.
2 Colm Toibin, *The Master* (London: Picador, 2005), p. 287.
3 Carol Shields, *Larry's Party* (London: 4th Estate, 1997), p. 249.
4 Shields, p. 260.

5 Shields, p. 261.
6 Shields, back cover.

28 The Longer Story

1 Henry James, in an 1888 letter to Robert Louis Stevenson, cited by Valerie
   Shaw, *The Short Story: A Critical Introduction* (Harlow: Longman's, 1983),
   p. 12.
2 Ailsa Cox, *Writing Short Stories* (Abingdon: Routledge, 2005), p. 3.
3 Alice Munro, 'The Jack Randa Hotel' in *Open Secrets* (London: Vintage,
   1995), p. 172.
4 Edgar Allan Poe, in a review of Nathaniel Hawthorne's *Twice-Told Tales*, first
   published in *Graham's Magazine* in 1842.
5 John Gardner, *The Art of Fiction: Notes on Craft for Young Writers* (New York:
   Vintage Books, 1991), p. 181.
6 Gardner, p. 183.
7 Cox, p. 6.
8 Alice Munro, pp. 166–7.

29 The Short Story Cycle

1 Robert Morgan, 'Only Connect,' http://dir.salon.com/story/books/bag/
   2000/11/03/morgan/index.xml, accessed 22 September 2005.
2 Susan Garland Mann, *The Short Story Cycle: A Genre Companion & Reference
   Guide* (Westport, Connecticut: Greenwood, 1989).

30 Structure – What Is It Good For?

1 George Polti, *36 Dramatic Situations* (Boston: The Writer Inc, 1999).
2 Joseph Campbell, *The Hero With A Thousand Faces* (London: Paladin, 1993).
3 Gareth Creer, *Big Sky* (London: Black Swan, 2002).

Afterword: How To Go The Distance

1 Richard Ford, 'The Beginning, As Viewed From The Middle' in Jenny
   Brown and Shona Munro (eds), *Writers Writing* (Edinburgh: Mainstream
   Publishing, 1993), p. 48.
2 Ford, p. 55.

3 George V. Higgins, *On Writing: Advice for Those Who Write to Publish (or Would Like To)* (London: Bloomsbury Publishing, 1991), p. 82.

4 Michael Norman, 'A Book in Search of a Buzz: The Marketing of a First Novel' in Jack Heffron (ed.), *The Best Writing on Writing Volume Two* (Cincinnati: Story Press, 1995), p. 43.

5 Source, a lecture on the writer's life given by novelist Amanda Craig at the City of London Girls' School, http://www.amandacraig.com/pages/journalism/lectures/a_writers_life.htm, accessed 17 January, 2006.

6 Kurt Vonnegut Jr, the distinguished American author of, amongst other novels, *Slaughterhouse Five* speaking to postgraduate writers at the University of Iowa, September 2001.

Bibliography

Fiction

Tim Akers and Jerry Moore (eds), *Short Stories for Students: Vol. 5* (Detroit: Gale, 1999).

Martin Amis, *Time's Arrow* (London: Vintage, 1991).

Margaret Atwood, *Bluebeard's Egg* (London: Vintage, 1980).

Alessandro Baricco, *Ocean Sea* (London: Hamish Hamilton, 1999).

Pat Barker, *Regeneration* (London: Penguin Books, 1992).

Elizabeth Bowen, *Collected Stories* (London: Cape, 1980).

Malcolm Bradbury (ed.), *The Penguin Book of Modern British Short Stories* (London: Penguin, 1985).

Angela Carter, *Nights at the Circus* (London: Picador, 1984).

Angela Carter, *Burning Your Boats* (London: Penguin, 1997).

Raymond Carver, *What We Talk About When We Talk About Love* (New York: Vintage, 1989).

Raymond Carver, *Where I'm Calling From: New and Selected Stories* (New York: Vintage, 1989).

Michael Chabon, *The Amazing Adventures of Kavalier & Clay* (New York: Picador USA, 2001).

Anne Charters, *The Story and Its Writer* (New York: St. Martin's Press, 1995).

Anton Chekhov (edited with an introduction by Richard Ford), *The Essential Tales of Chekhov* (New York: HarperCollins, 2000).

Anton Chekhov (trans. by Robert Payne), *Forty Stories* (New York: Vintage, 1991).

Gareth Creer, *Big Sky* (London: Black Swan, 2002).

Helen Dunmore, *A Spell Of Winter* (London: Viking, 1995).

George Eliot, *Silas Marner* (Harmondsworth: Penguin Books, 1967).

William Faulkner, *Selected Short Stories* (New York: Modern Library, 1993).

Susan Fletcher, *Eve Green* (London: Harper Perennial, 2005).

Jonathan Safran Foer, *Everything Is Illuminated* (London: Penguin Books, 2003).

Richard Ford, *Independence Day* (London: The Harvill Press, 1995).

Richard Ford (ed.), *Granta Book of the American Short Story* (London: Granta, 1992).

Michael Frayn, *Spies* (London: Faber and Faber, 2002).

Romesh Gunesekera, 'The Hole' in *Granta 50*, Summer 1995.

David Guterson, *Snow Falling on Cedars* (London: Bloomsbury, 1995).

Mark Haddon, *The Curious Incident of the Dog in the Night* (London: Vintage, 2004).

L.P. Hartley, *The Go Between* (London: Penguin, 2004).

Ernest Hemingway, *The Essential Hemingway* (Harmondsworth: Penguin books, 1964).

Alice Hoffman, *Here on Earth* (London: Vintage, 1998).

Washington Irving, *Rip Van Winkle* (London: Puffin Books, 1996).

Henry James, *What Maisie Knew* (London: Everyman, 1997).

James Joyce, *Dubliners* (Harmondsworth: Penguin Books, 1971).

Daren King, *Tom Boler* (London: Jonathan Cape, 2005).

Hermione Lee (ed.), *The Secret Self: A Century of Short Stories by Women* (London: Everyman, 1993).

Andrea Levy, *Small Island* (London: Review, 2005).

Cormac McCarthy, *All the Pretty Horses* (London: Picador, 1993).

Ian McEwan, *Enduring Love* (Vintage, London, 1998).

Jay McInerney (ed.), *The Penguin Book of New American Voices* (London: Penguin Books, 1995).

Duncan Minshull (ed.), *Telling Stories* (London: Sceptre, 1992).

Alice Munro, *Open Secrets* (London: Vintage, 1995).

Vladimir Nabokov, *Pnin* (New York: Vintage, 1989).

Joyce Carol Oates (ed.), *The Oxford Book of the American Short Story* (Oxford: OUP, 1995).

Joyce Carol Oates (ed.), *Telling Stories* (New York: W.W. Norton & Co., 1997).

Tim O'Brien, *The Things They Carried* (New York: Broadway, 1998).

Flannery O'Connor, *Everything That Rises Must Converge* (Harmondsworth: Penguin Books, 1975).

David Park, *Swallowing the Sun* (London: Bloomsbury Publishing, 2004).

Michele Roberts, *The Mistress Class* (London: Virago Press, 2004).

Manda Scott, *Boudica: Dreaming the Eagle* (London: Bantam, 2003).

Carol Shields, *Larry's Party* (London: Forth Estate, 1998).

Anita Shreve, *Sea Glass* (London: Abacus, 2002).

Zadie Smith, *Martha and Hanwell* (London: Penguin Books, 2005).

Robert Stone (ed.), *The Best American Short Stories 1992* (Boston: Houghton Mifflin Company, 1992).

Amy Tan, *The Joy Luck Club* (London: Minerva, 1989).

Rupert Thompson, *Air and Fire* (London: Penguin Books, 1993).

Colm Toibin, *The Master* (London: Picador, 2005).

Rose Tremain, *The Colour* (London: Vintage, 2003).

William Trevor, *The Stories of William Trevor* (Harmondsworth: Penguin Books, 1983).

Mark Twain, *The Adventures of Huckleberry Finn* (London: Penguin Classics, 1884).

Anne Tyler, *Back When We Were Grown-Ups* (London: Vintage, 2001).

John Updike (ed.), *The Best American Short Stories of the Century* (London: Houghton-Mifflin, 1999).

David Foster Wallace, *Brief Interviews with Hideous Men* (New York: Little Brown, 1999).

Sarah Waters, *Affinity* (London: Virago, 2000).

Irvine Welsh, *Trainspotting* (London: Minerva 1994).

Jeanette Winterson, *Sexing the Cherry* (London: Vintage, 1989).

Tobias Wolff, *Collected Stories* (London: Bloomsbury, 1997).
Tobias Wolff (ed.), *The Picador Book of Contemporary American Short Stories* (London: Picador, 1994).

Memoir

Augusten Burroughs, *Running with Scissors* (London: Atlantic Books, 2004).
Bob Dylan, *Chronicles Volume 1* (London: Simon & Shuster, 2004).
Francis Spufford, *The Child That Books Built* (London: Faber and Faber, 2002).

Biography

Alexander Masters, *Stuart: A Life Backwards* (London: Fourth Estate, 2005).

Poetry

Gerard Manley Hopkins, *Poetry and Prose* (London: Everyman, 1998).
Emily Dickinson (edited by Thomas H. Johnson), *The Complete Poems of Emily Dickinson* (London: Faber and Faber, 1975).

Craft, Criticism And So On

Tom Bailey (ed.), *On Writing Short Stories* (New York: Oxford University Press, 2000).
Michael Baldwin, *The Way to Write Short Stories* (London: Elm Tree Books, 1996).
Julia Bell and Paul Magrs, *The Creative Writing Coursebook* (Basingstoke: Macmillan, 2001).
Madison Smartt Bell, *Narrative Design: A Writer's Guide to Structure* (New York: Norton, 1997).
Jack M. Bickham, *Writing the Short Story: A Hands-On Guide for Creating Captivating Short Fiction* (Cincinnati: Writer's Digest Books, 1994).
Will Blythe (ed.), *Why I Write: Thoughts on the Craft of Fiction* (London: Little, Brown, 1998).
Clare Boylan (ed.), *The Agony and the Ego: The Art and Strategy of Fiction Writing Explored* (Harmondsworth: Penguin Books, 1993).
Dorothea Brande, *Becoming a Writer* (New York: Harcourt Brace & Company, 1934).
Rita Mae Brown, *Starting from Scratch: A Different Kind of Writers' Manual* (New York: Bantam, 1989).

Jenny Brown and Shona Munro (eds), *Writers Writing* (Edinburgh: Mainstream Publishing, 1993).

Janet Burroway, *Writing Fiction: A Guide to Narrative Craft, Sixth Edition* (New York: Longman, 2003).

Joseph Campbell, *The Hero with a Thousand Faces* (London: Paladin, 1993).

Orson Scott Card, *Characters and Viewpoint* (London: Robinson Publishing, 1990).

Guy Claxton, *Hare Brain, Tortoise Mind: Why Intelligence Increases When You Think Less* (London: 4th Estate, 1998).

J.M. and M.J. Cohen (eds), *The Penguin Dictionary of Twentieth Century Quotations* (London: Penguin Books, 1995).

Barnaby Conrad (ed.), *The Complete Guide to Writing Fiction* (Cincinnati: Writer's Digest Books, 1990).

Kevin Conroy-Scott, *Screenwriters' Masterclass* (London: Faber and Faber, 2005).

Ailsa Cox, *Writing Short Stories* (Abingdon: Routledge, 2005).

Ansen Dibell, *Plot* (London: Robinson Publishing, 1990).

Joan Didion, *Slouching Towards Bethlehem* (London: Flamingo, 2001).

Jonathan Franzen, *How to Be Alone* (London: 4th Estate, 2002).

James N. Frey, *How to Write a Damned Good Novel* (Basingstoke: Macmillan Publishers Limited, 1988).

John Gardner, *The Art of Fiction: Notes on Craft for Young Writers* (New York: Vintage, 1991).

Natalie Goldburg, *Wild Mind* (London: Rider, 1991).

William Goldman, *Which Lie Did I Tell?* (London: Bloomsbury, 2000).

Robert Graham, Heather Leach, Helen Newall and John Singleton (eds), *The Road to Somewhere: A Creative Writing Companion* (Basingstoke: Palgrave, 2005).

John Haffenden (ed.), *Novelists in Interview* (London: Methuen, 1985).

Oakley Hall, *The Art and Craft of Novel Writing* (Cincinnati: Story Press, 1989).

Ernest Hemingway, *A Movable Feast* (London: Arrow, 1994).

Jack Heffron (ed.), *The Best Writing on Writing Volume Two* (Cincinnati: Story Press, 1995).

George V. Higgins, *On Writing: Advice for Those Who Write to Publish (or Would Like to)* (London: Bloomsbury, 1991).

Stephen King, *On Writing* (London: New English Library, 2000).

Anne Lamott, *Bird By Bird – Some Instructions on Writing and Life* (New York, Anchor Books, 1995).

Bonnie Lyons and Bill Oliver (eds), *Passion and Craft: Conversations with Notable Writers* (Chicago: University of Illinois Press, 1998).

Robert McKee, *Story* (London: Methuen, 1998).

Susan Garland Mann, *The Short Story Cycle: A Genre Companion & Reference Guide* (Westport, Connecticut: Greenwood, 1989).

Sharon Monteith, Jenny Newman and Pat Wheeler (eds), *Contemporary British and Irish Fiction: An Introduction Through Interviews* (London: Arnold, 2004).

Jennifer Moon, *Learning Journals: A Handbook for Academics, Students and Professional Development* (London: Kogan Page, 1999).

Gary F. Moring, *The Complete Idiot's Guide to Understanding Einstein* (Indianapolis: Alpha Books, 2000).

Jenny Newman, Edmund Cusick and Aileen La Tourette (eds), *The Writer's Workbook, Second Edition* (London: Arnold, 2004).

Josip Novakovich, *Fiction Writer's Workshop* (Cincinnati: Story Press, 1995).

Sean O'Faolain, *The Lonely Voice* (London: Macmillan, 1993).

Patricia T. O'Connor, *Words Fail Me: What Everyone Who Writes Should Know About Writing* (New York: Harcourt Brace and Company, 1999).

Larry W. Phillips (ed.), *Ernest Hemingway on Writing* (New York: Simon and Schuster, 2002).

George Plimpton (ed.), *The Writer's Chapbook* (New York: Penguin Books, 1992).

George Polti, *36 Dramatic Situations* (Boston: The Writer Inc., 1999).

Daniel Price, *How to Make a Journal of Your Life* (Berkeley: Ten Speed Press, 1999).

Tristine Rainer, The New Diary.

Daniel J. Schwarz (ed.), *The Dead*: Case *Studies in Contemporary Criticism* (New York: Bedford Division of St. Martin's Press, 1994).

Valerie Shaw, *The Short Story: A Critical Introduction* (London: Longman, 1983).

William I. Strunk and E.B. White (eds), *The Elements of Style* (Allyn and Bacon, 1999).

John Updike, *More Matter: Essays and Criticism* (New York: Fawcett Books, 2000).

Christopher Vogler, *The Writer's Journey* (London: Pan, 1999).

Eudora Welty, *The Eye of the Story* (New York: Random House, 1978).

Oscar Wilde, *The Critic as Artist: With Some Remarks on the Importance of Doing Nothing and Discussing Everything* (Los Angeles: Sun & Moon Books, 1997).

Index

Index of Writing Exercises